IMAGES
of America

ST. JOSEPH COUNTY'S HISTORIC RIVER COUNTRY

IMAGES
of America

ST. JOSEPH COUNTY'S HISTORIC RIVER COUNTRY

Jane Simon Ammeson

ARCADIA
PUBLISHING

ISBN 978-0-7385-3383-4

Published by Arcadia Publishing
Charleston, South Carolina

Printed in the United States of America

Library of Congress Control Number: 2005920197

For all general information, please contact Arcadia Publishing:
Telephone 843-853-2070
Fax 843-853-0044
E-mail sales@arcadiapublishing.com
For customer service and orders:
Toll-Free 1-888-313-2665

Visit us on the Internet at www.arcadiapublishing.com

Contents

ACKNOWLEDGMENTS

A book like this results from collaboration between the author and those who are willing to share their valuable tales of local history and their treasure troves of wonderful photos. There are many who made this book possible—whose pride in their communities and determination to keep history alive led them to talk to me and to contribute the photographs to this book.

It is heartening to realize how many people believe in the history of their towns and are willing to work hard at preserving it. They are the people who make a book like this possible. In alphabetical order and not order of importance, I wish to give hearty and heartfelt thanks to the following: Geff and Cheryl Clark, owners of the Mendon Country Inn; the Colon Public Library; Dick Cripe; Bill Dehn; Vic Eichler; David Farrell; Larry Frank; the Governor Barry House Museum; Robert Hair; Larry Humphreys; Katherine Langworthy; the Mendon Public Library; Tim Peterson; the Historic Sue Silliman House Museum, owned and operated by Abiel Fellows DAR; the Three Rivers Public Library; M.E.Vercler, MD; and Steve Zarza.

And thank you to my family: my husband, Charlie, and my children, Evan and Nia, for making do with pizza for dinner on nights when I was researching in libraries and hunting for the photographs that appear in this book.

Introduction

Historic St. Joseph County, with its meandering waterways and small scenic lakes, has the most navigable streams of any county in Michigan. Because of this, several of the state's earliest and largest inland communities were located here. The river ways were superhighways in the days when roads were just rutted paths through the forests. Both Native Americans and French explorers used the rivers and the streams to move from village to village and to transport their goods to the large ports that opened up onto the Great Lakes.

The rivers were also the location of early industrial enterprises, including mills. The 131-year-old Rawson's King Mill still stands above a millpond on a little crook of Nottawa Creek near a cascading waterfall. The pristine Nottawa Creek ambles here, dividing the land into small islands that are accessible by bridges. Though the mill wheel continues to turn, it has been almost a century since lumber cut in the mill was floated down the creek to the St. Joseph River, which flows west running into Lake Michigan at St. Joseph, Michigan. Once the wood arrived at this busy port town, it could be shipped to many destinations, including Milwaukee, and notably, Chicago, where it was used to help rebuild the city after the great fire. The mill was later converted into a gristmill to grind locally-grown wheat into flour.

There are other portals to the past still here. The Sue Silliman House, a blacksmith shop in the early 1870s, is now a museum in Three Rivers, a town whose name reflects the fact that it is situated where three rivers converge. A late 19th-century Georgian manor, built perched above the river by the Marantette family, remains standing in Mendon. It is the site of a trading post built by Patrick Marantette, which was in business as early as 1821. Just upstream is the old 1843 stagecoach inn, called the Wakeman House, now a bed and breakfast. Nearby, St. Edwards Catholic Church, built with stones donated by parishioners in 1905, remains a focal point in town. In the resort town of nearby Nottawa, children get to spend a day at the Nottawa Stone School, a one-room schoolhouse in use from 1870 to 1961, to learn what education was like back then.

Almost all of the small towns here, including Mendon, Sturgis, Colon, and Three Rivers, boast Carnegie libraries built in the late 1800s and early 1900s through the largesse of philanthropist Andrew Carnegie.

One of the few remaining covered bridges in Michigan crosses the St. Joseph River near Centerville, the county seat. The bridge, built in 1887, at 282 feet with three 94-foot spans, is the longest covered bridge in the state. In downtown Centreville, the county courthouse, which is on the National Register of Historic Places, sits on the old-fashioned town square and is as busy today as it was when it was built in 1900 (the first courthouse in this location was erected in 1842). Mottville's 270-foot Camelback Bridge, erected in 1922, is now a pedestrian pathway across the St. Joseph.

Unfortunately, some of the past is almost gone. The old 1850s era Hoffman Mill can be seen just in bits and parts—and the Native American village, which early French fur traders described as stretching for miles and miles along the banks of the St. Joseph River, has completely disappeared.

Some of the county's most prestigious personalities exist now just in memory and in faded photos, but at one time, they lived here in all their glory.

Magician Harry Blackstone loved to fish, and so he chose Colon as a place to relax when he wasn't on the road. Other magicians migrated to Colon, now known as the Magic Capital of the World. Abbott's Magic, a magic tricks business for both professionals and amateurs, opened in 1936 and is still owned by the same family. Blackstone is buried outside of Colon in Lakeside Cemetery.

With her sweeping broad-brimmed hats and majestic appearance, Mendon native Madame Emma Peek Marantette was every inch a show woman. Famed as an equestrian, she had her own railroad car and toured the country. As a professional horsewoman, she garnered a high jump record of 7 feet, 10 and one-half inches—while riding sidesaddle.

Potawatomi Indian Chief Wahbememe (also known as Chief White Pigeon) ran 150 miles to warn white settlers that they were going to be attacked. He saved the village, now named White Pigeon after him, but died from the exertion.

Like all communities, those in St. Joseph County had their share of tragedies—fires roared through the towns, rivers flooded, and men marched off to war.

St. Joseph County is also home to the largest Amish population in Michigan, and it is typical to see horses pulling buggies trotting along the rolling country roads, or to watch Amish housewives hang their laundry out to dry every Monday. And it is the first region in the state to offer paddling enthusiasts a chance to paddle into history—as part of the Michigan Heritage Water Trails—a series of historic markers that illuminate the past for canoers and kayakers.

And St. Joseph County still has enough woods to harbor a family of mountain lions which every once in awhile—say three or four years—are sighted.

To visit St. Joseph County is a chance to connect to the past.

One

Enjoying the Waters

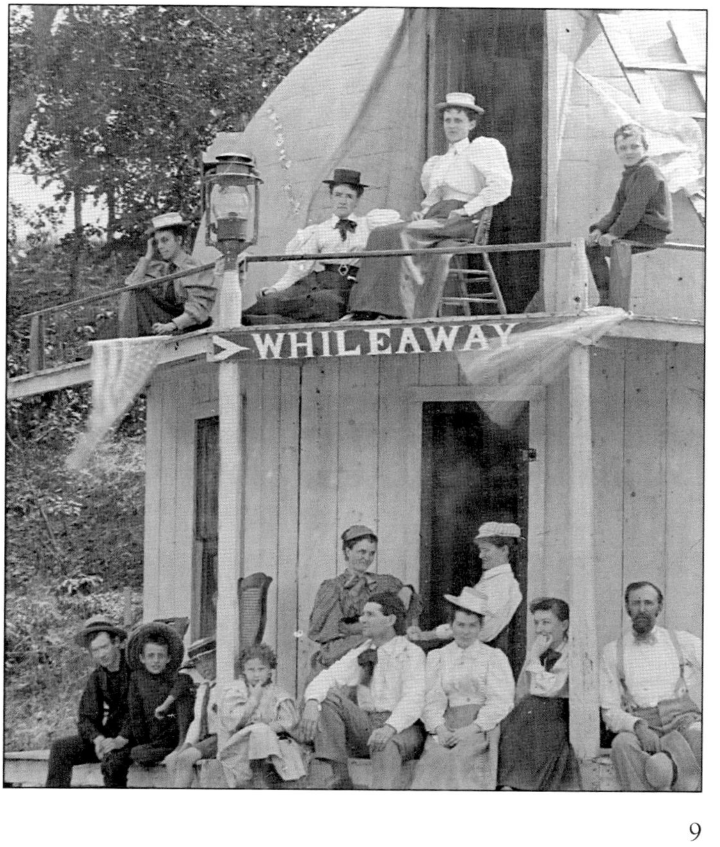

Visitors came from all over Michigan and beyond to enjoy the pretty lakes and rivers of St. Joseph County. Whileaway Cabin, one of the earliest cottages on Corey Lake, dates back to at least 1892. According to Ann Haradine Langefeld and Betty Haradine Sarhatt in the book *Hooked on Corey Lake*, compiled by Lynn Cassady, the dome on the cabin was part of an old water tower in Three Rivers, transported and placed on top of Whileaway to create an extra bedroom. This picture is dated 1894. By 1916, the cabin's name had changed to The Dome. (Three Rivers Public Library Collection.)

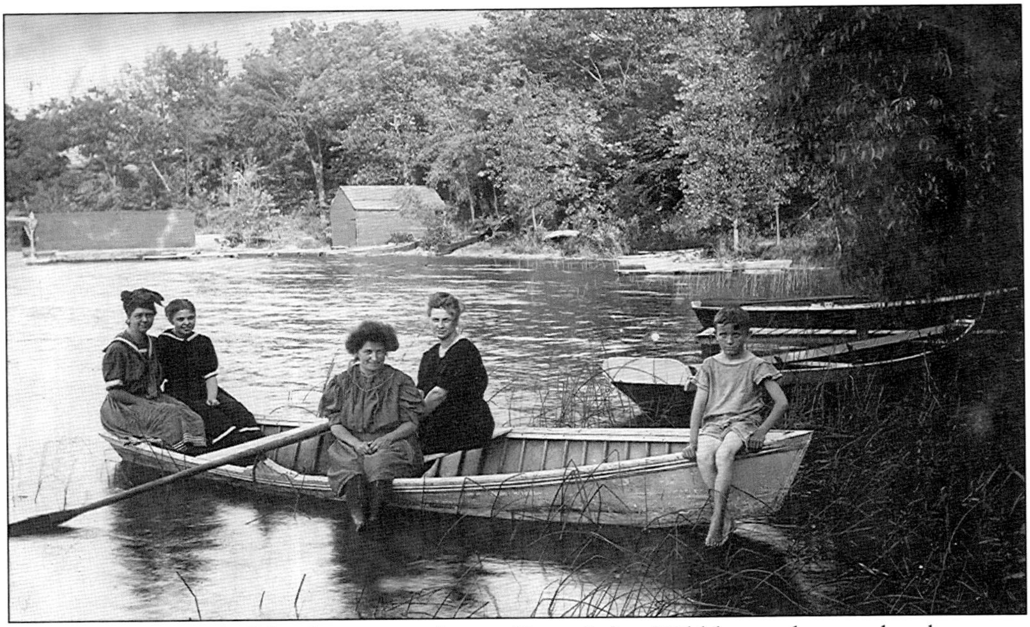

Water recreation of all kinds was popular on Corey Lake. Wild bears, deer, and wolves were frequently found in the woods surrounding the lake, which is why Chief Sangamon and his tribe hunted the area around Corey Lake. (Three Rivers Public Library Collection.)

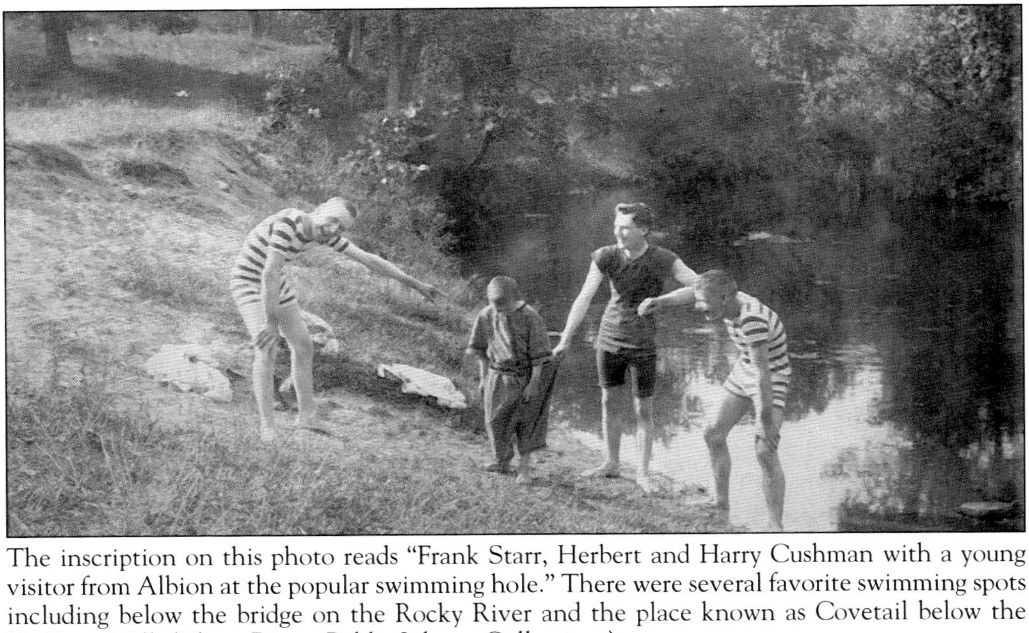

The inscription on this photo reads "Frank Starr, Herbert and Harry Cushman with a young visitor from Albion at the popular swimming hole." There were several favorite swimming spots including below the bridge on the Rocky River and the place known as Covetail below the Hoffman Mill. (Three Rivers Public Library Collection.)

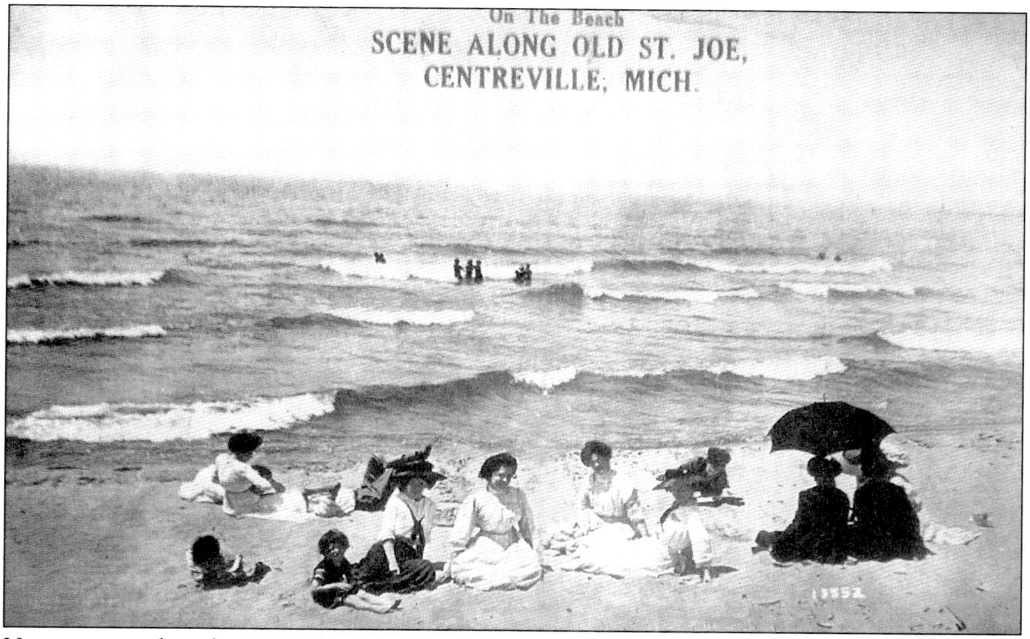

Humorous and trick postcards were popular back in the late 1800s and early 1900s and this might be one of them. Though it says it's a scene along the Old St. Joseph River in Centreville, the river is never this wide nor wavy. The scene could be Lake Michigan, some 60 miles away, or one of the resort lakes such as Corey or Klinger. (Dick Cripe Collection.)

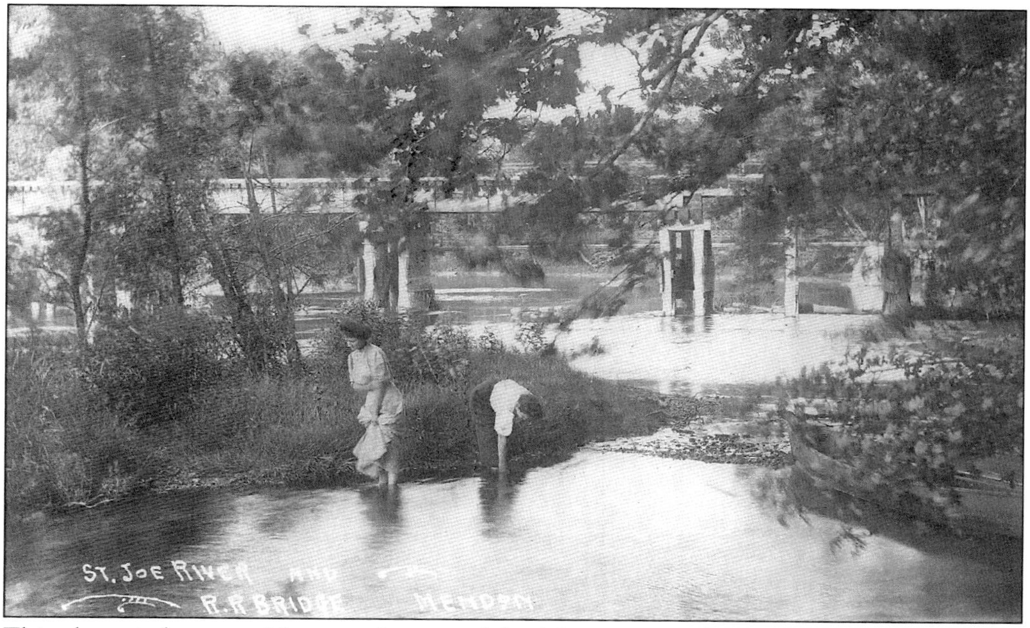

This photo is from an old postcard sent to John Marantette in Pierpont, South Dakota. The Marantettes were a well-established family in St. Joseph County. The postcard, which is dated Sunday July 11th, reads "Dear John I wonder how you are day to day. Received your nice card. Donna M." (Mendon Country Inn Collection.)

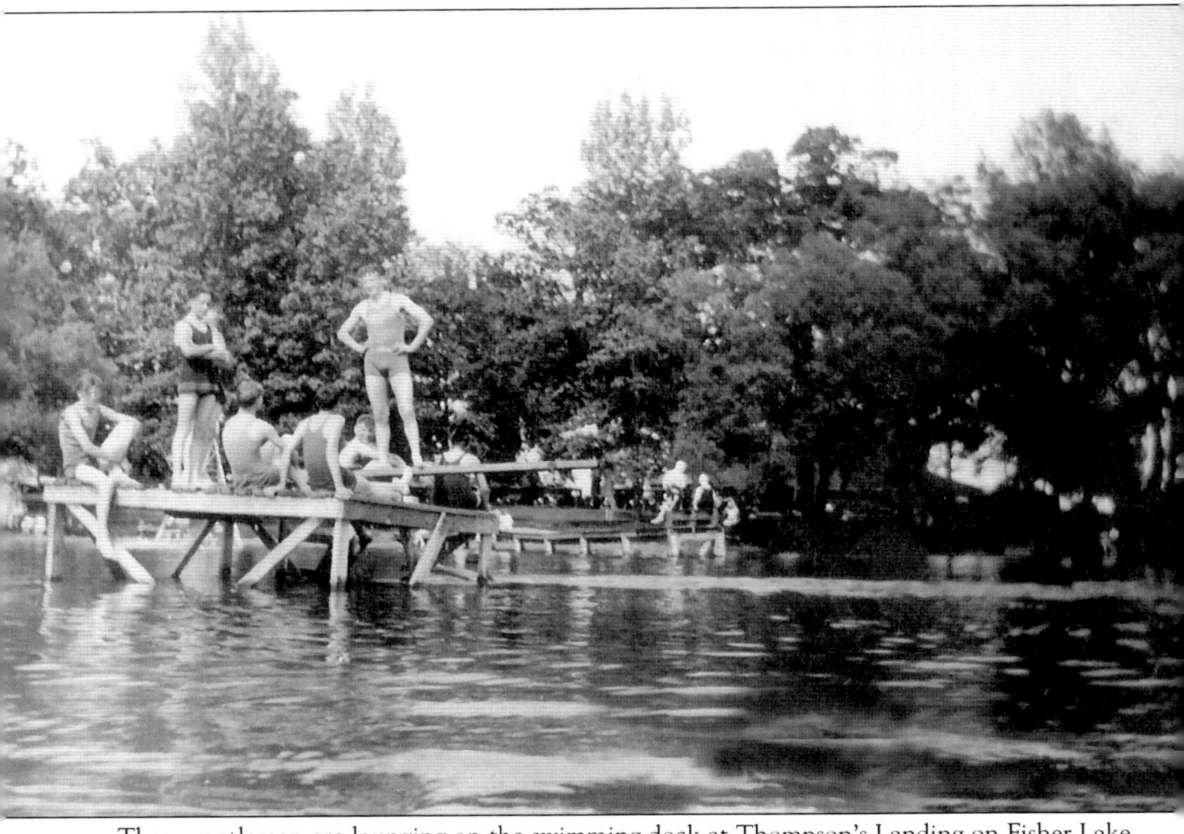

These gentlemen are lounging on the swimming dock at Thompson's Landing on Fisher Lake. The lake was named after Jonas and Leonard Fisher, who helped the first settler on the eastern shores of the lake, Harvey Kinney, build his log cabin. The lake was first settled in 1833 when settlers reneged on a agreement with Native Americans not to settle there until later. In 1834 there was a "fever an' ague" epidemic at the lake. According to contemporary reports, these scratchy wool bathing suits, besides being scratchy, took forever to dry. (Sue Silliman House Museum Collection.)

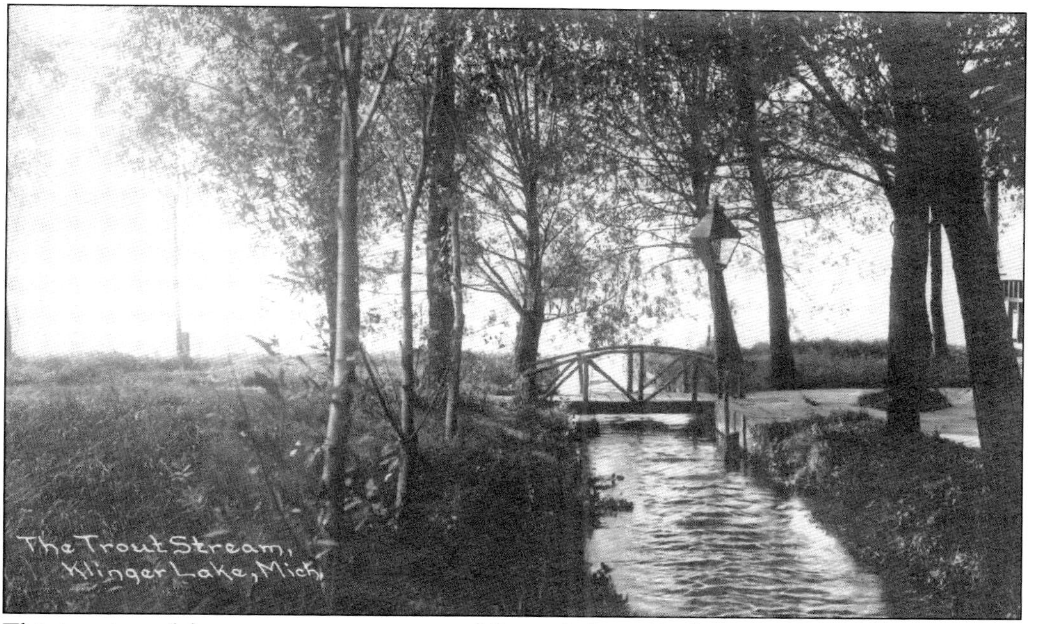

This is a view of the trout stream as it enters Klinger Lake at Benham Beach. (Sturgis Historical Society Collection.)

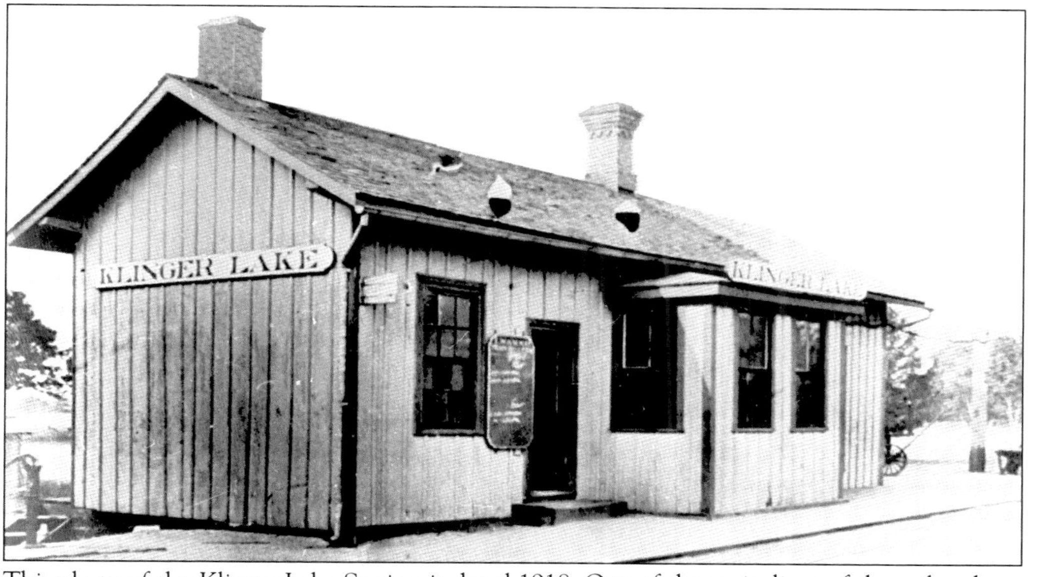

This photo of the Klinger Lake Station is dated 1918. One of the main lines of the railroad ran along the southern edge of Klinger Lake, drawing people from Chicago, to the west, and all the way from Buffalo, New York, to the east. In 1903, the Lake Shore and Michigan Southern Railroad listed the Oakwood Tavern in its Klinger Lake listings. The price was $5.50 per week for adults and $4 per week for children. So many people traveled to Oakwood that a flag stop was established within walking distance of the resort, even though the train made a stop at the Klinger Lake station in the village of Klinger not too far away. (Sturgis Historical Society Collection)

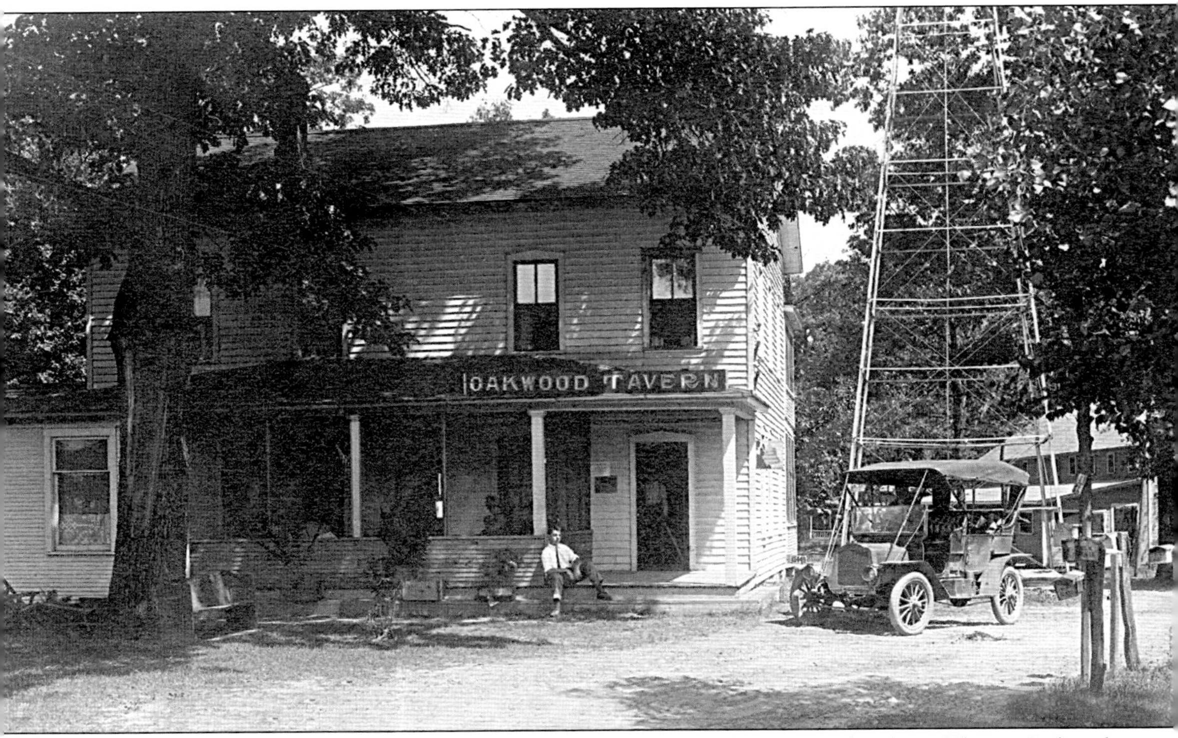

According to St. Joseph County historian Robert Hair, who wrote a book on Klinger Lake, this postcard of the Oakwood Tavern was mailed in Sturgis on December 6, 1910. Klinger Lake was such a popular destination that, according to the June 20, 1907 edition of the *Sturgis Times*, over 800 round-trip tickets from Sturgis to the lake had already been sold that season. (Sturgis Historical Society Collection.)

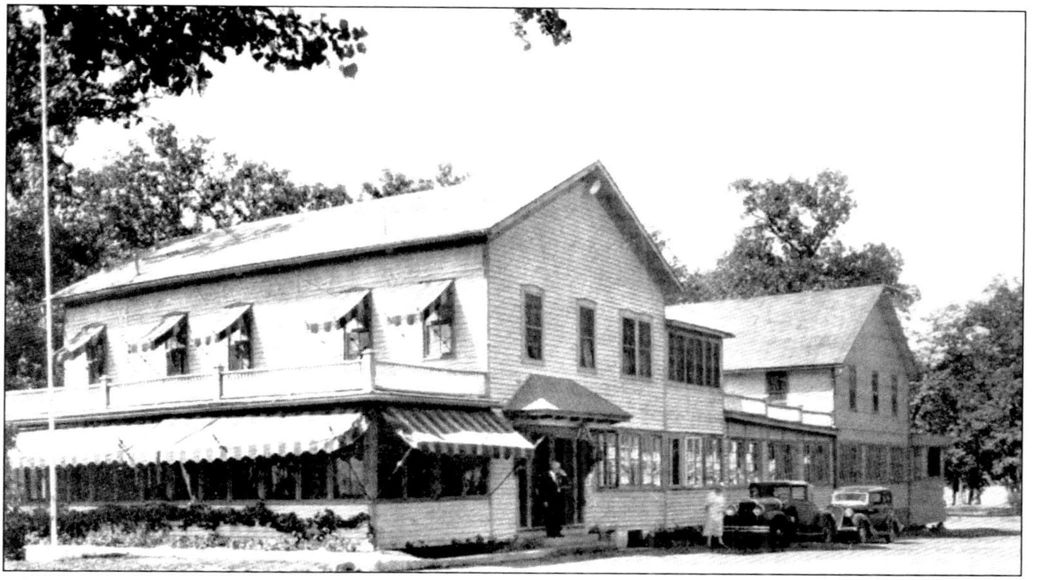

This is another view of the Oakwood Tavern on Klinger Lake. According to historian Robert Hair, around 1875 (long before this photo was taken), a White Pigeon resident named "Cash" Whiteman, whose father ran the bank in White Pigeon, built a saloon known as the Island House on pilings on a 50-foot-square island in the lake. "By squatting on the island," writes Hair in his book on the lake, "Whiteman avoided paying a license fee for serving beer and soft drinks." (Sturgis Historical Society Collection.)

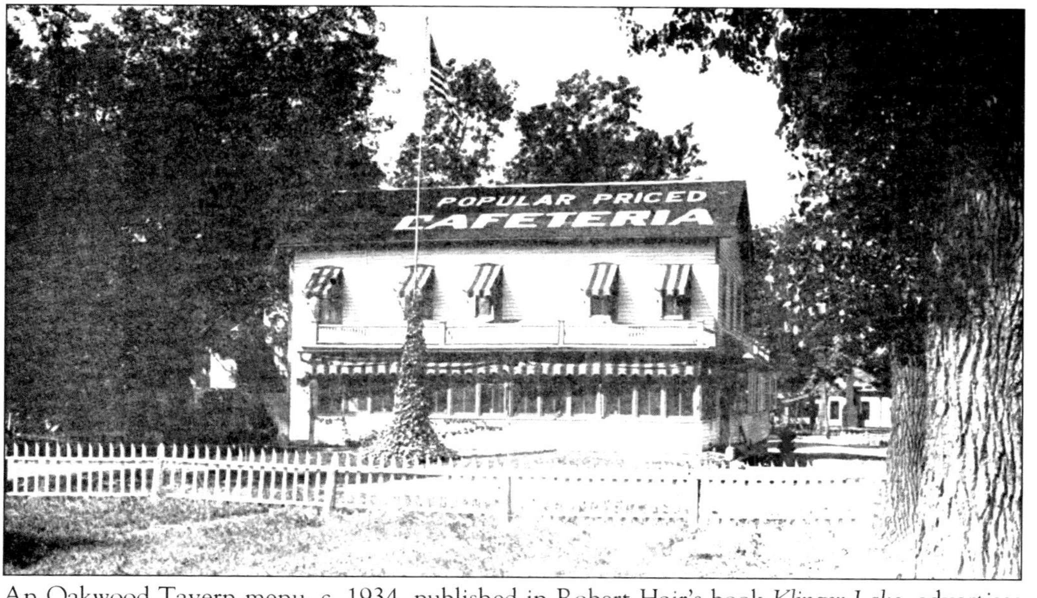

An Oakwood Tavern menu, c. 1934, published in Robert Hair's book *Klinger Lake*, advertises a small steak for 50¢, while a side order of potatoes Lyonnaise would add another 20¢ to the bill. But a bottle (sold in quart sizes) of Pommery & Grecco imported champagne cost $8.50. (Sturgis Historical Society Collection.)

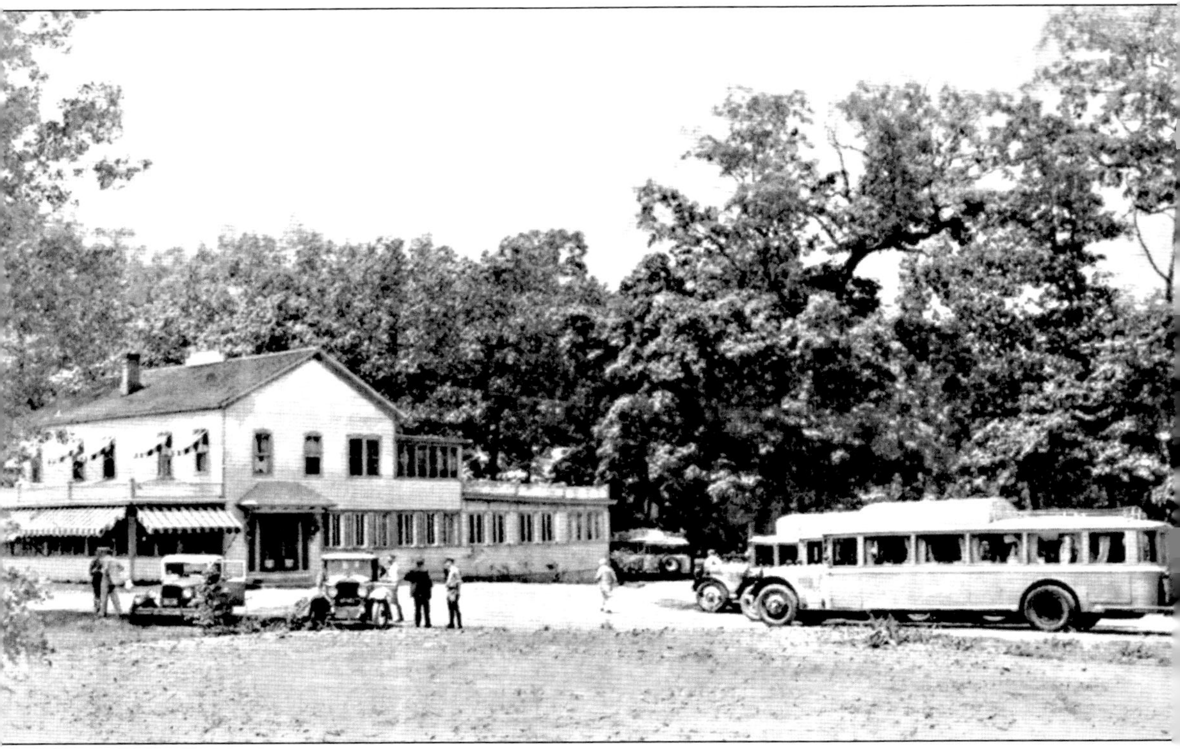

After the end of Prohibition, Greyhound busses frequently made stops at the Oakwood Tavern. There was even a sandwich titled the Greyhound Drivers Special—a combination of chicken salad and bacon, which sold for 30¢. The Greyhound Special—hot egg, tomato, and onion—also cost 30¢. (Sturgis Historical Society Collection.)

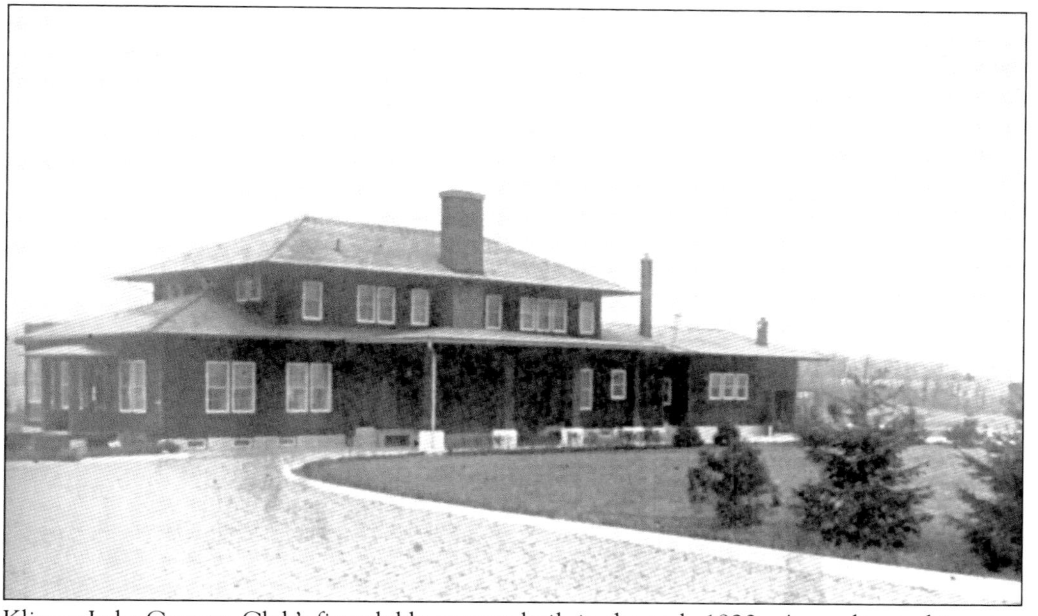

Klinger Lake Country Club's first clubhouse was built in the early 1920s. According to historian Robert Hair, the idea for the golf club is credited to William A. Calvin, a lumber dealer from Sturgis who first played golf while in Florida shortly after World War. I. The clubhouse was destroyed by fire one early Saturday morning on July 31, 1937, and a new one built on this site. (Sturgis Historical Society Collection.)

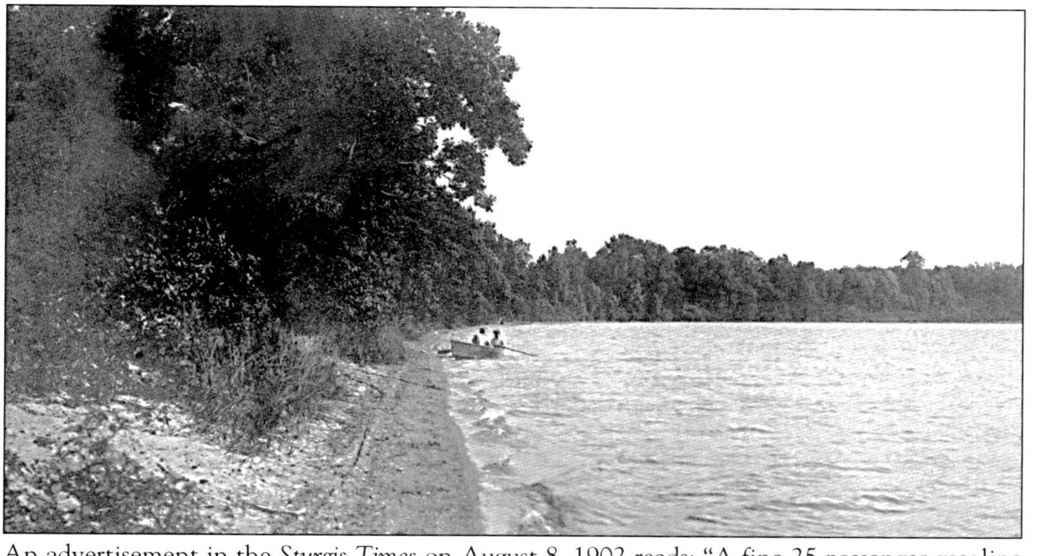

An advertisement in the *Sturgis Times* on August 8, 1902 reads: "A fine 25 passenger gasoline launch has been placed at the disposal of pleasure seekers at Klinger Lake by Capt. A.A. McLauchlin of Coldwater. A powerful 3-cylinder, 18 h.p. engine drives the launch at high speed and makes a tour of the lake one of the pleasantest features of recreation at this beautiful resort. Capt. McLauchlin also has a large number of fine rowboats at Mineral Springs resort to let for fishing and pleasure." Note the wagon trail that parallels the shoreline. (Sturgis Historical Society Collection.)

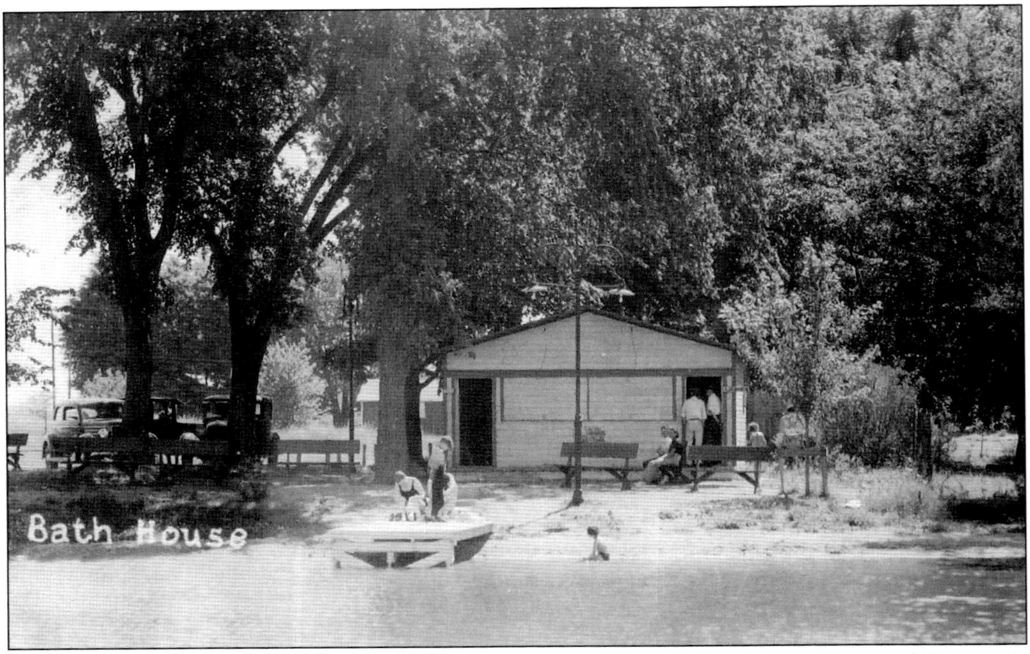

Sand Lake in Nottawa was also a popular destination. The old Sand Lake Men and Women's Bath House, shown here in a photo from the 1930s, was just recently torn down. (Steve Zazra Collection.)

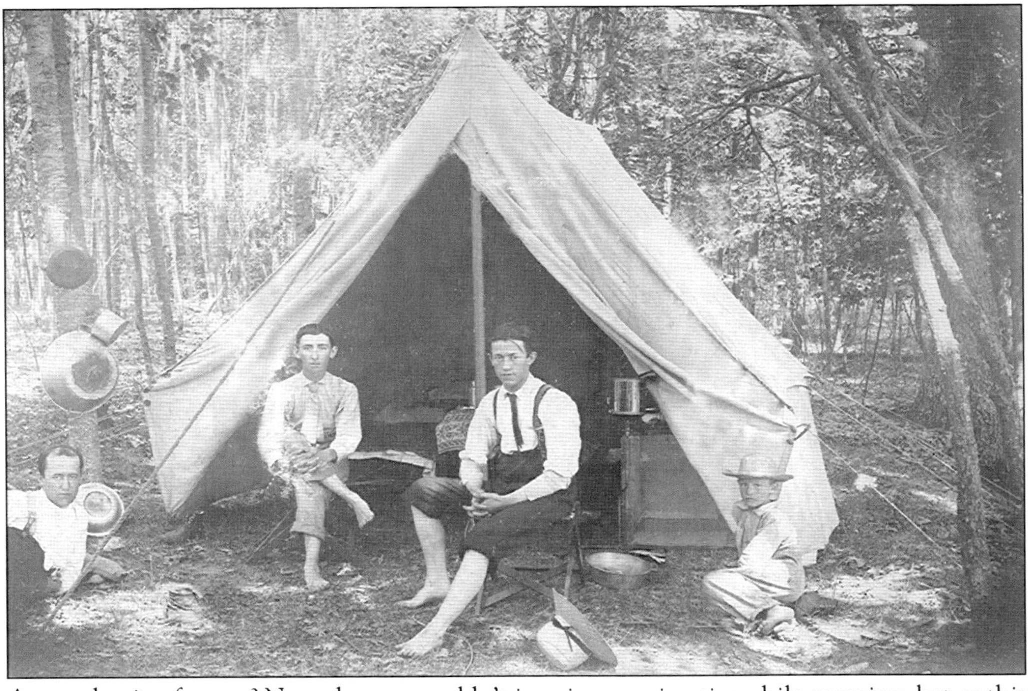

Are we having fun yet? Nowadays we couldn't imagine wearing ties while camping, but as this photo, courtesy of the Three Rivers Public Library, shows, it certainly seems the norm back in the early 1900s.

Two

PERSONALITIES

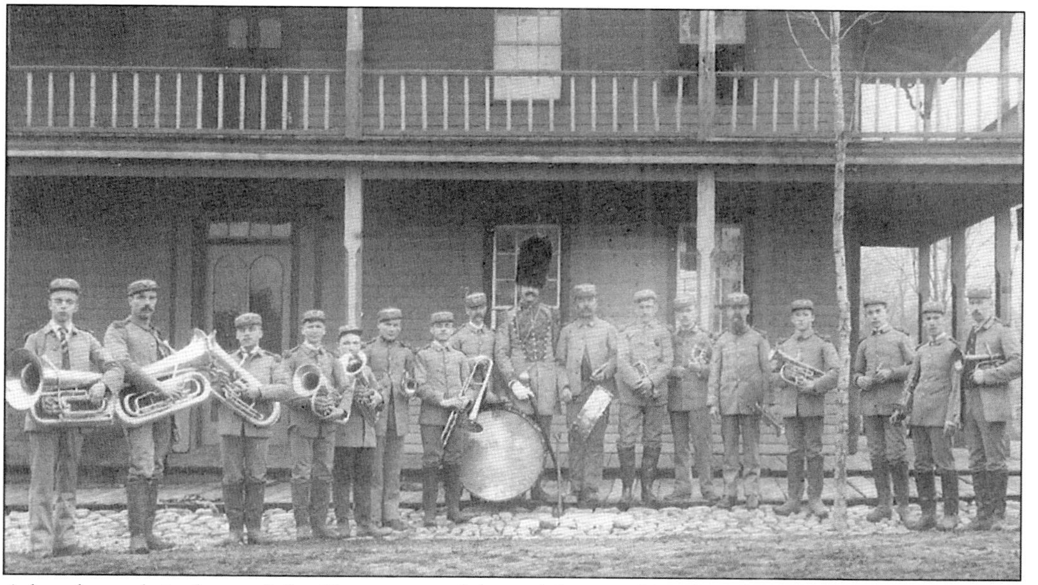

A band stands in front of the Constantine Mineral Springs Hotel in the 1880s. The bandleader was Frank Crossette, who, according to Dr. M.E.Vercler of Constantine, was an extremely talented musician who at a very young age could write marches and other musical compositions as easily as others could write words. Constantine had one of the earliest bands and orchestras in this part of the state and their band was so highly regarded that they traveled to the state capital in Lansing to play for the governor's inauguration. The town was a popular tourist destination because of its location on the St. Joseph River and its beneficial mineral waters. (Governor Barry House Collection.)

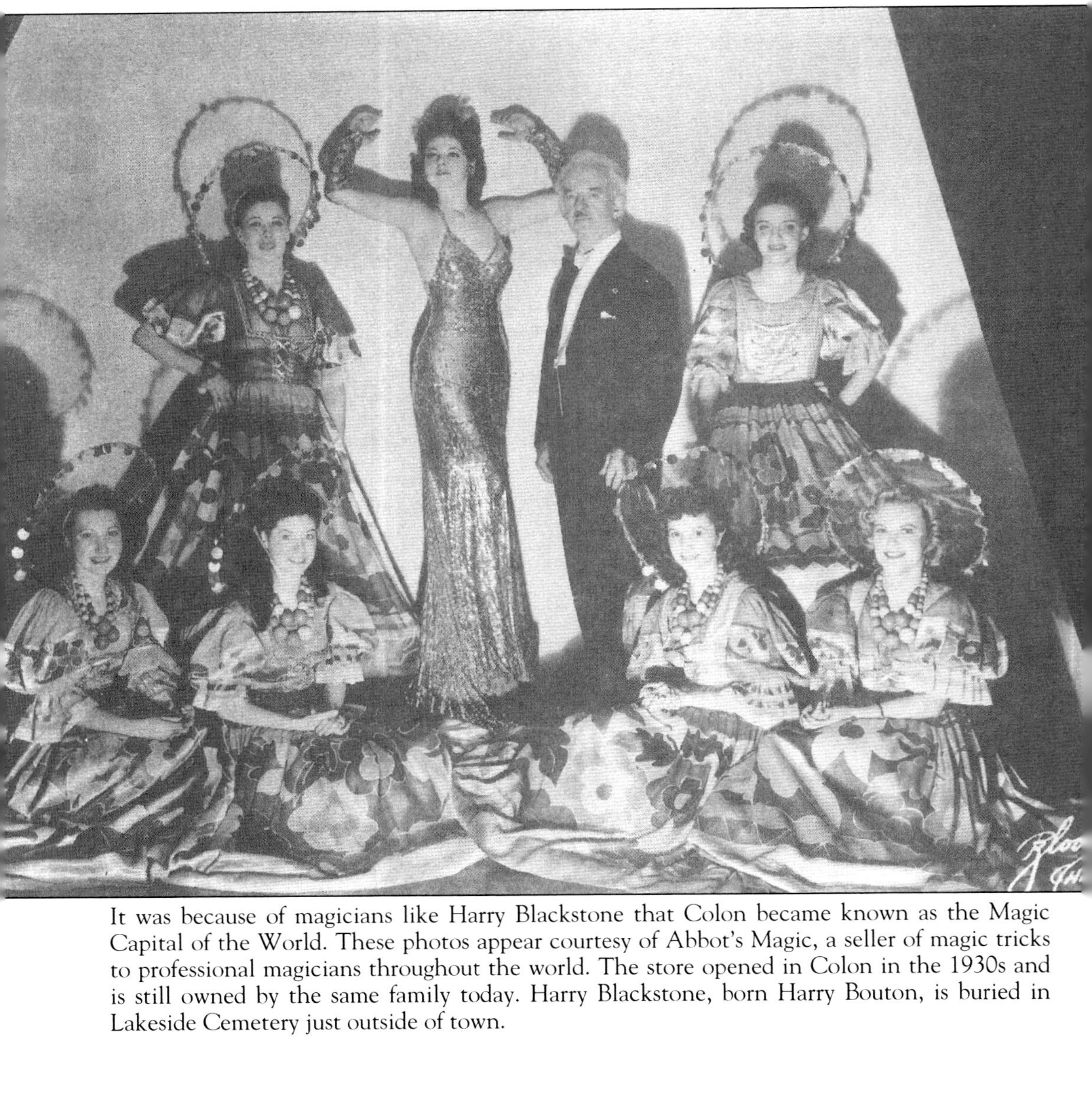

It was because of magicians like Harry Blackstone that Colon became known as the Magic Capital of the World. These photos appear courtesy of Abbot's Magic, a seller of magic tricks to professional magicians throughout the world. The store opened in Colon in the 1930s and is still owned by the same family today. Harry Blackstone, born Harry Bouton, is buried in Lakeside Cemetery just outside of town.

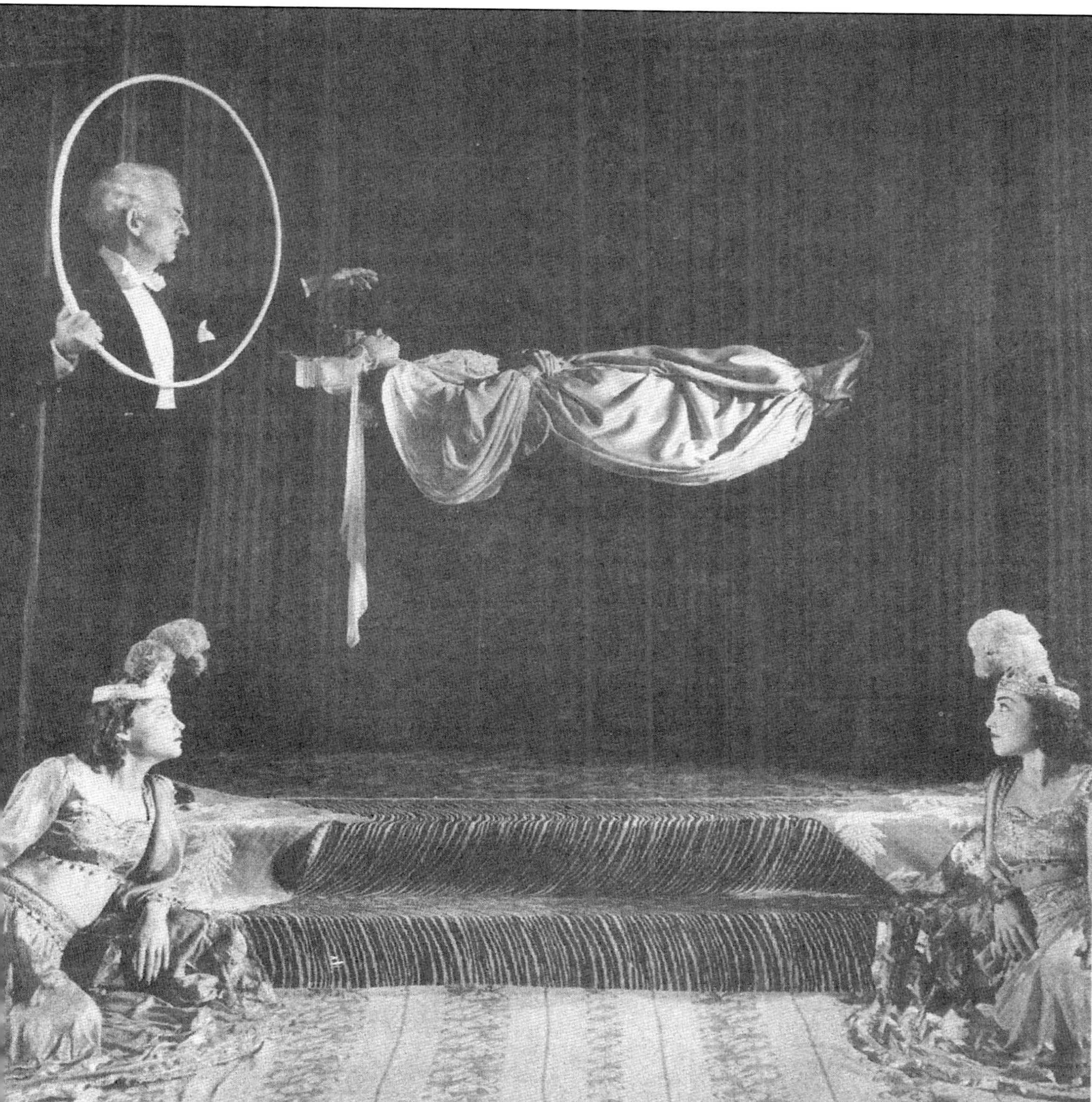

Harry Blackstone was probably the most well-known magician in America in the 1930s. Many of his tricks have become classics, but probably the best one was performed in 1942 when Blackstone was performing at the Lincoln Theater in Decatur, Illinois. During the middle of his performance he told his audience that in order to see his next trick they would have to quietly leave the theater and go into the street. Blackstone helped the audience leave the building. Only when they were outside did they learn that the trick had been played on them in order to assure their safety—Blackstone, knowing the theater was on fire, had managed to avert chaos and panic with his "trick." (Abbott's Magic.)

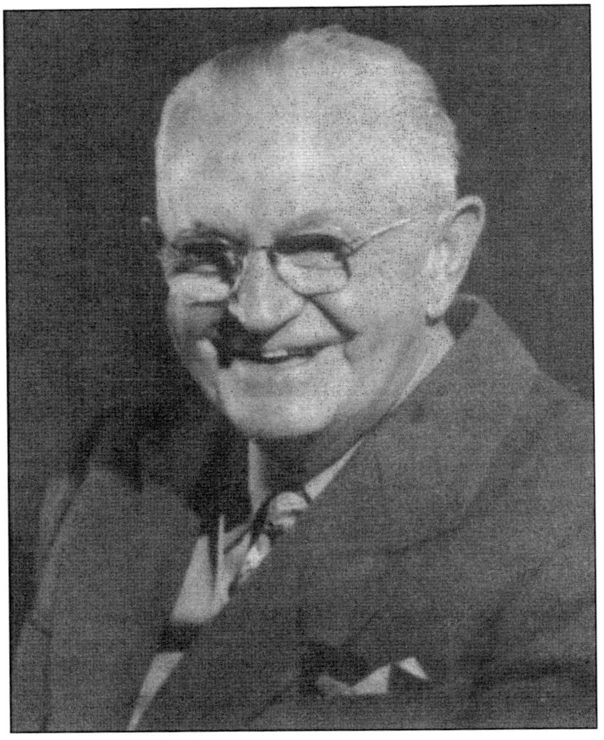

Donald Monk was born in Colon on March 23, 1894. He was a band director and vaudeville star who helped to give Bob Hope his start. Of himself, he wrote: "At age 8, I did my first show playing clarinet in the local church and performing a couple tricks of magic. I took a bow, backed up a couple of steps and fell into a Baptismal tank. If there had been water in it, I would have been a Baptist." (Abbott's Magic.)

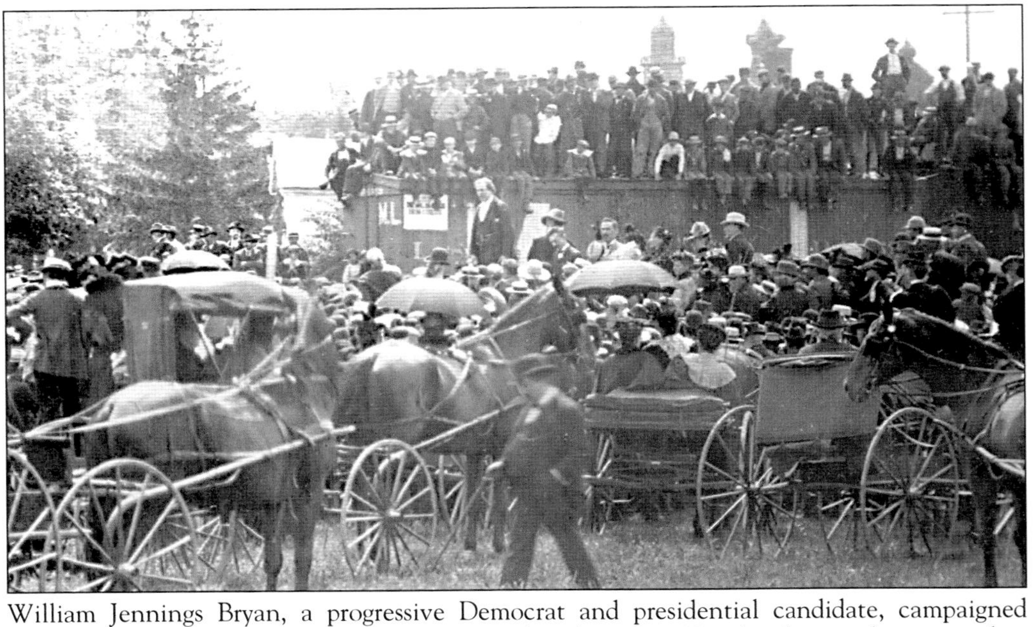

William Jennings Bryan, a progressive Democrat and presidential candidate, campaigned throughout the Midwest in the late 1800s and early 1900s. He also frequently appeared at the Chautauquas, which were popular in Michigan and Indiana. Chautauqua is an Iroquois word that means "two moccasins tied together," or "jumping fish." This name was given to an institution which sought to provide higher education opportunities through lectures, concerts, and public events. Traveling Chautauqaus also featured oratory, drama, and music.

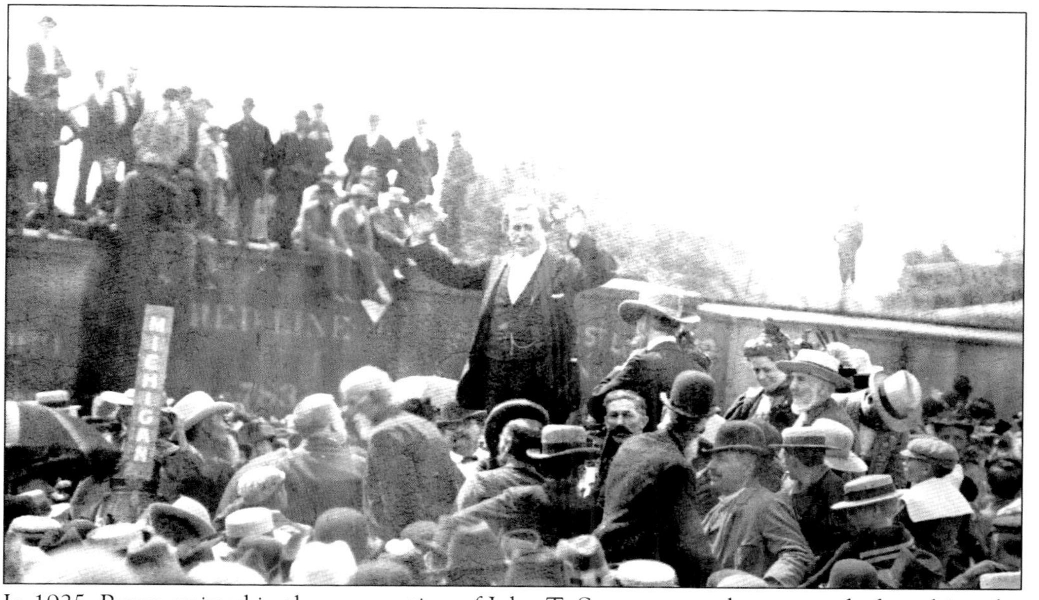

In 1925, Bryan assisted in the prosecution of John T. Scopes, a teacher accused of teaching the theory of evolution in school. Shortly after winning his case, Bryan died. It was his opponent—and the losing attorney—Clarence Darrow, who is best remembered from the trial. (Sturgis Historical Society Collection.)

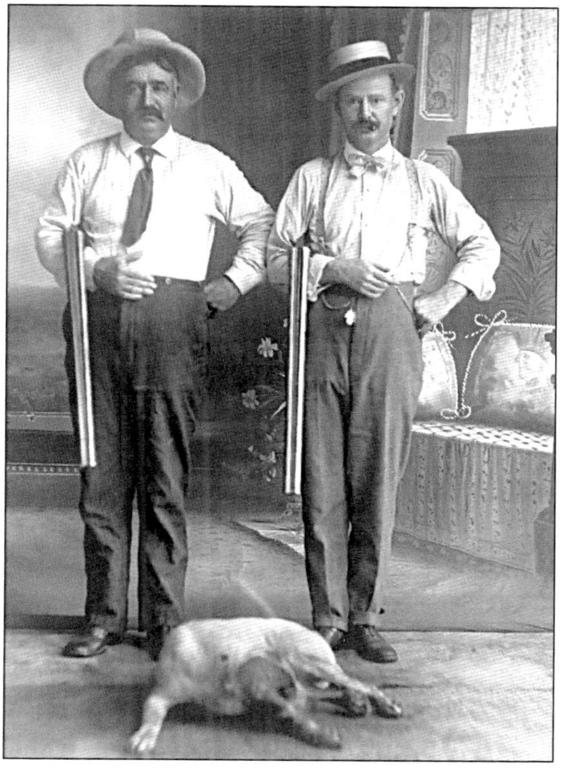

Dapper with their broad-brimmed hats, these two men pose with their guns and their dog. St. Joseph County, with its abundant woods and prairies, is a favorite region for hunters even today, but back then the land was so full of timber wolves and prairie coyotes that a bounty was placed on them. (Three Rivers Library collection.)

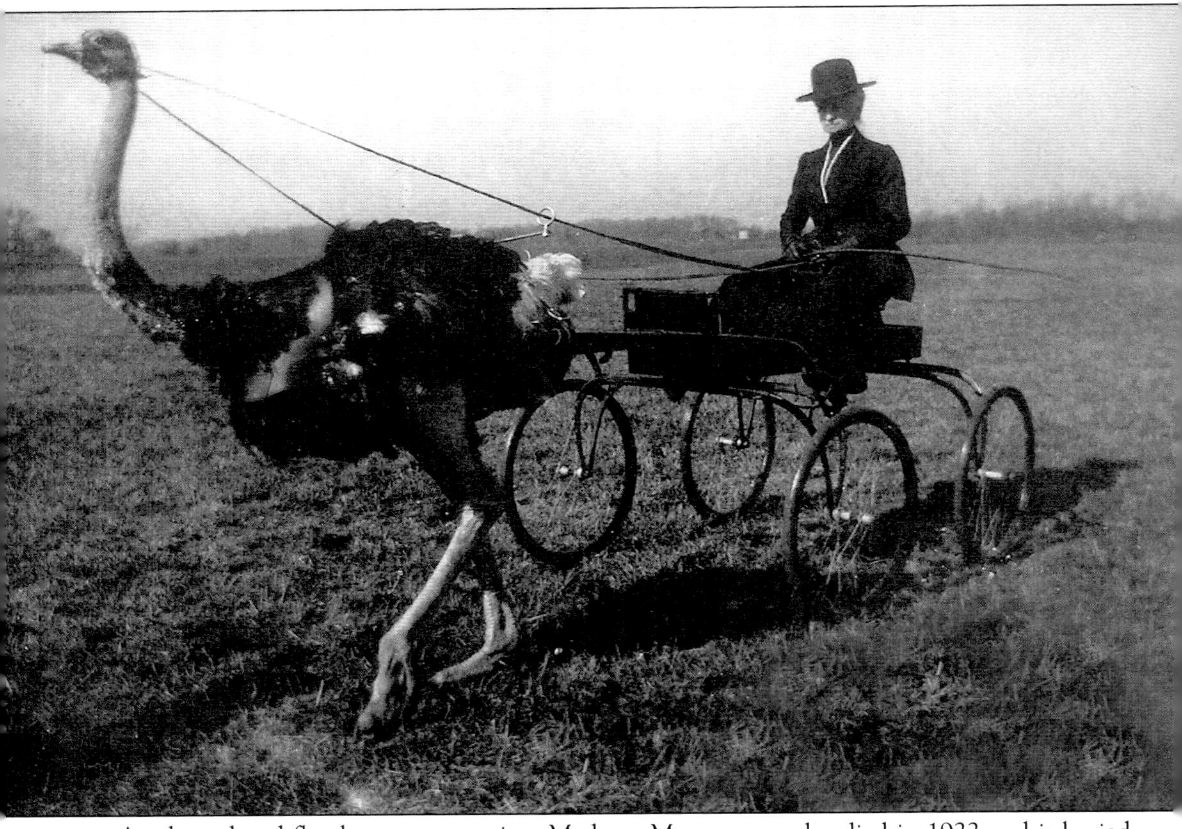

A talented and flamboyant equestrian, Madame Marantette, who died in 1922 and is buried, along with her dog, in the St. Edwards Catholic Cemetery in Mendon, set the high jump record of 7 feet and 10 and one-quarter inches while riding sidesaddle. Her trotting ostrich, Gaucho, may be the only ostrich ever trained to drive hitched with a horse—also owned by the Madame. Gaucho. The horse, Bonnie Anne, established a record in Detroit in 1913. (Dick Cripe Collection.)

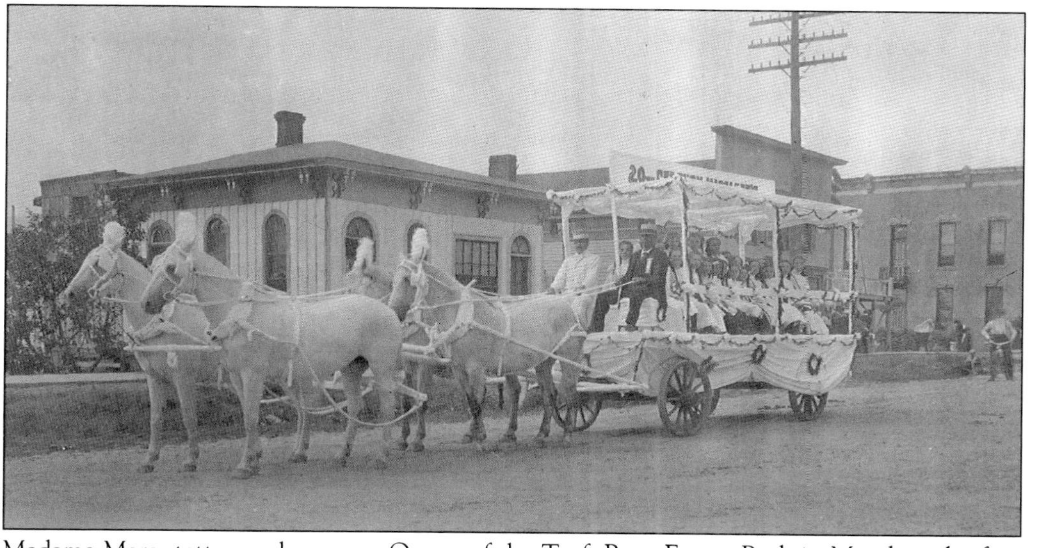

Madame Marantette was known as Queen of the Turf. Born Emma Peek in Mendon, she first married a Marantette, of the very well-known Mendon family and then, later, married Colonel D.H. Harris. According to an old newspaper article, in 1855 she made her first appearance as the driver of a team of thoroughbred running horses at Poughkeepsie, New York, where she made a mile in 1:49. Later that year, she broke her own record. (Dick Cripe Collection.)

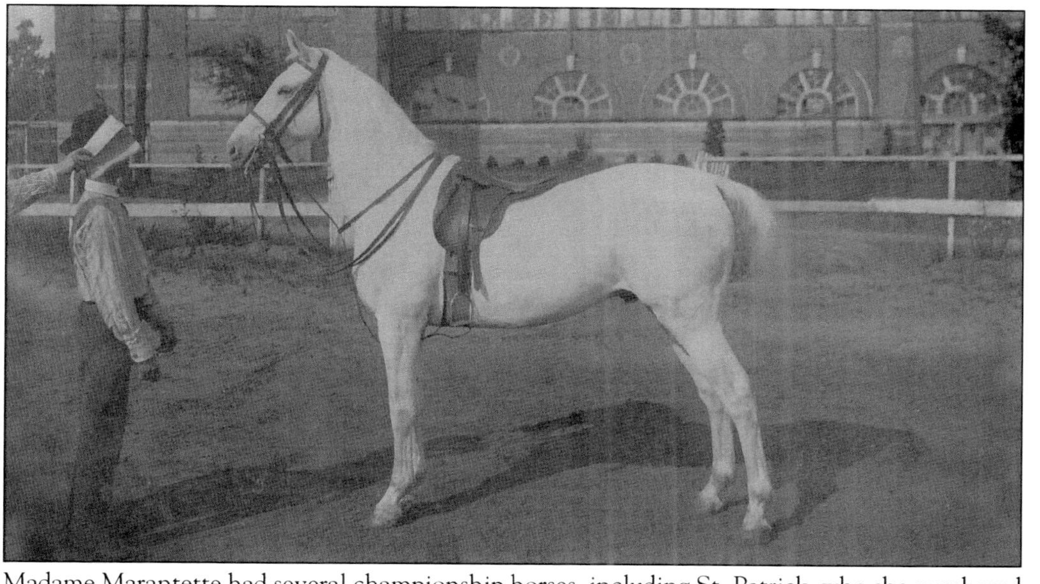

Madame Marantette had several championship horses, including St. Patrick, who she purchased in Dublin, Ireland, and Sunflower and Chief Geronimo, who she bought while in Saudi Arabia. This is one of her horses but his name is unknown to us. Madame was known throughout the country for her expertise with horses, and she traveled to England with the Barnum and Bailey Circus. According to www.findagrave.com, a year after her death, when the circus passed through town, they made a stop and the performers marched to St. Edward's Cemetery in Mendon to pay their respects and place a wreath on her grave. (Dick Cripe Collection.)

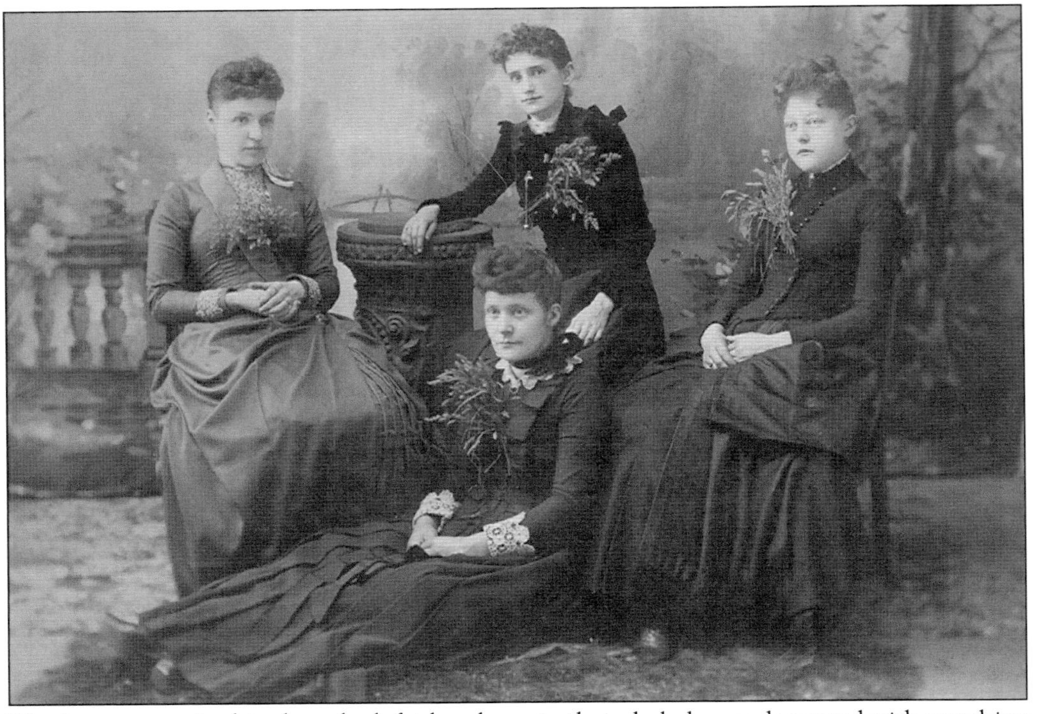

The four women in this photo look fairly solemn in their dark dresses decorated with matching corsages. (Three Rivers Library Collection.)

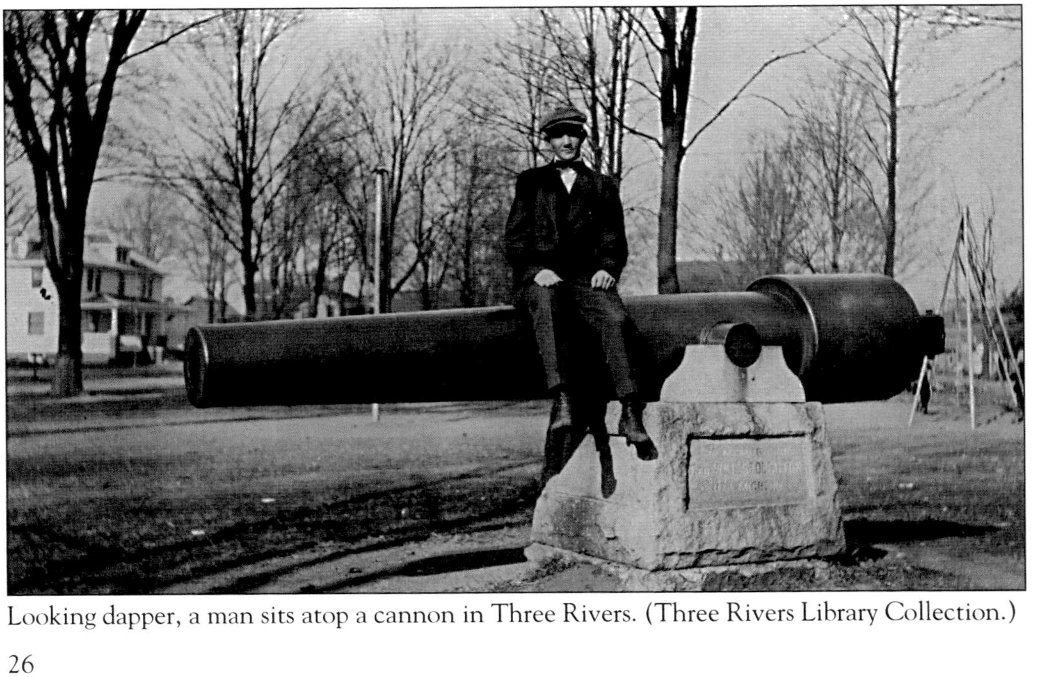

Looking dapper, a man sits atop a cannon in Three Rivers. (Three Rivers Library Collection.)

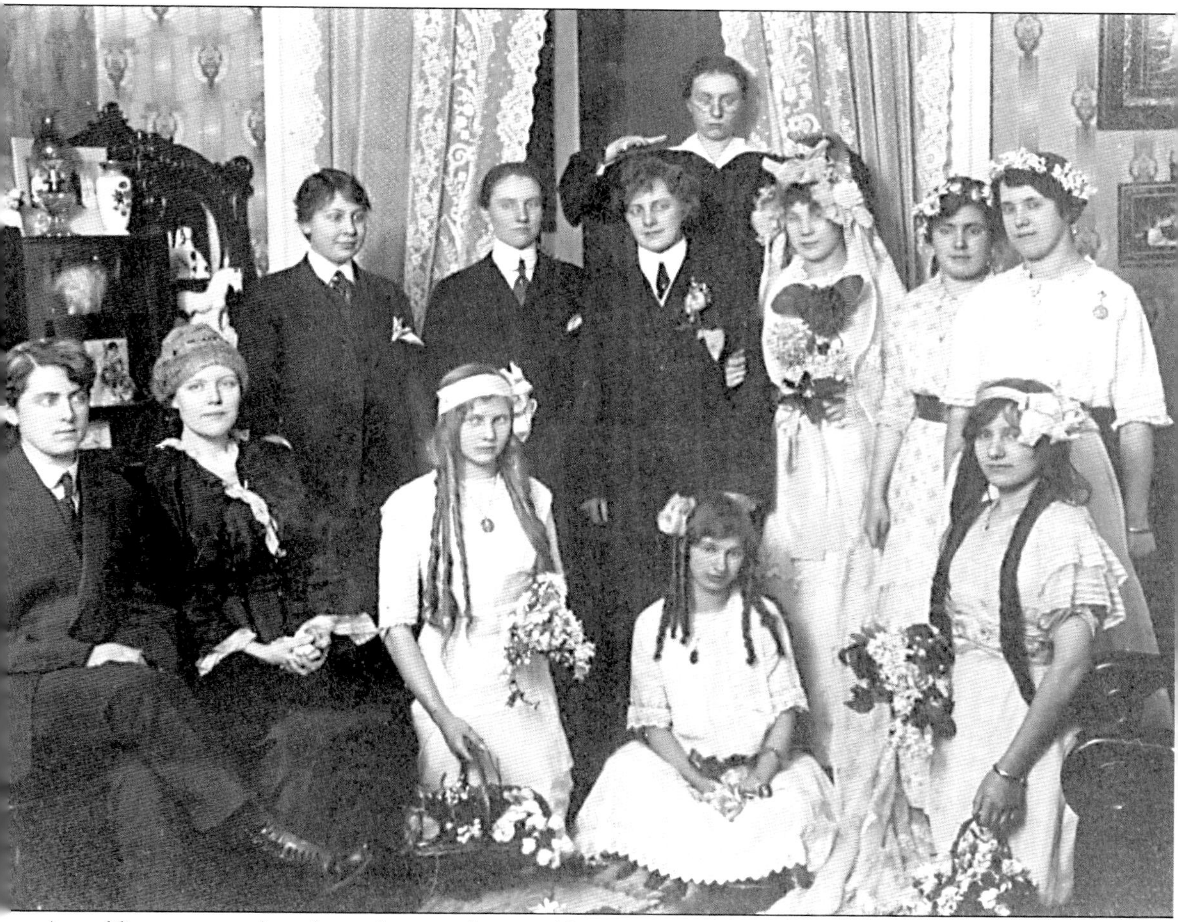

A wedding party gathers for a photo in Sturgis. (Sturgis Historical Society Collection.)

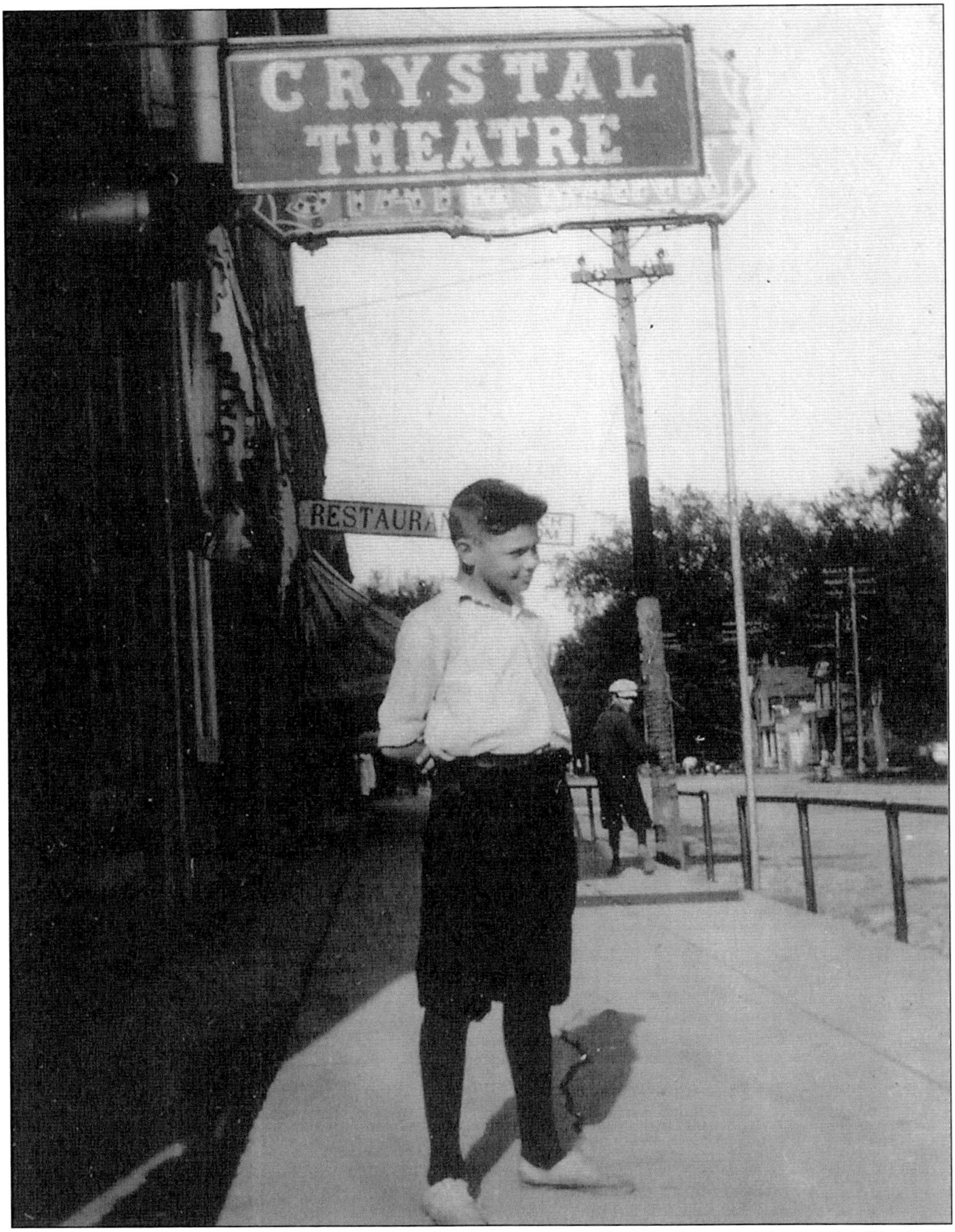

This is a photo of Ed Mosher as a young boy. Born in Centreville, Mosher was educated at Ypsilanti High School because his parents, according to historian Dick Cripe, believed that he would have a better education there than at the local school. He then attended the University of Michigan and Columbia University, and additionally studied in Europe as a violinist. Mosher coordinated music for the Dearborn Public School system in Dearborn, Michigan. When he retired, he returned to Centreville, where he passed away at the age of 97. (Dick Cripe Collection.)

This photo of a nurse was taken in the late 1800s in Three Rivers. (Butch Davis Collection.)

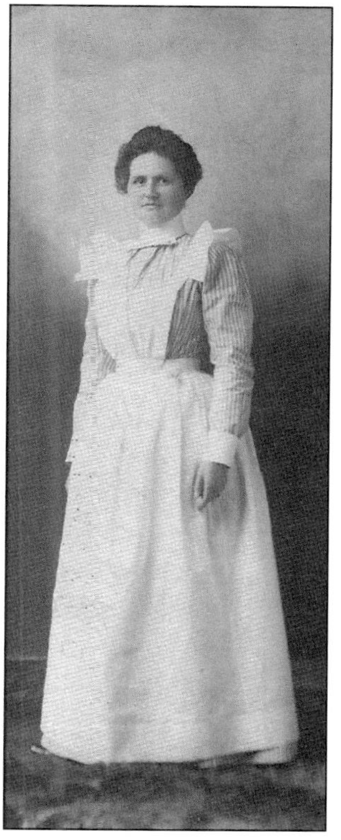

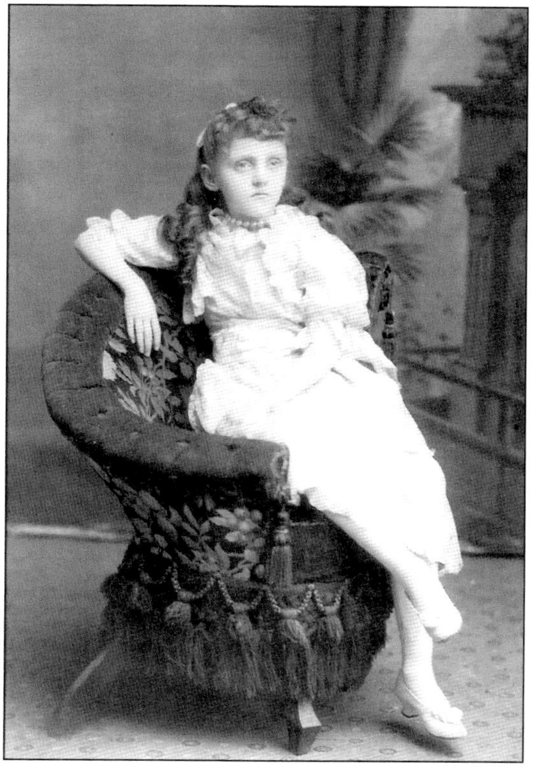

An unknown girl stares pensively towards the camera. The chair and her attire date the photo to the late 1800s. (Governor Barry House Collection.)

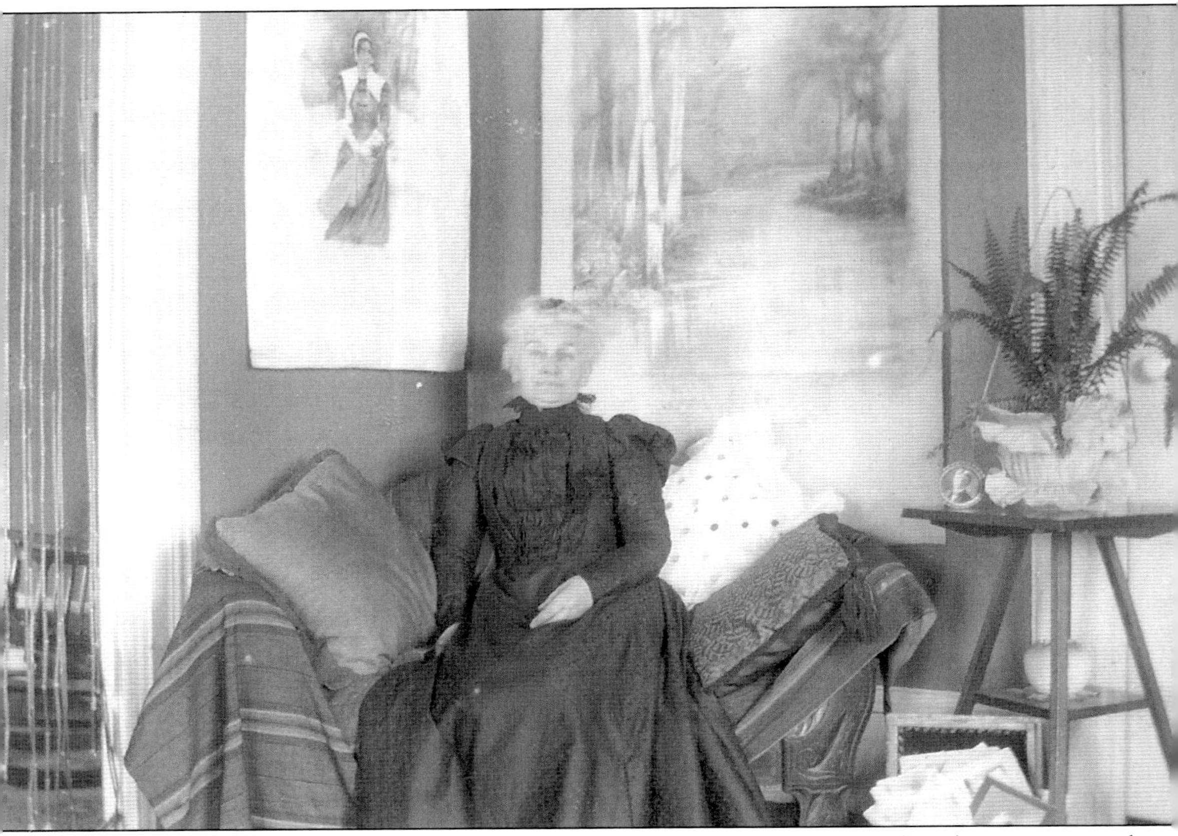

Mary Silliman is pictured in a moment of repose. She and her husband Arthur were pivotal in the development of Three Rivers, and their home, now a museum and named after their daughter, still stands on the St. Joseph River. (Sue Silliman House Museum Collection.)

This photo shows Arthur Silliman, an early pioneer in the area. In an excerpt from his daughter Sue's book, *St. Joseph in Homespun*, she describes the family immigration to this county: "The Silliman family left White Deer Valley, Pennsylvania, in 1847 and were four weeks in covered wagons on the way. The odd diary kept by the father, Alexander Silliman, includes even the prescriptions given by the family doctor, anticipating all the ills to which the flesh is heir. We do not know whether these directions were the cause or cure of conditions mentioned in a letter by Thomas Silliman, the oldest son. 'We are in the Black Swamp. Father has the pleurisy, was bled, is better; Mother, Mary Jane and Arthur are having chills; Brady has one every other day. James is keeping up on Jane's alterative.'" Eventually the family arrived and settled on the old Buckhorn road. (Sue Silliman House Museum Collection.)

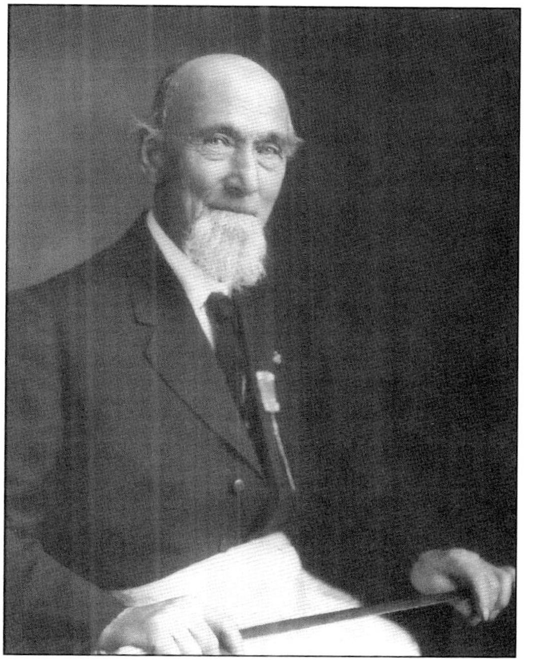

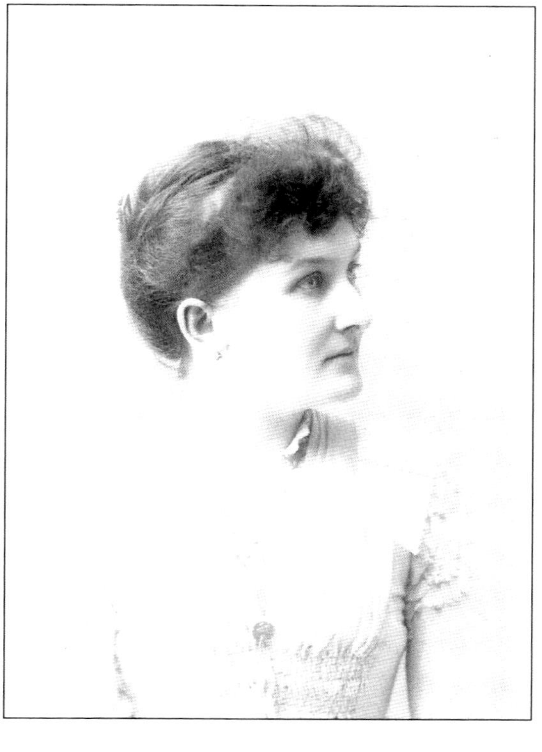

Sue Silliman was a Three Rivers librarian and historian for 42 years. During that time she also served on national, state, and local boards of the Daughters of the American Revolution. Before passing away in 1945, she donated her papers, the books she wrote, including *St. Joseph in Homespun*, published in 1931, and her home, to the people of Three Rivers. To this day, she remains highly regarded. (Sue Silliman House Museum Collection.)

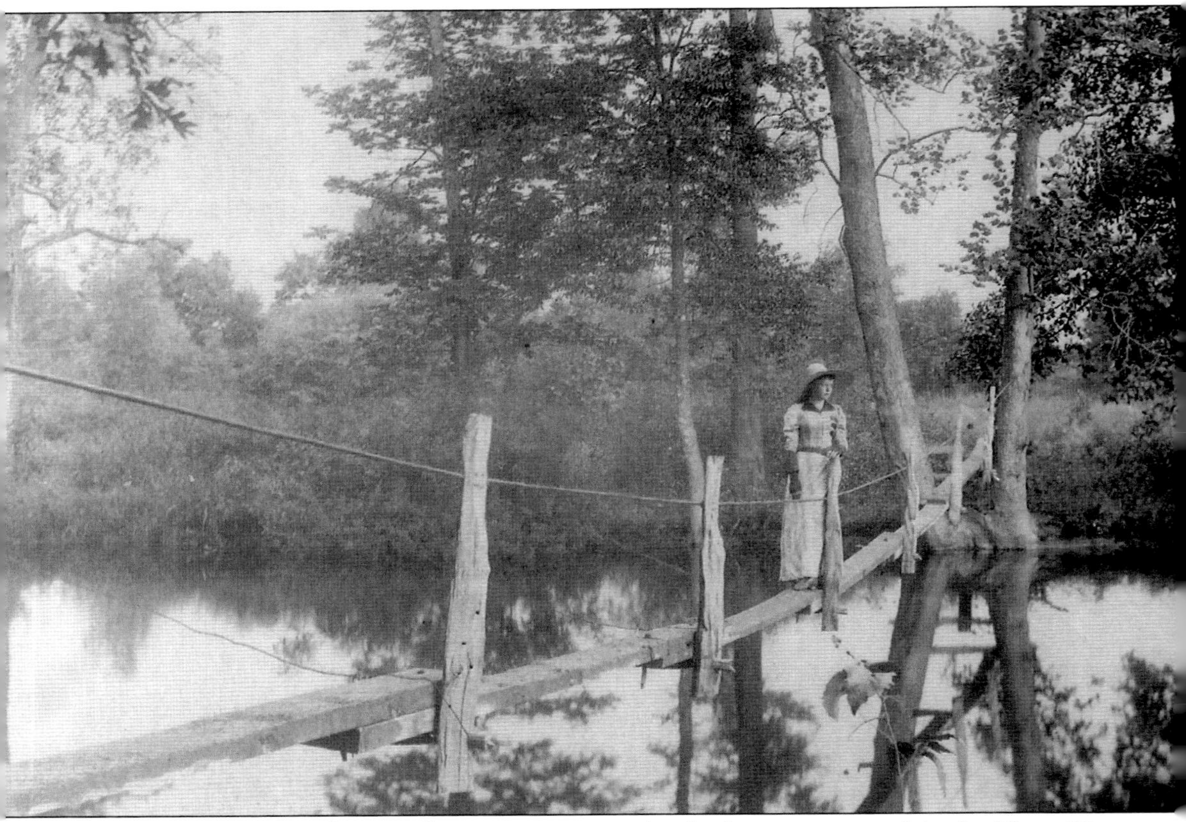

A young woman takes a walk on a narrow wooden bridge across a pond in the Three Rivers area. This photo, most likely taken in the late 1800s, shows how much clothing has changed in the last century or so. (Sue Silliman House Museum Collection.)

This is a photo of Frank Hepner of Centreville. Frank and his brother, Chris, manufactured hot air balloons, building their first in an area barn. As their balloons became more popular, they moved their business to the corner of Chicago Road and Nottawa Street in Sturgis. (Dick Cripe Collection.)

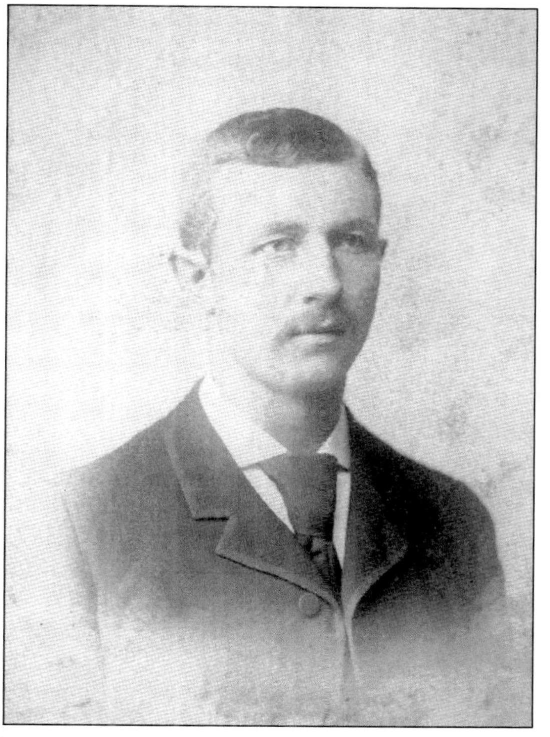

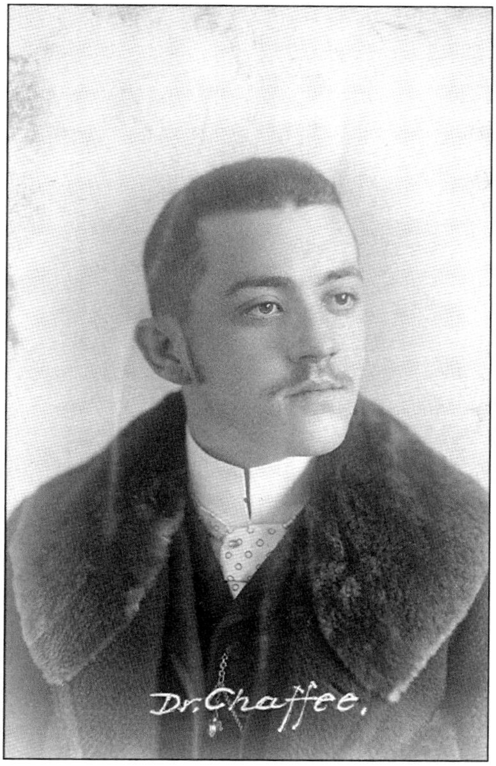

This is a photo of Dr. Walter Chaffe of Three Rivers. (Three Rivers Library Collection.)

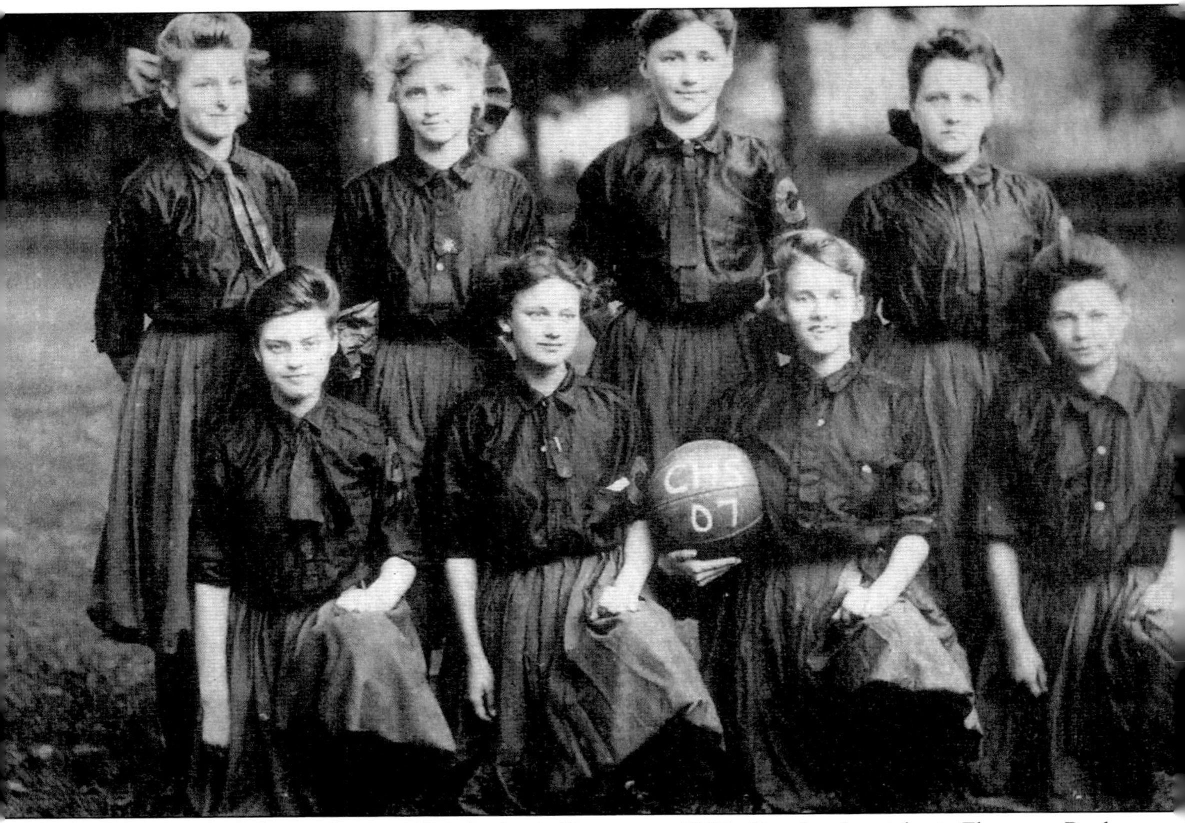

This photo shows Centreville's basketball team in 1907. On the far right is Florence Butler, whose name became Hall after she was married. Dick Cripe describes her as a strong community member who was first the Latin teacher and then later the school principal at Centreville. Her sister's husband, Lester Schrader, along with another local man, Howard Bucknell, rescued the financially failing county fair after it went bankrupt. (Dick Cripe Collection.)

Three

City Life

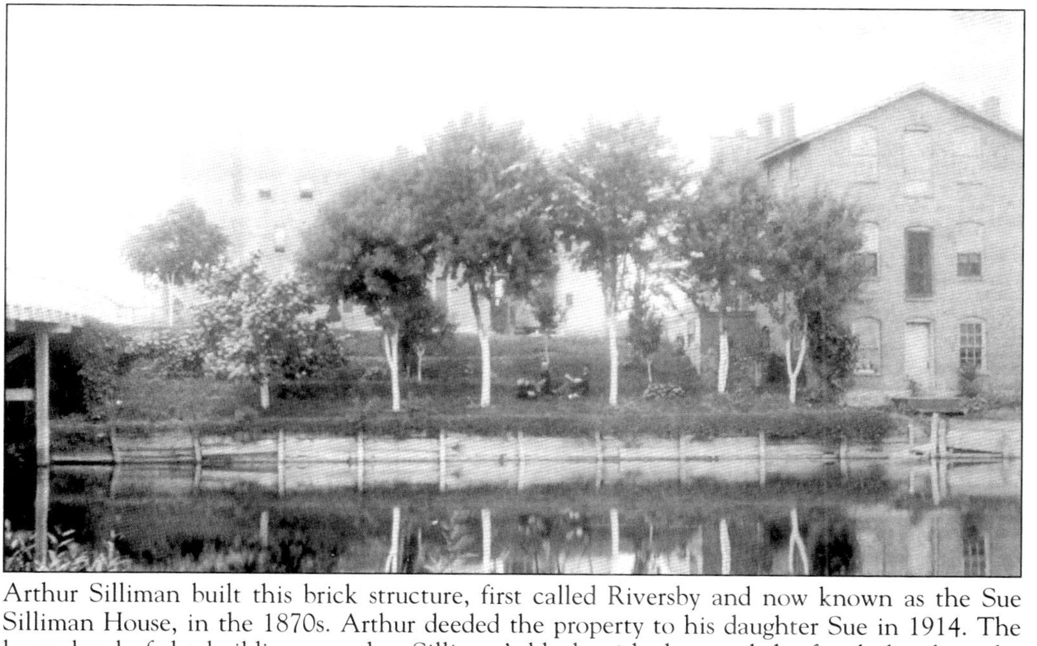

Arthur Silliman built this brick structure, first called Riversby and now known as the Sue Silliman House, in the 1870s. Arthur deeded the property to his daughter Sue in 1914. The lower level of the building served as Silliman's blacksmith shop and the family lived on the upper stories. Situated on the St. Joseph River, the home is near the place where a Potawatomi Indian trail crossed the St. Joseph. It is on the Michigan Register of Historic Places. (Sue Silliman House Museum Collection.)

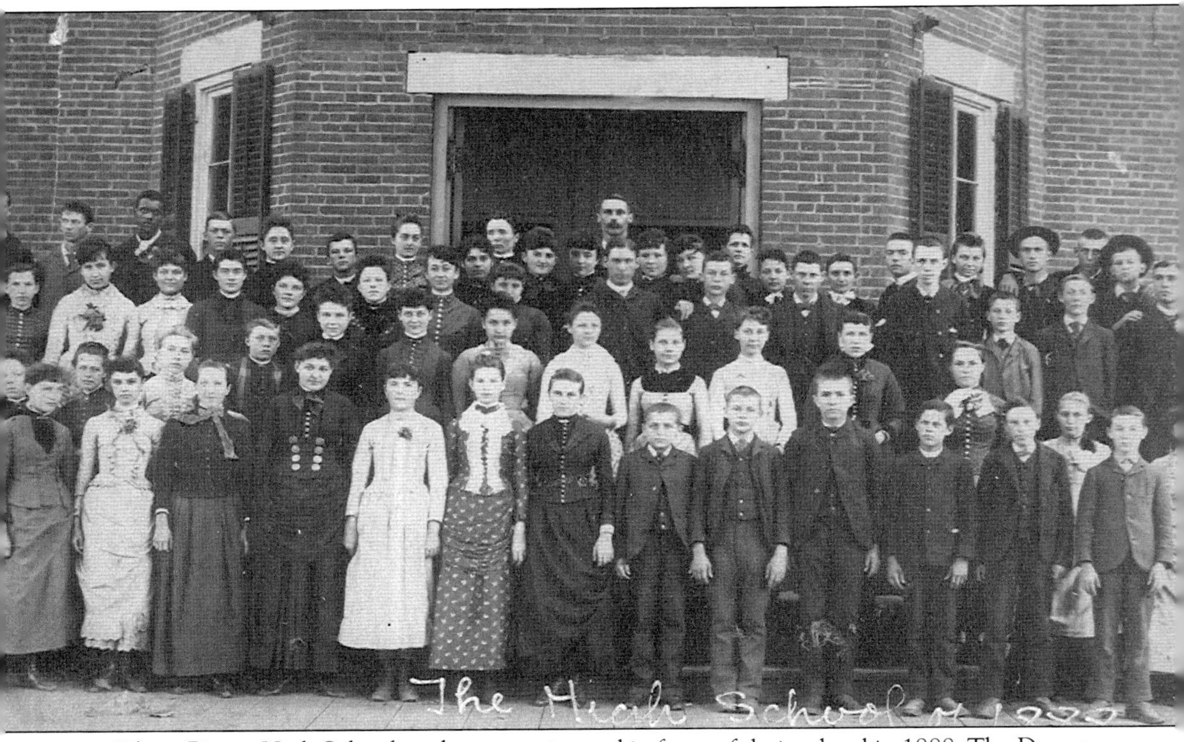

Three Rivers High School students are pictured in front of their school in 1888. The Downtown Three Rivers Commercial Historic District is on both the Michigan and the National Registers of Historic Places. (Three Rivers Library Collection.)

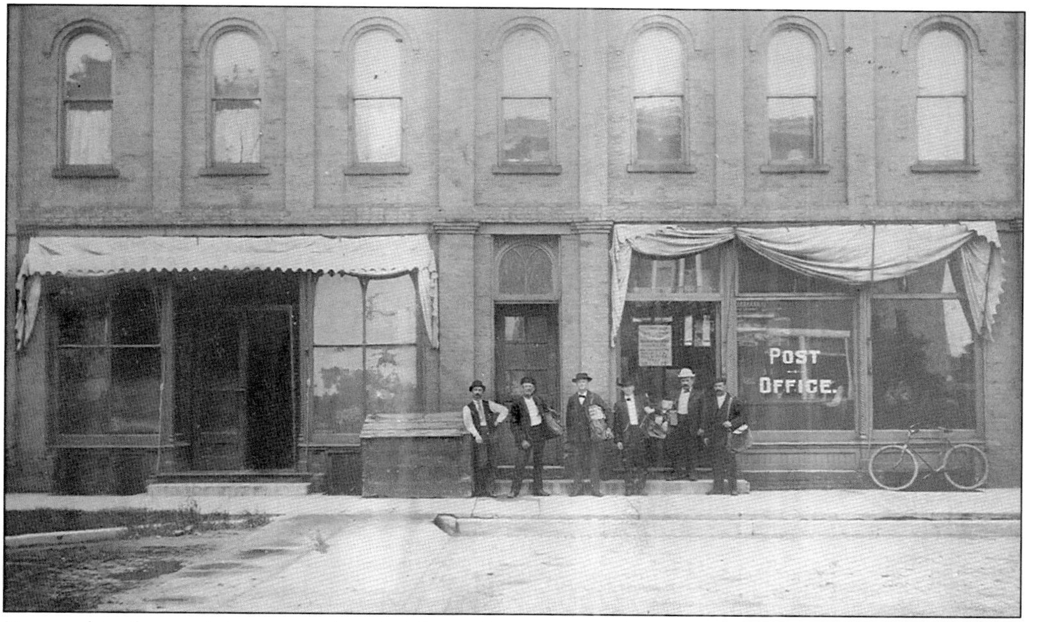

Pictured in front of the post office in Three Rivers, according to a note attached to the photo, are rural carriers "Zete" Walton, William Brewer, John Fulcher, Morris Wetherbee, Jim Waltz, and Charles Bittings. (Three Rivers Library Collection.)

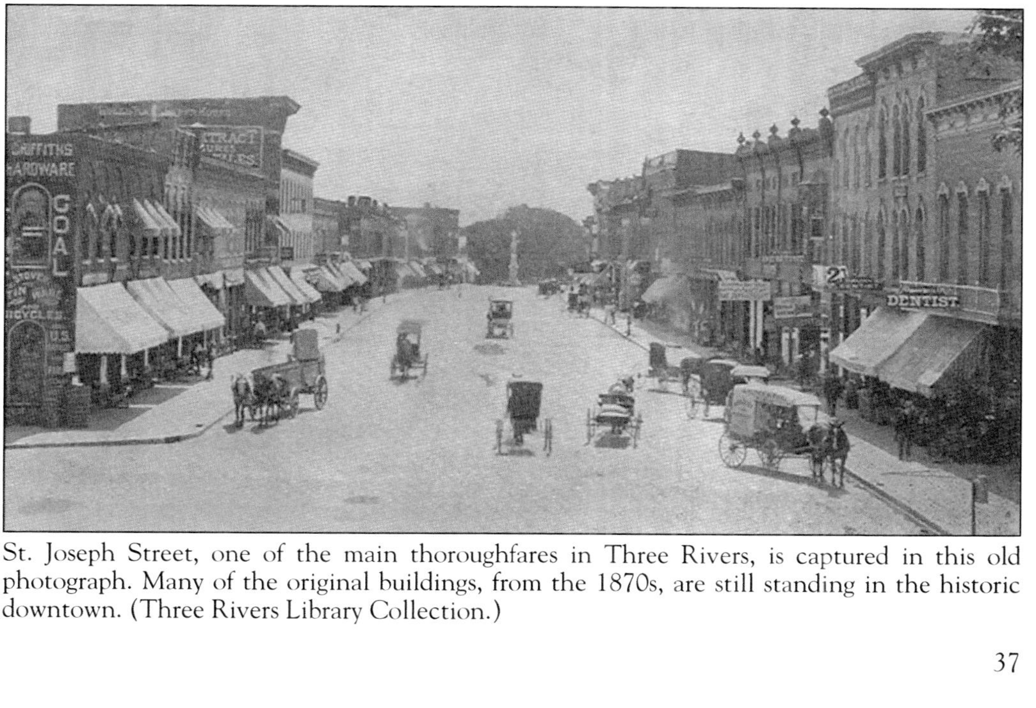

St. Joseph Street, one of the main thoroughfares in Three Rivers, is captured in this old photograph. Many of the original buildings, from the 1870s, are still standing in the historic downtown. (Three Rivers Library Collection.)

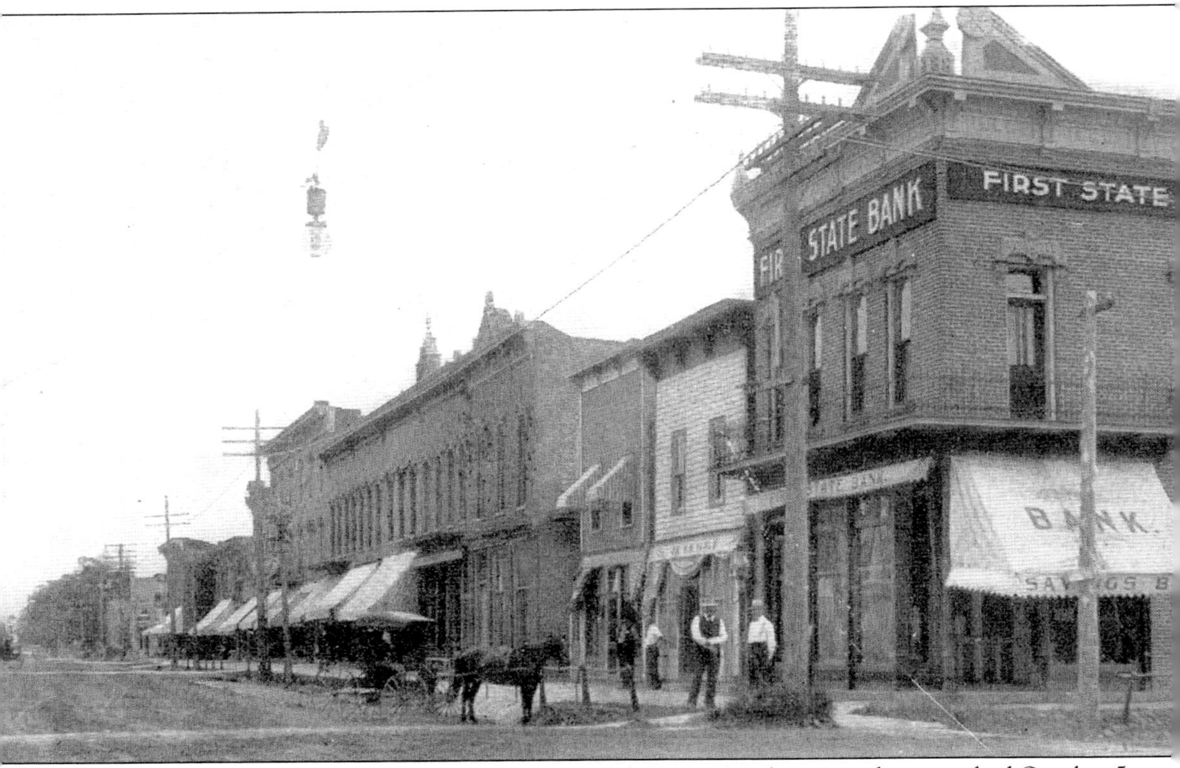

This postcard, sent to Frances Marantette in Kalamazoo, Michigan, and postmarked October 5, 1911 reads: "Am sending card to McC today, I will him you would appreciate a card like mine. Does her know your address?" The postcard provides a view of the north side of Main Street in downtown Mendon. (Mendon Country Inn Collection.)

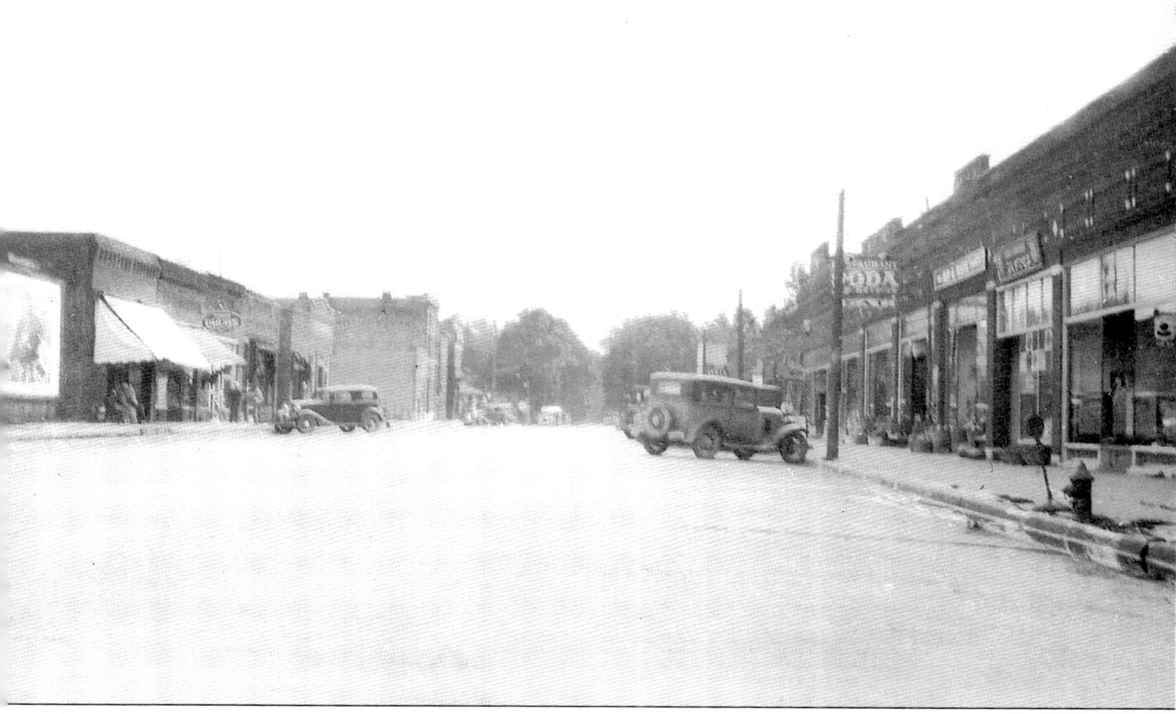

This image shows Main Street in Mendon looking east. Many of these buildings are still standing. (Mendon Country Inn Collection.)

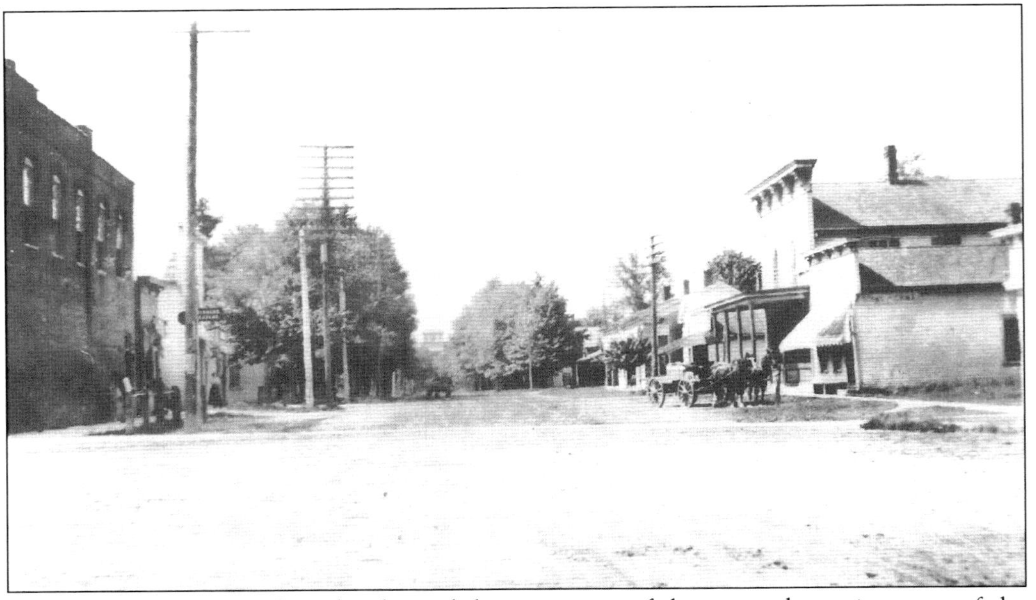

Colon had three major fires that burned down sections of the town, destroying most of the wood buildings seen in this photo. According to historian David Farrell, this photo shows one of the last of the wood buildings, which would later burn in a different fire. The view looks north on State Street, the main road in town. (Community Historical Society.)

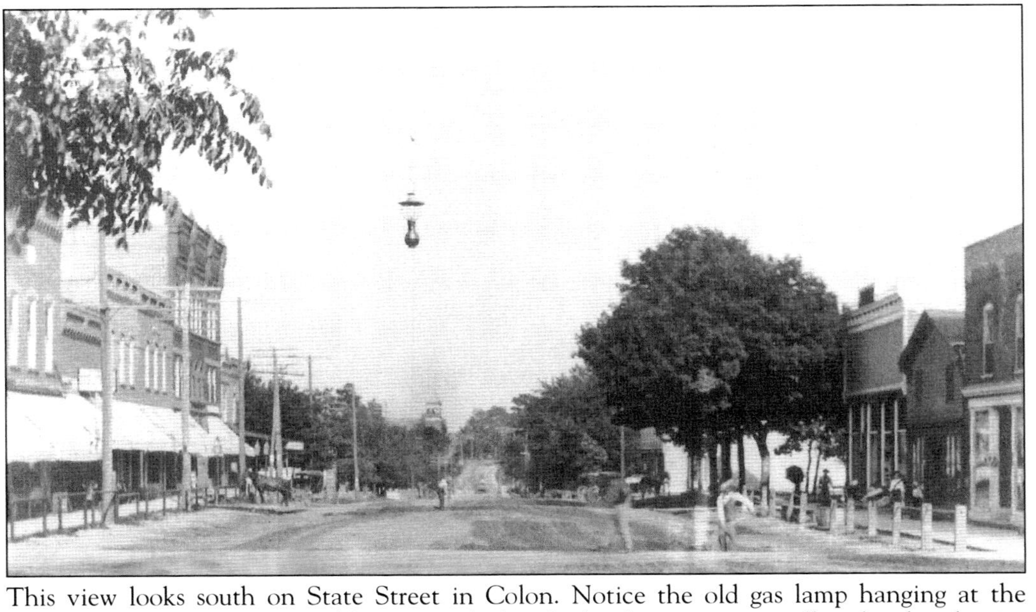

This view looks south on State Street in Colon. Notice the old gas lamp hanging at the intersection and the horses and buggies parked at the hitching posts, as well as the church spire in the distance. In the last half of the 19th century, the prosperity of Colon and its surrounding area was built, in part, on agricultural endeavors. According to a thesis written by Patrick West, the agricultural products shipped from Colon on the Michigan Central Railroad in 1876 included 745 barrels of flour, 26 cars of hogs, six cars of sheep, five cars of cattle, and 46,450 bushels of grain. (Community Historical Society.)

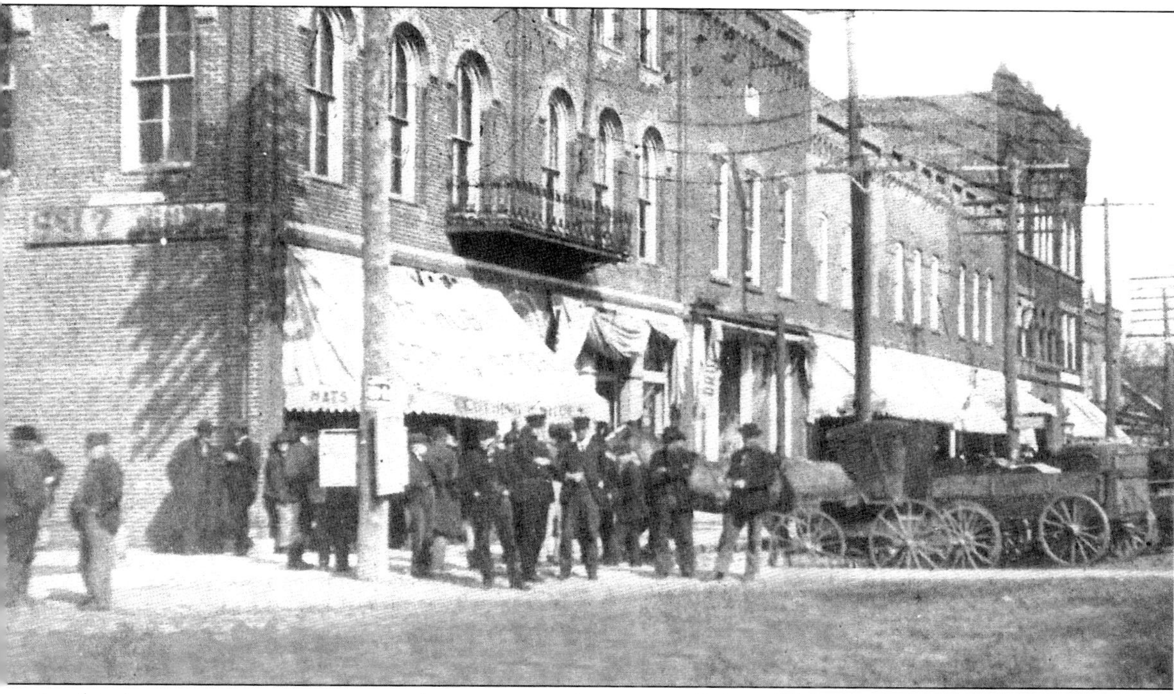

In this image, men congregate at the corner in downtown Colon. The corner building, with its beautiful Palladium arched windows, is still standing. Nestled between two lakes, the small town of Colon was once a mill town. It was also famed for the magicians who lived there and for a magic-tricks business, called Abbott's Magic, which was founded by Australian Percy Abbot. Abbot sold a partnership in the business to Recil Bourdner, another magician, in 1932. The Bourdner family acquired the entire business in 1959, and the store is still located near the Carnegie Library in the downtown area. (Community Historical Society.)

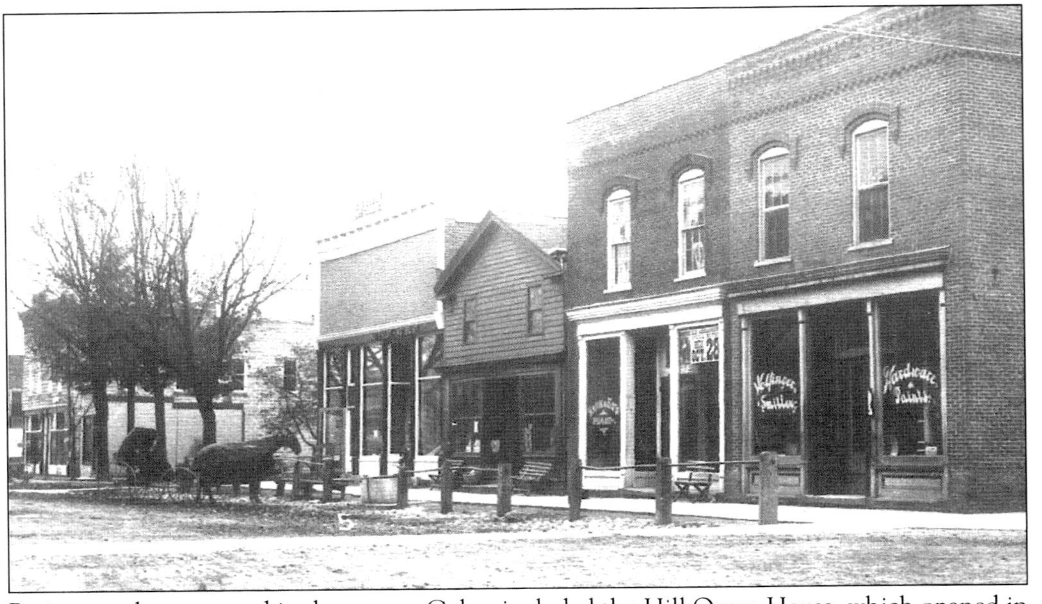

Businesses that operated in downtown Colon included the Hill Opera House, which opened in 1897. The Hills were a prominent family and owned a bank, a knitting factory, and a mercantile store. Also downtown were Wolfinger & Smitley's Hardware and the St. Joseph Hotel, which also had a livery stable nearby, as was common in those times. (Community Historical Society.)

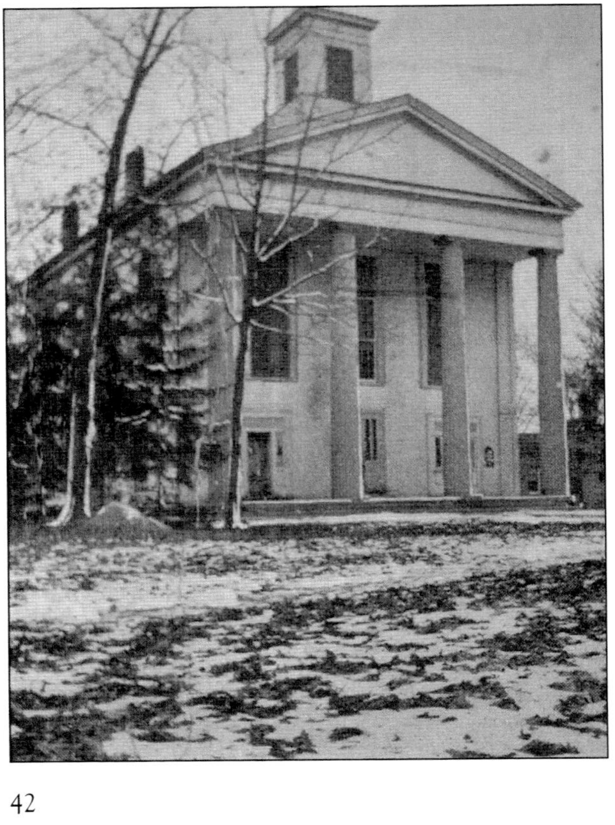

The original Greek Revival-style county courthouse in Centreville is pictured as it looked in 1842. The first courthouse in Centreville, according to the county's website, was the leased upper room of the two-story frame building, constructed and owned by Thomas W. Langley in 1832. The building, located on the corner of Main and Clark Streets, served county officials and the courts until the first courthouse was erected in the fall of 1842 at a cost of $43,200. According to Centreville historian Dick Cripe, the bell (note the belfry) most likely served as a rallying signal for fires, floods, and celebrations. (Dick Cripe Collection.)

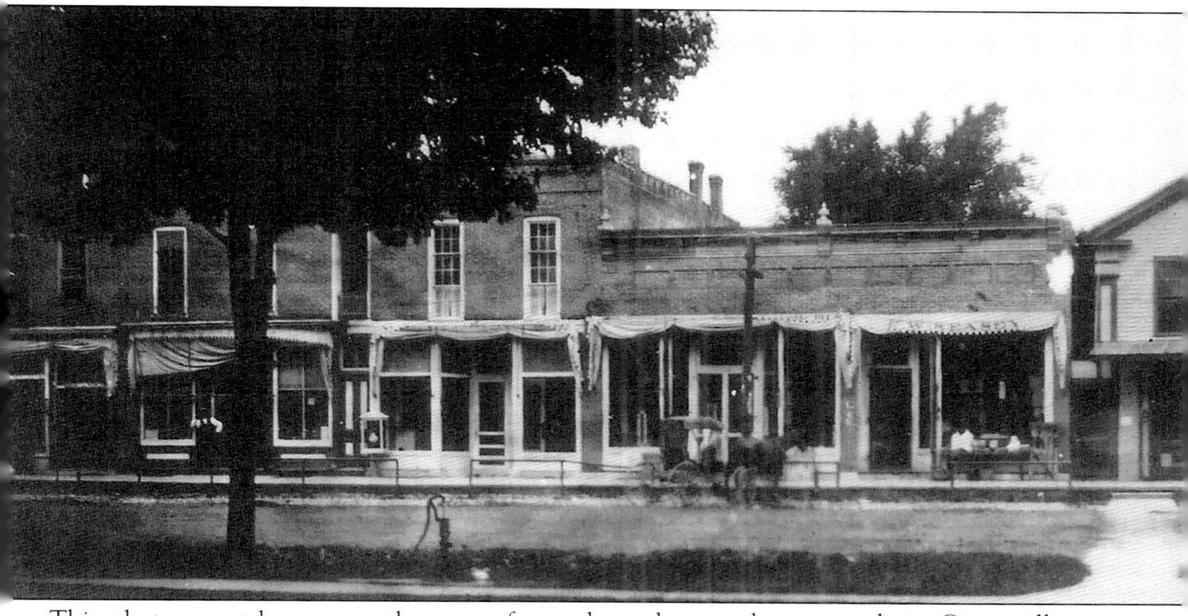

This photo was taken across the street from where the courthouse stands in Centreville. According to historian Dick Cripe, this is a view of downtown Centreville before fire decimated many of these wooden buildings. The buildings on the left survived the fire, the buildings on the right did not. All the wooden buildings were destroyed while the brick ones survived. (Dick Cripe Collection.)

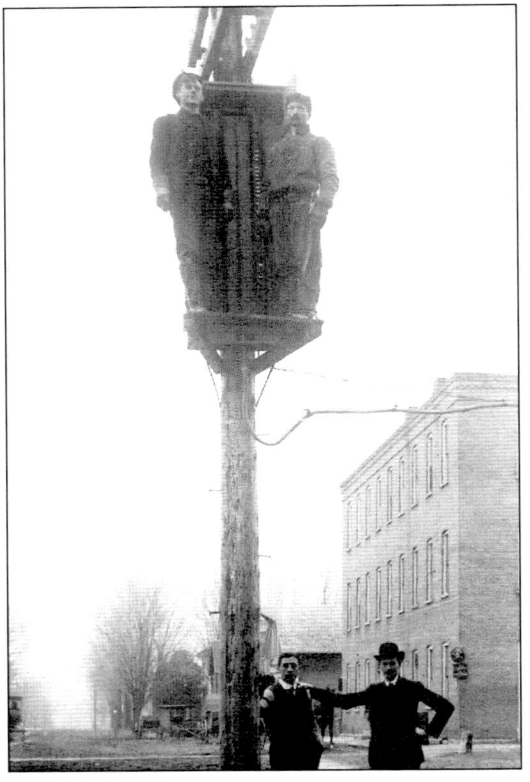

Historian Dick Cripe has determined that this photo of a telephone relay station in Centreville was taken prior to 1914, as that was the year that the Hart Hotel, shown in the background, burned down. (Dick Cripe Collection.)

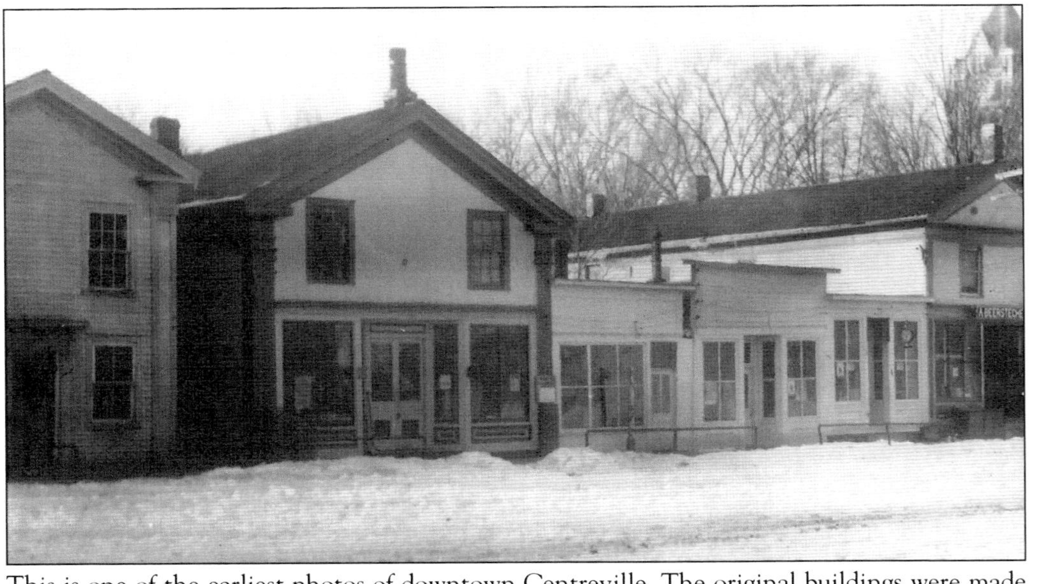

This is one of the earliest photos of downtown Centreville. The original buildings were made of wood and were destroyed by several fires that decimated the downtown. Centreville's plat was recorded on November 7, 1831. The village was surveyed and laid out by its four original proprietors: Robert Clark Jr., Electra W. Dean, Charles Nobel, and Dennis B. Miller. (Dick Cripe Collection.)

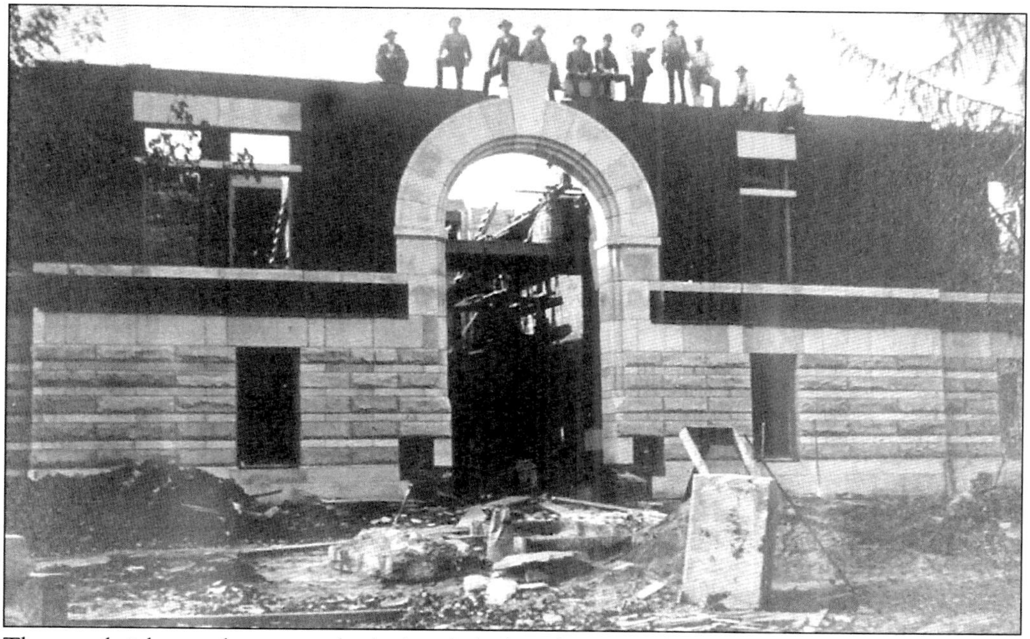

The new brick courthouse was built shortly before the turn of the last century. The courthouse opened for business in 1900 and is still in use today. Among the first couples to be married there were John W. Fletcher and Sarah Knox, on September 18, 1831, and the parents of Ed Mosher. The first recorded deaths were George Buck and Levi Waterman, who were killed when a well they were digging collapsed in 1829. (Dick Cripe Collection.)

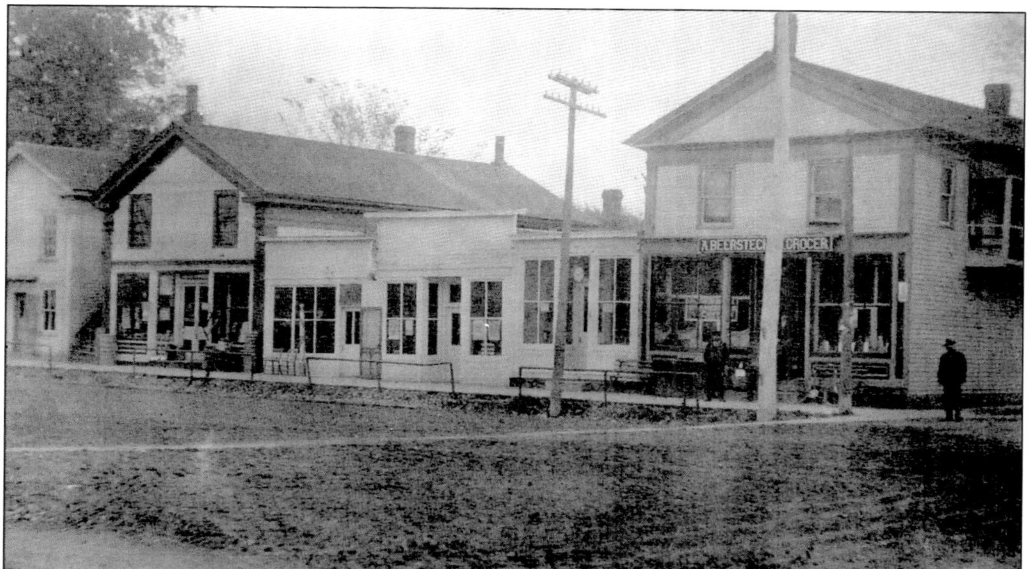

Note the store of grocer A. Beerstitcher, which was for a long time the main grocery store downtown. The store later was called the County Seat Market and then became part of the Village Market chain. The Beerstitcher family were longtime residents of Centreville. (Dick Cripe Collection.)

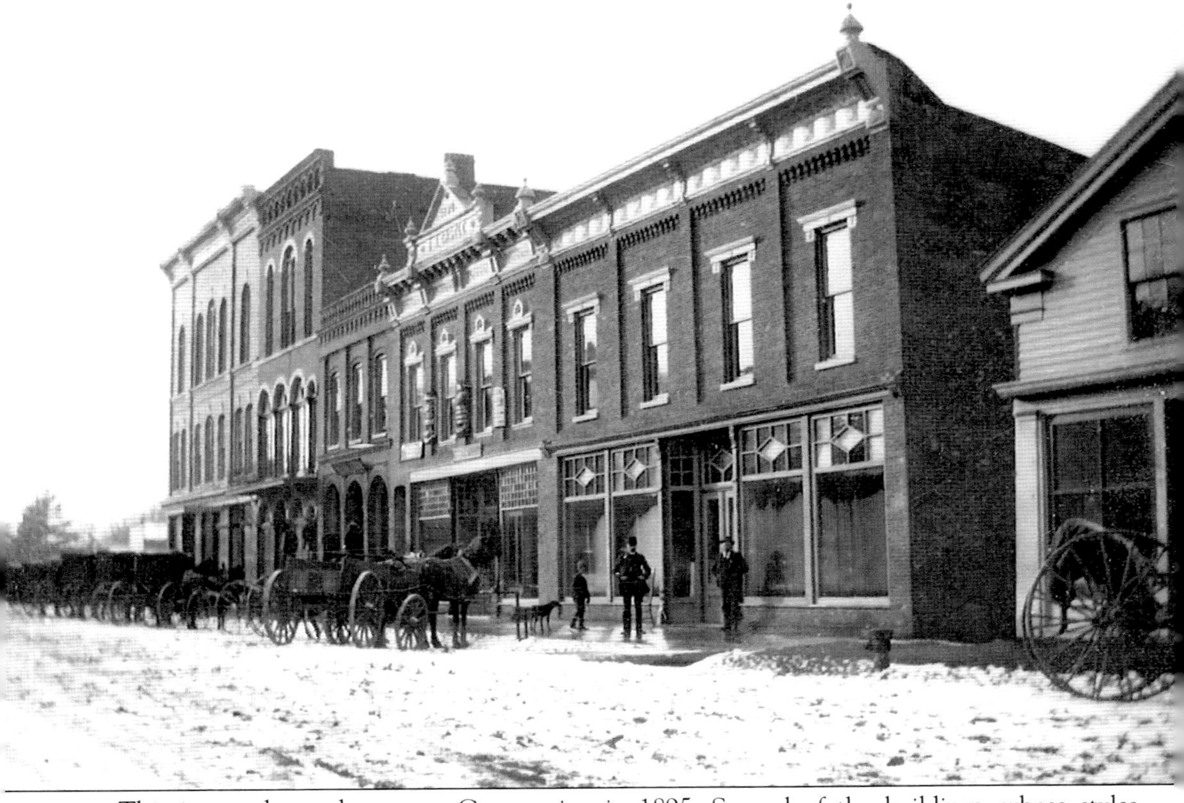

This image shows downtown Constantine in 1895. Several of the buildings, whose styles include Gothic, Italianate, and Greek Revival, are still standing in the historic downtown. Two of the state governors came from Constantine, including John Barry, who served three terms as governor, beginning in 1841, and whose house, located just north of the river, is now a museum. Besides his career as a politician, Barry was an astute businessman, who in 1845 built a warehouse on piles over the river. This sped up the process of loading and unloading boats, facilitating transportation and trade. (Governor Barry House Collection.)

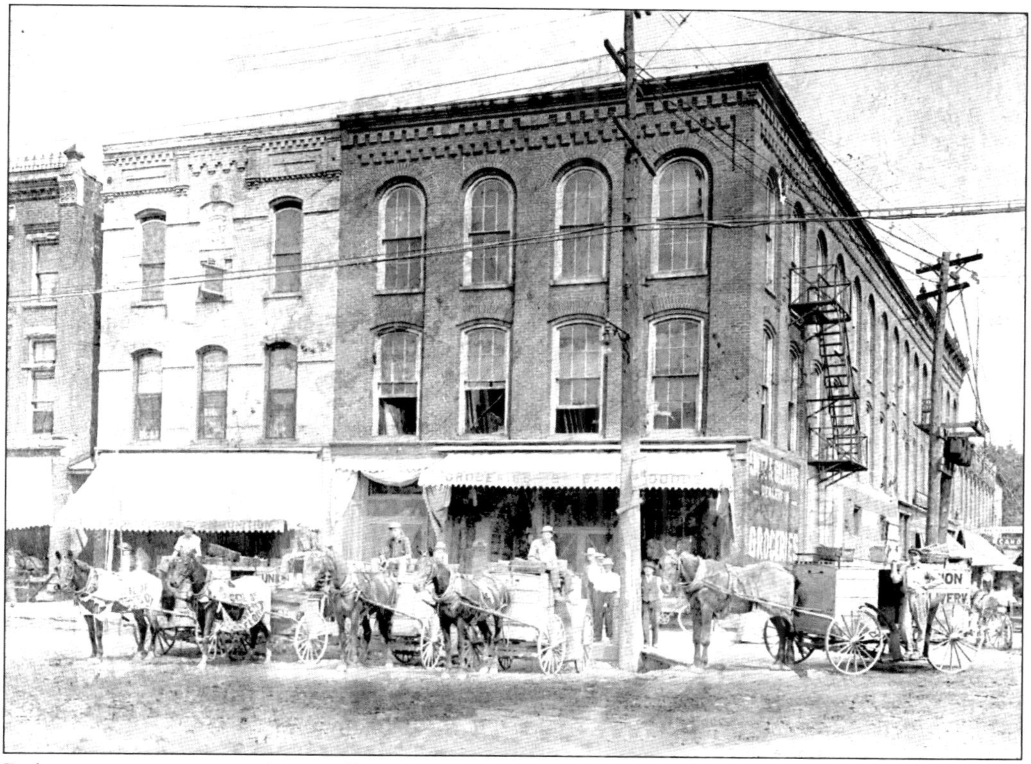

Delivery wagons get ready to roll out in downtown Sturgis. Sturgis was founded by Judge John Sturgis, who moved there from Monroe, Michigan in 1828 and built a log cabin. By the mid-1800s the city was booming. (Sturgis Historical Society Collection.)

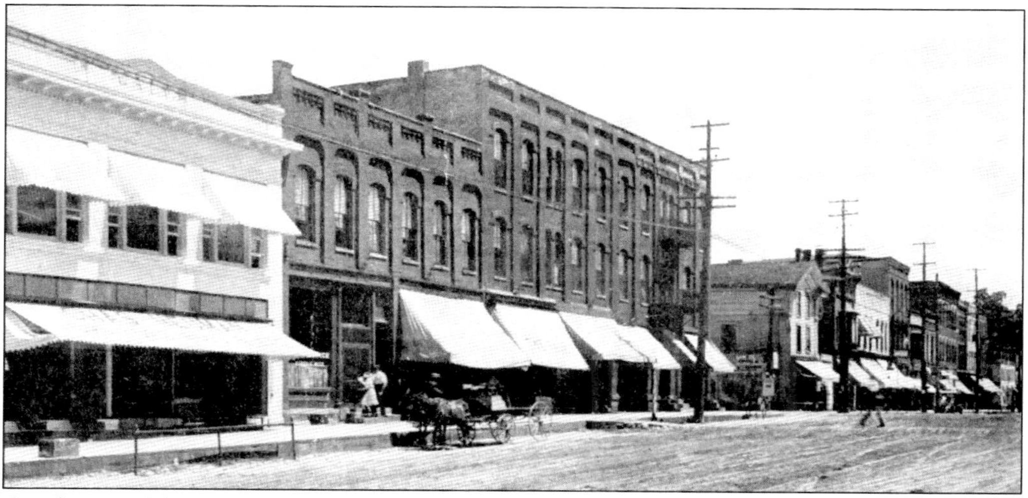

Goods were delivered via horse and wagon, as this photo taken in Sturgis shows, but unpaved dirt roads made getting from place to place difficult. The streets were unpaved even in the early 1910s. (Sturgis Historical Society Collection.)

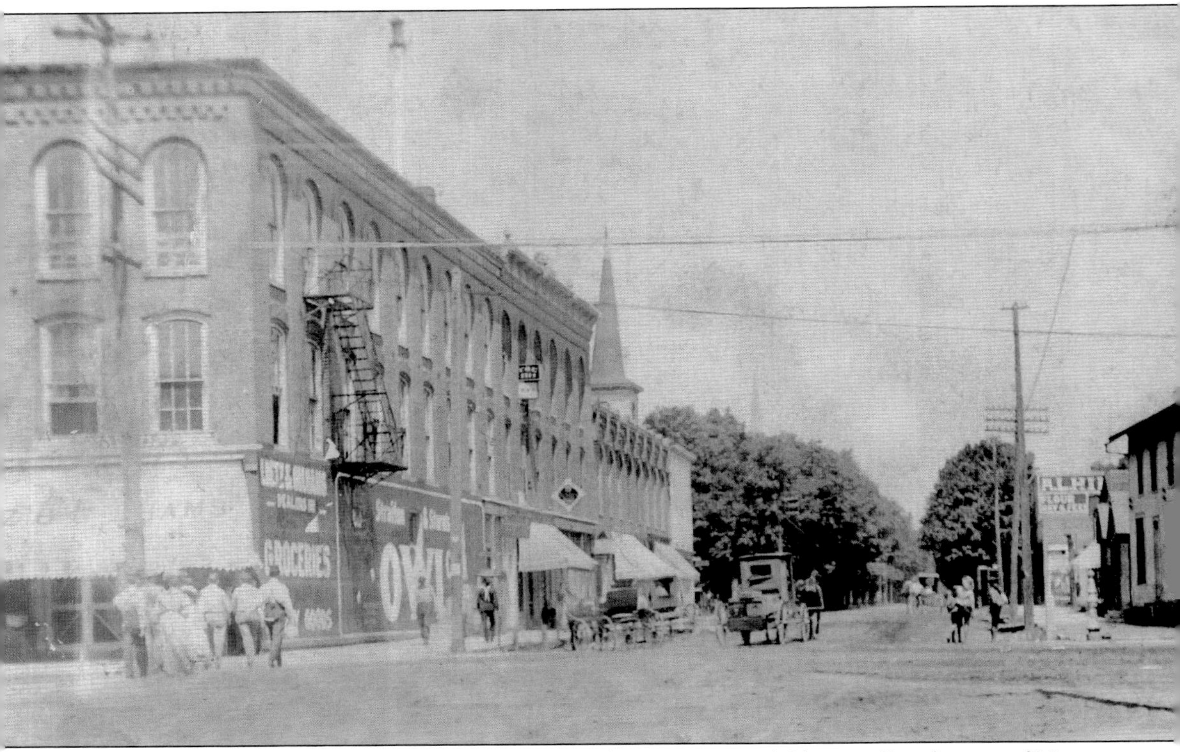

According to historian Robert Hair, the northwest corner of Chicago Road, west of Nottawa, housed a series of grocery stores up until 1963. This photo was taken *c.* 1900s, when Loetz & Gilhams Grocers was in business. (Sturgis Historical Society Collection.)

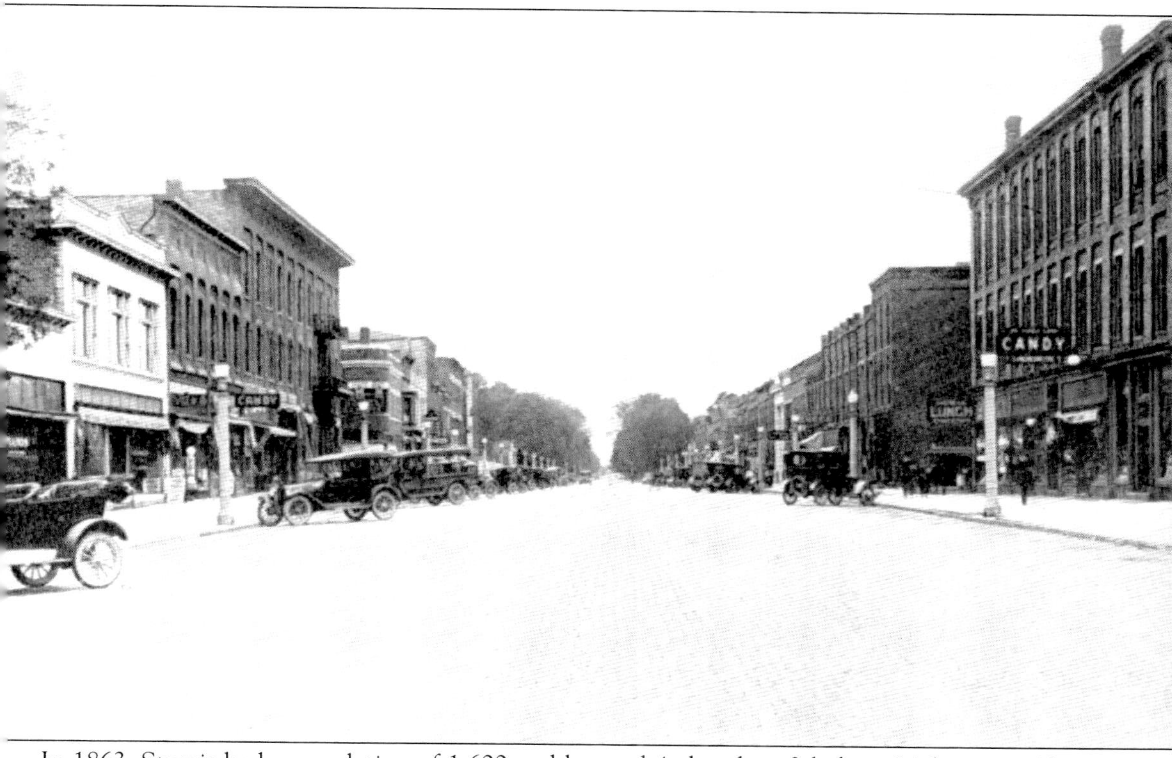

In 1863, Sturgis had a population of 1,600 and boasted 4 churches, 3 lodges, 14 factories, 12 stores, 1 bank, and 1 flour mill—despite a major fire in 1859. This photo was taken on Chicago Street, looking east. (Sturgis Historical Society Collection.)

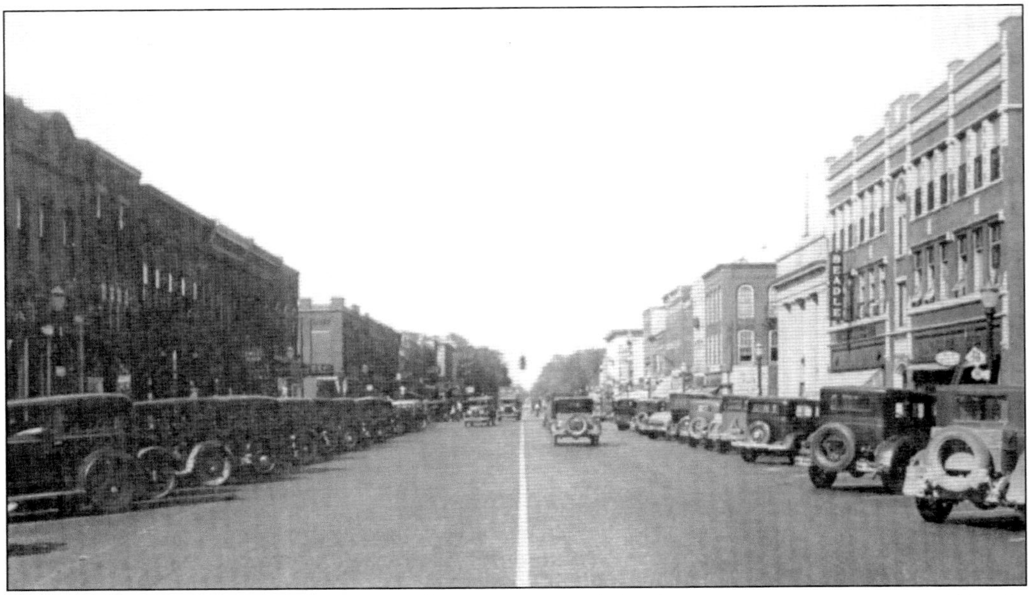

Chicago Street was one of the first roads in Sturgis, and the downtown soon grew around it. At one time called Chicago Drive, it was established in 1832 as a military road. Horses still ruled the road when Dr. John Moe, a Sturgis physician, purchased the city's first car with an internal combustion engine in 1902. (Sturgis Historical Society Collection.)

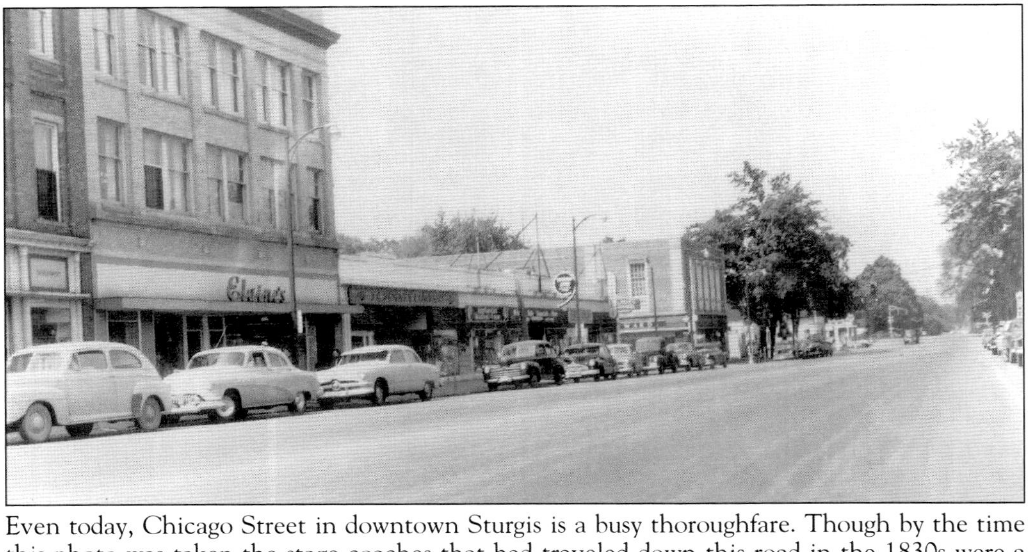

Even today, Chicago Street in downtown Sturgis is a busy thoroughfare. Though by the time this photo was taken the stage coaches that had traveled down this road in the 1830s were a distant memory, Chicago Street has always been important to the community. Its name reflects its original purpose—connecting Detroit to Chicago for the transportation of passengers and goods. (Sturgis Historical Society Collection.)

The Sturgis National Bank building, located at 114 West Chicago Road, was built in 1914. (Sturgis Historical Society Collection.)

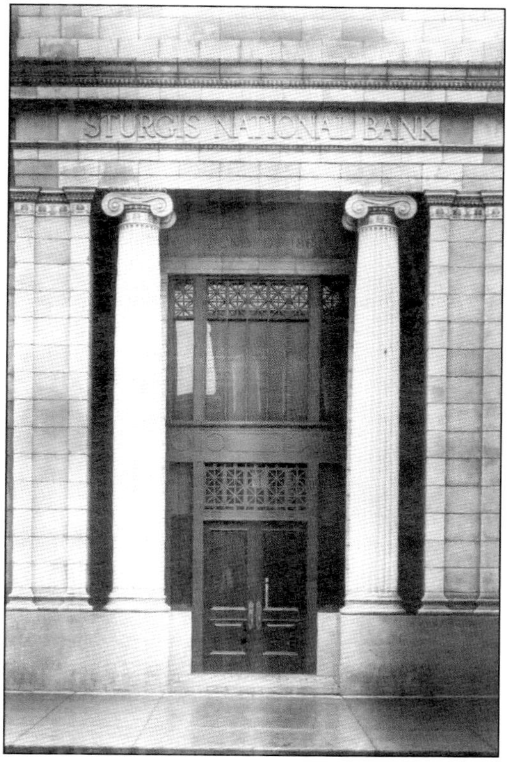

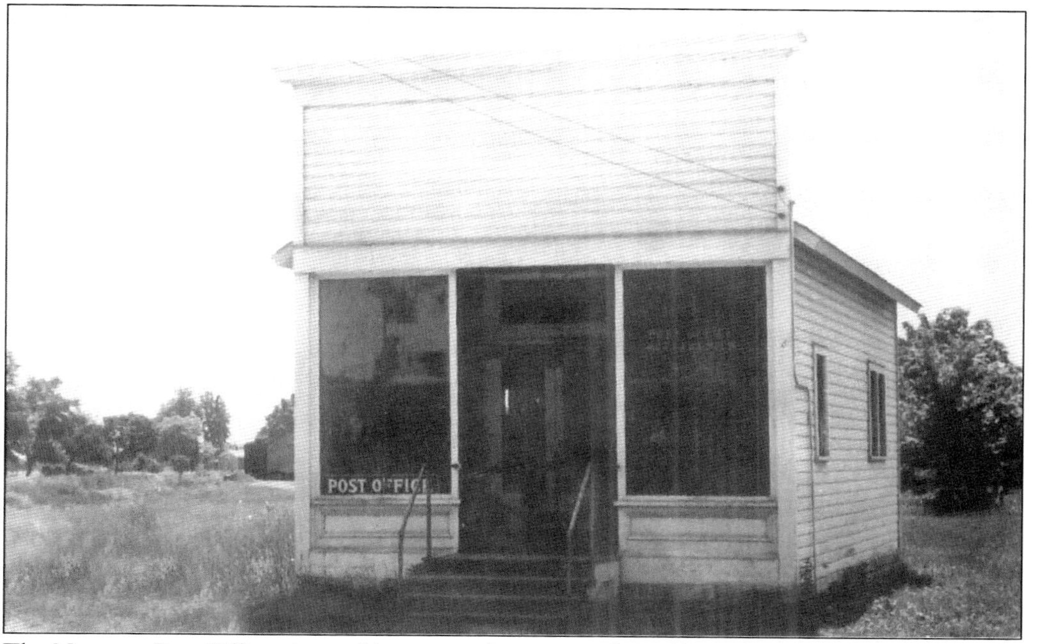

The Nottawa Post Office pictured here is no longer standing. (Steve Zazra Collection.)

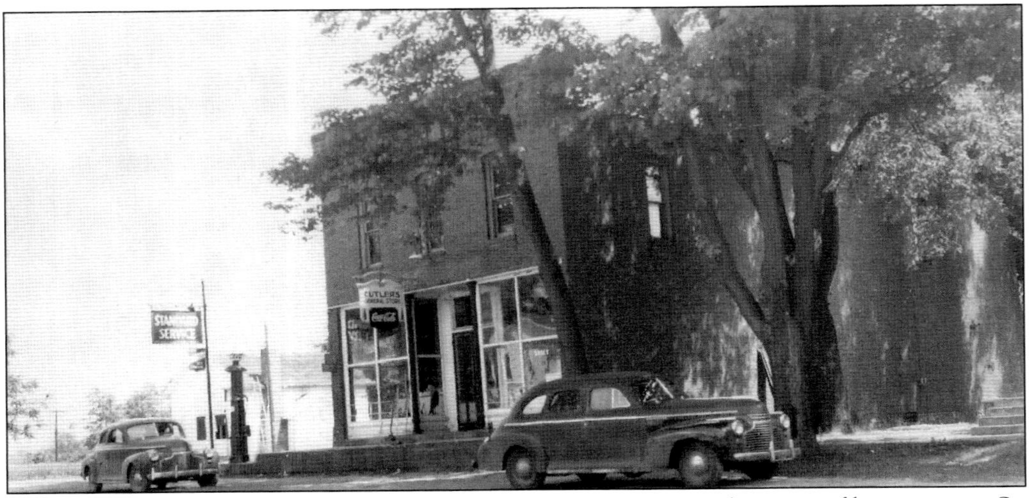

This is an image of Cutler's General Store in Nottawa. In a 1930s directory of businesses in St. Joseph County, the phone number for Cutler's store, which advertised having "everything for the home or lake cottage," was 176-F11. (Steve Zazra Collection.)

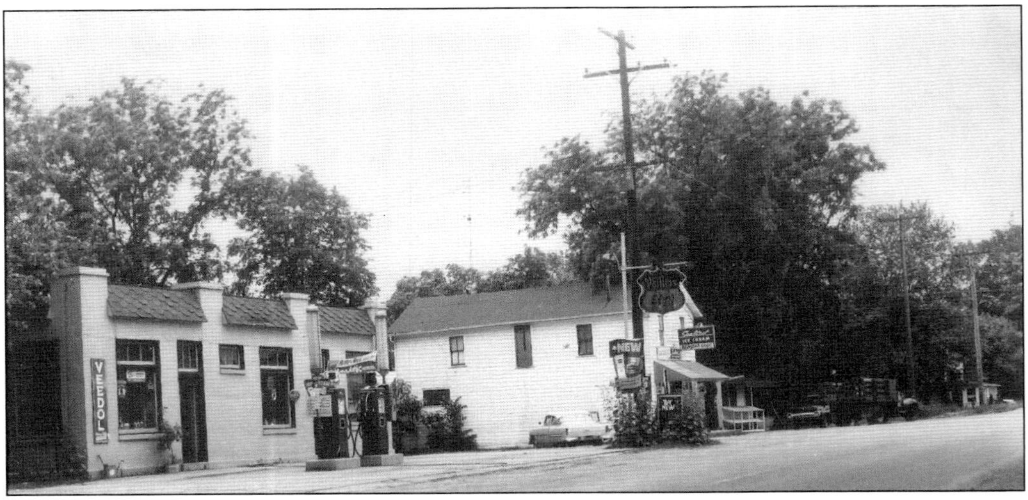

At one time, the White Star Service Station was owned by Bill Post. An early forerunner to today's convenience stores, it served as a place to stop for gas and to shop in the adjacent store. (Steve Zarza Collection.)

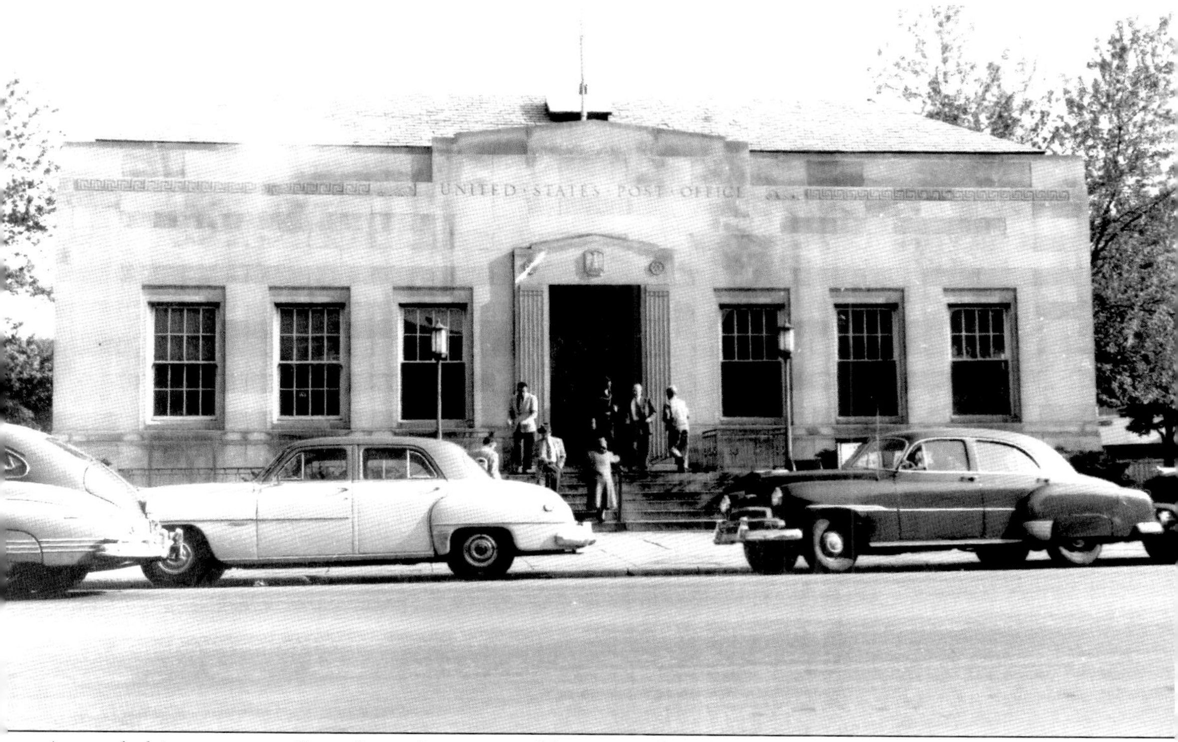

A much bigger post office than the one in Nottawa, the classic streamlined design of the Sturgis Post Office is also reflected in the style of the cars parked out front. (Sturgis Historical Society Collection.)

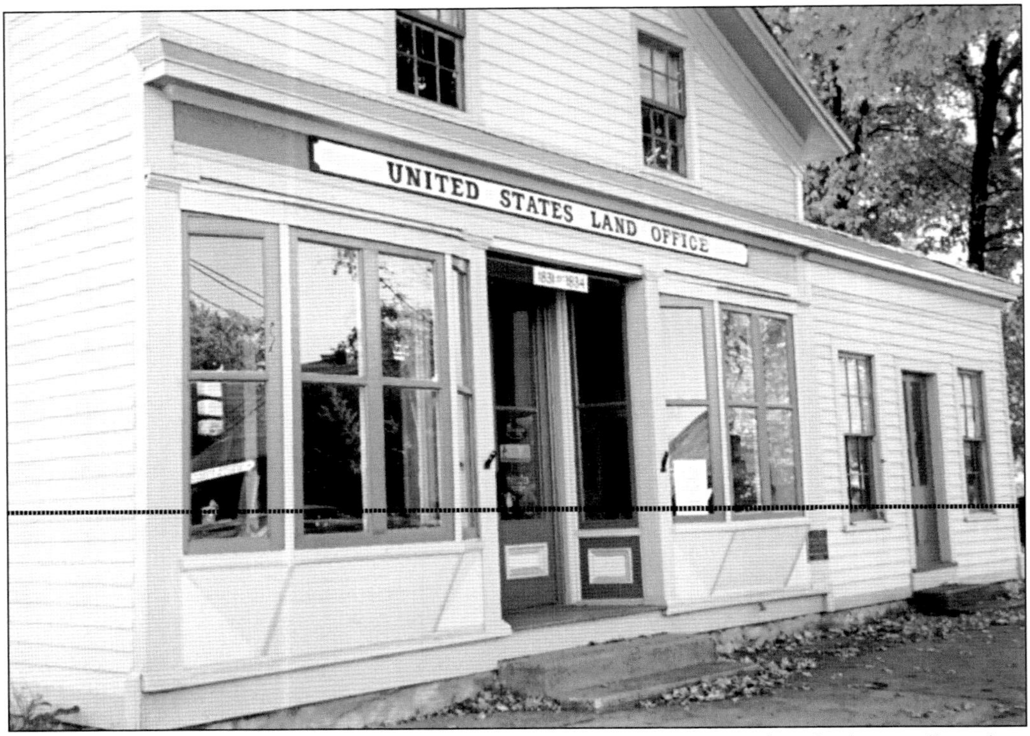

The White Pigeon Prairie Land Office opened in 1831. Before, settlers had to walk, ride a horse, or take a wagon to Monroe, Michigan, to do their land transactions. Among those who requested that a land office be opened in St. Joseph County were John Sturgis, Peter Klinger, Richard Meek, Arba Heald, and Luther Newton. (Sturgis Historical Society Collection.)

Four

Frivolities and Fun

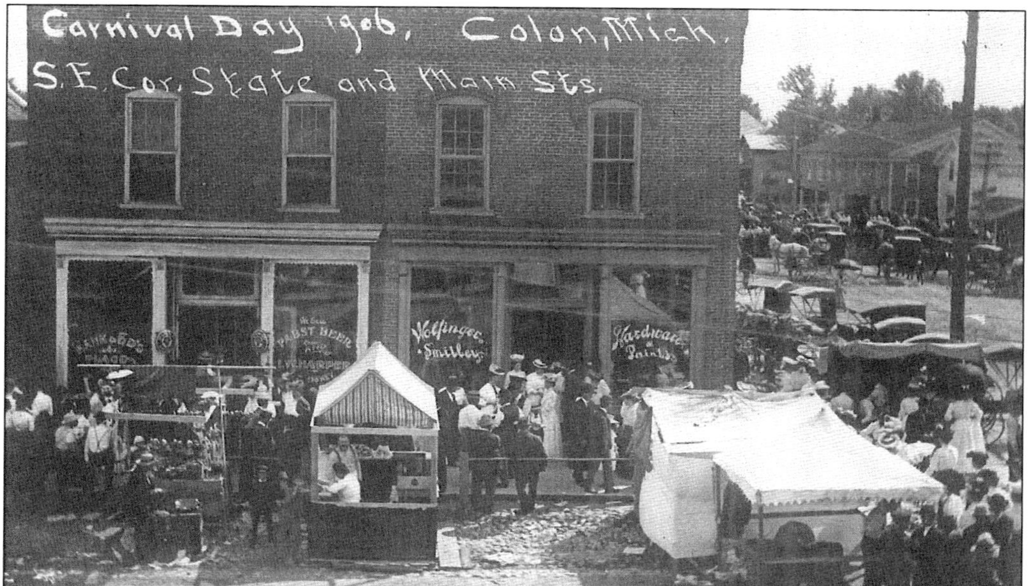

This is a 1906 photo of Carnival Day in Colon, showing the southeast corner of State and Main. According to historian David Farrell of Colon, a glimpse of the old Lakeview Hotel can be seen in the upper right hand corner of the photo. Notice the Wolfinger & Smitley Hardware Store, where a group of people have congregated. There is still a hardware store in that location all these years later. (Community Historical Society.)

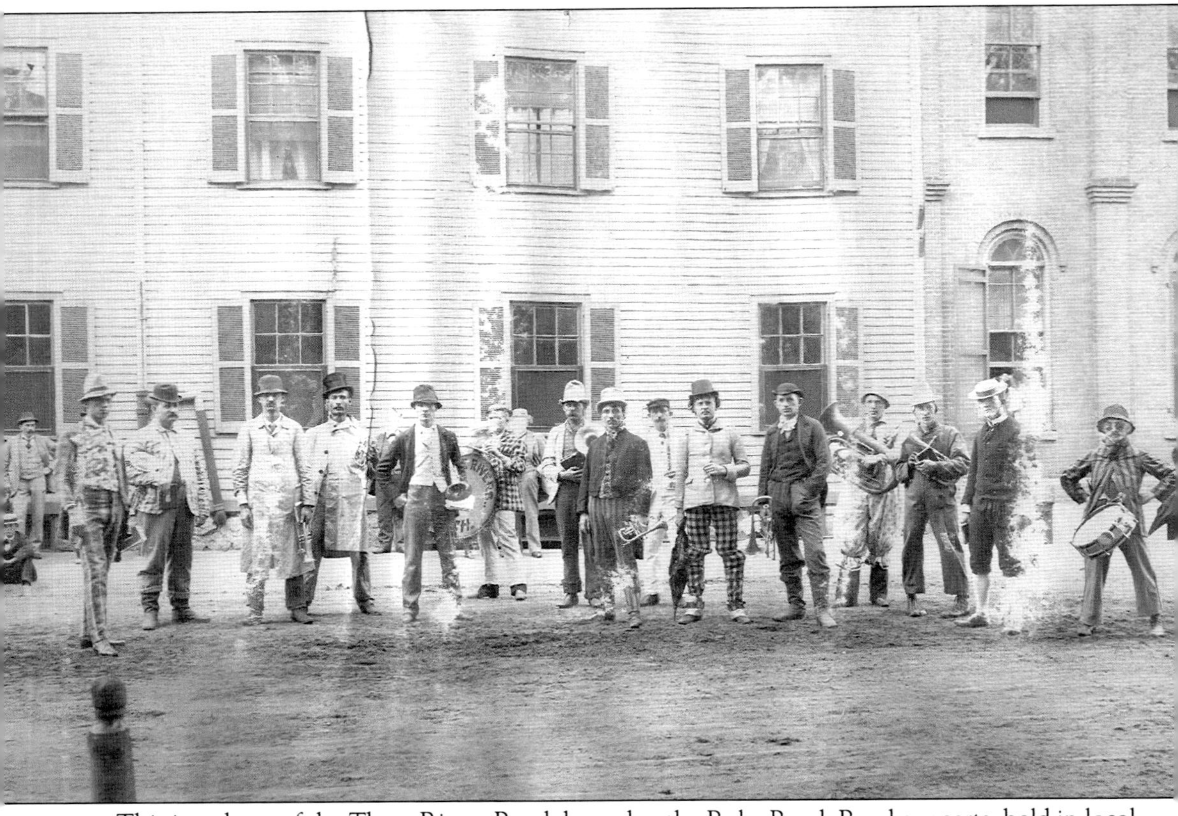

This is a photo of the Three Rivers Band dressed as the Rube Band. Band concerts, held in local parks, were the perfect way to spend a Sunday afternoon or early weekday evening. From left to right are as follows: Will Timm, Henry Arnold, Guy Bodley, Eugene Schall, Norman Hawes, Rudy Colver, Asher Belote, W.J. Predmore, Gus Arnold, Charles Burch, and B. Elliott. (Three Rivers Library Collection.)

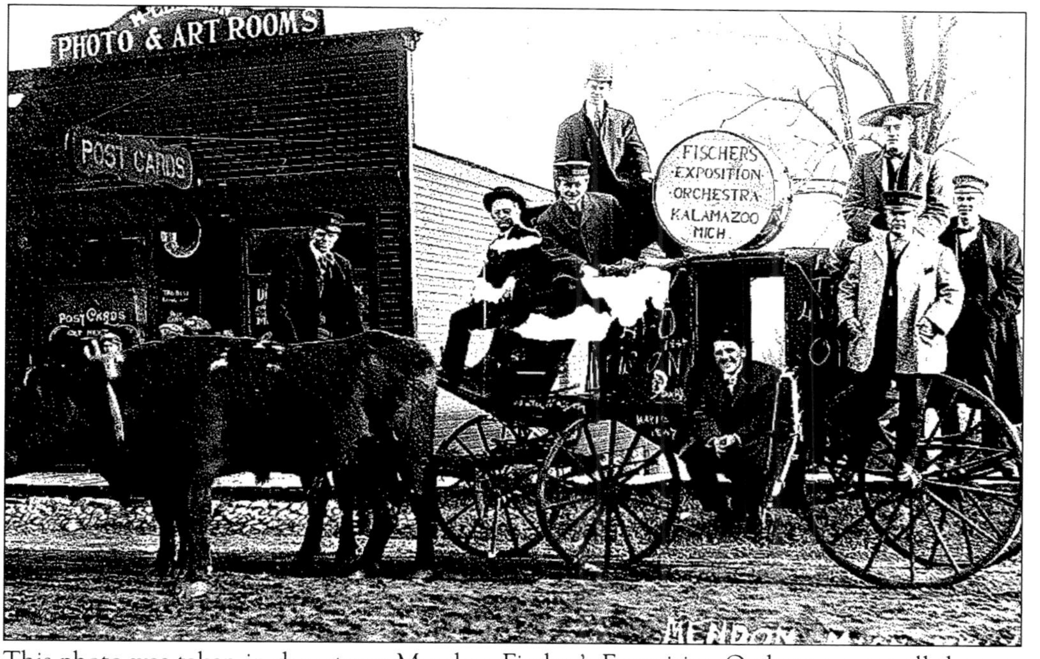

This photo was taken in downtown Mendon. Fischer's Exposition Orchestra came all the way from Kalamazoo to play. Note the dirt streets. Most roads weren't paved until well into the early 1900s. (Mendon Country Inn Collection.)

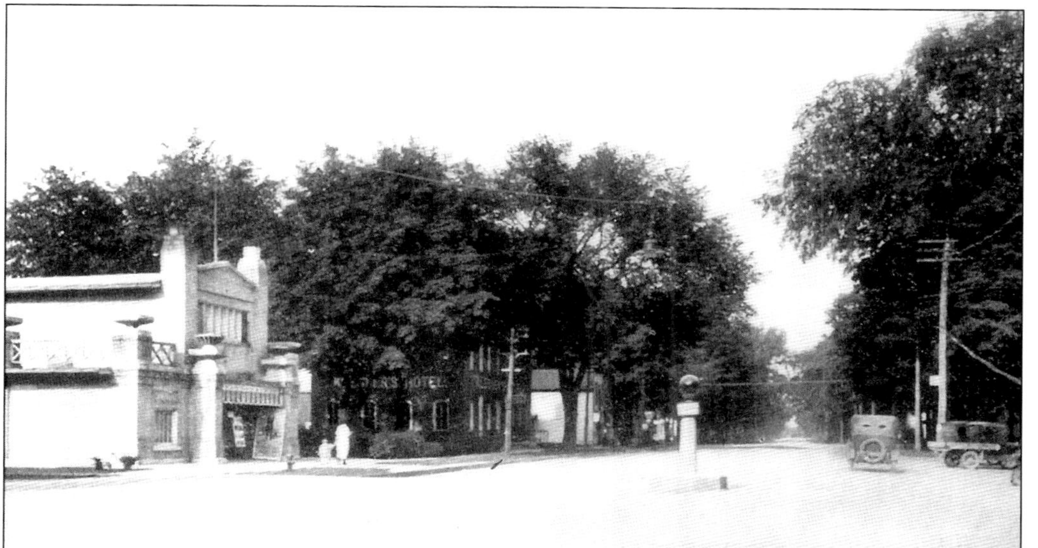

This is a photo of the Centreville Community Theatre. Note the safety island, one of two, in the street. According to Dick Cripe, there is a local legend that the city discontinued use of the safety islands when a man under the influence drove into both of them during the 1920s. (Dick Cripe Collection.)

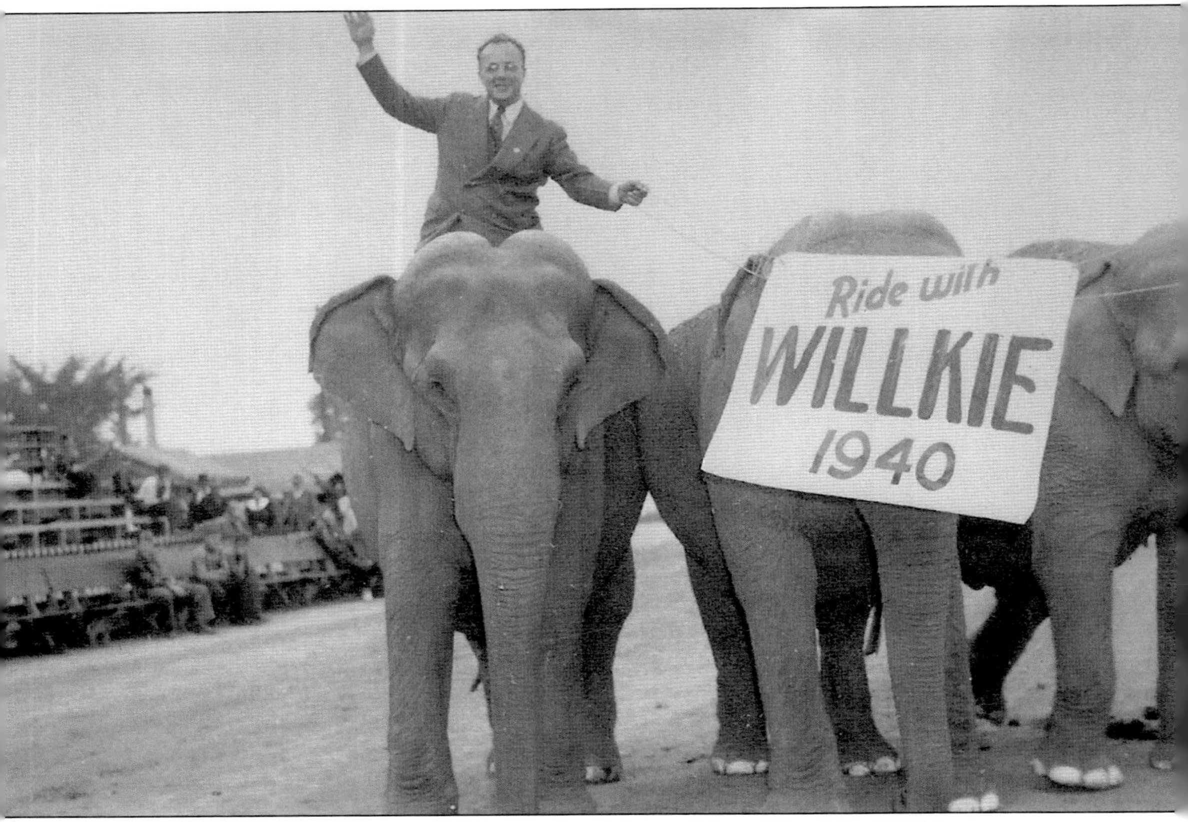

According to Dick Cripe, 1940 presidential candidate Wendell Willkie never came to Centreville. This photo was taken at the St. Joseph County Fairground's grandstand and depicts an enthusiastic supporter. (Dick Cripe Collection.)

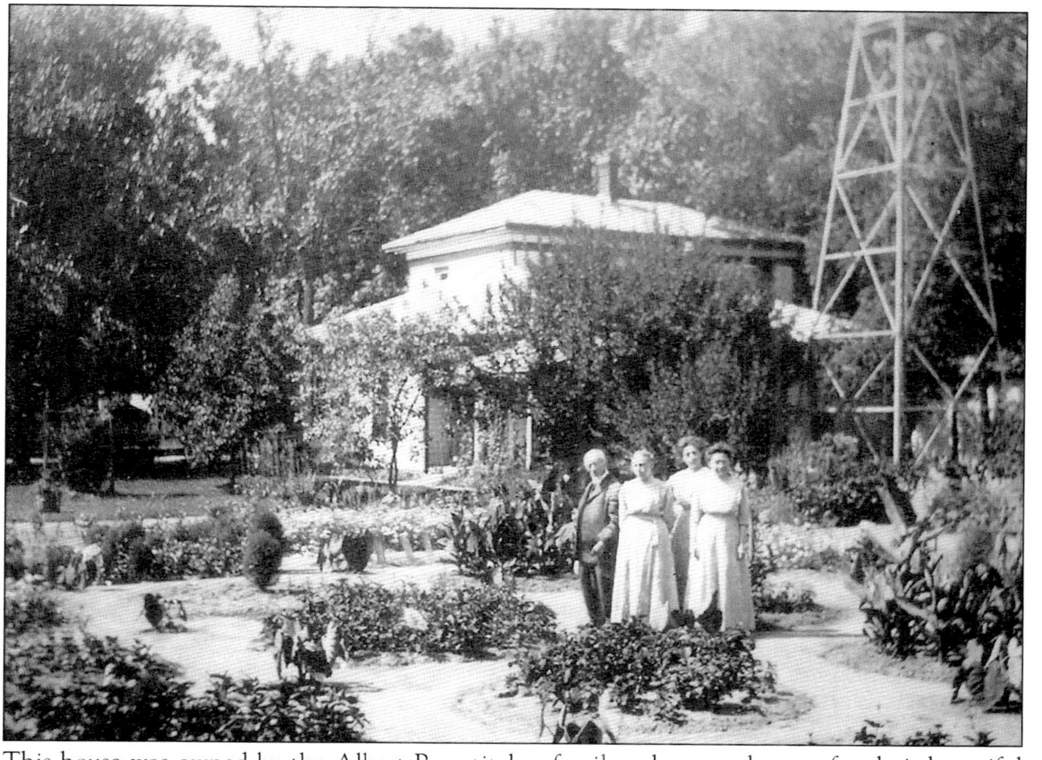

This house was owned by the Albert Beerstitcher family, who were known for their beautiful gardens. The home was probably built in the 1870s. A magnolia tree in this garden is still standing, as is the house. (Dick Cripe Collection.)

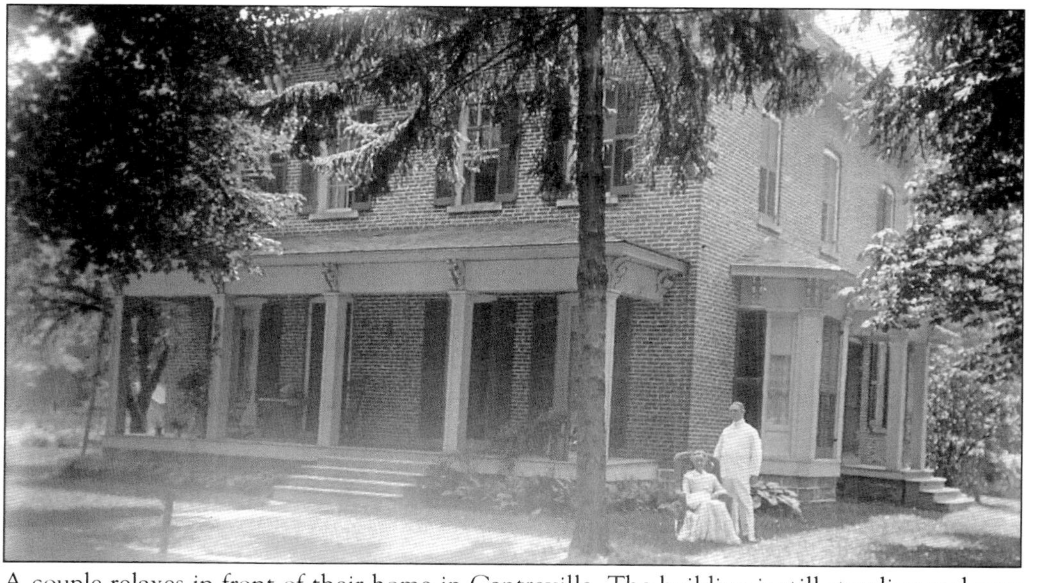

A couple relaxes in front of their home in Centreville. The building is still standing and now serves as the Ely Funeral Home. (Dick Cripe Collection.)

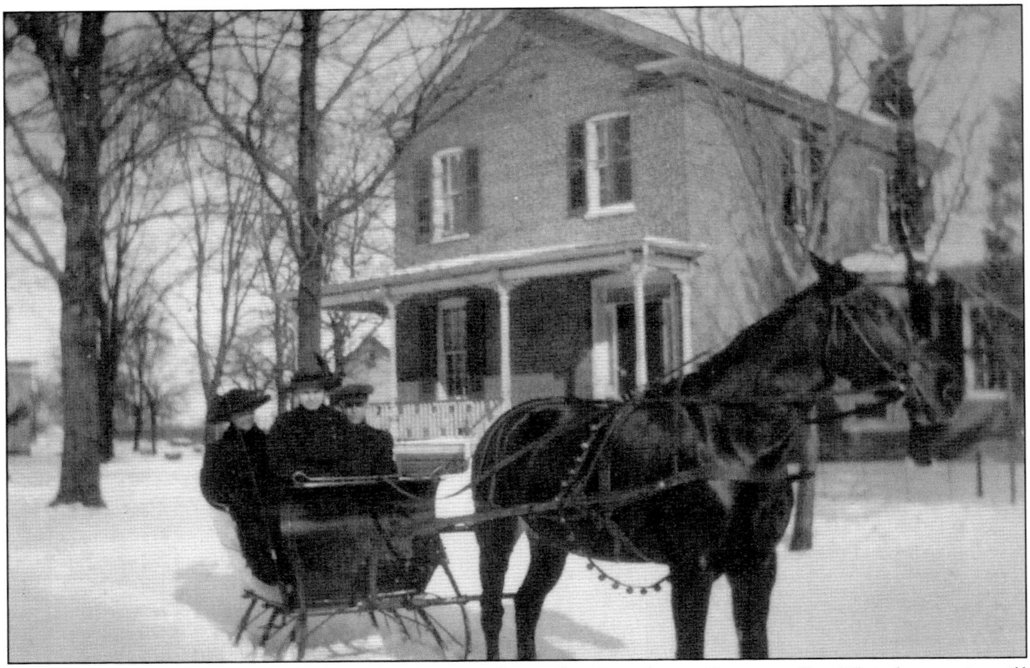

Bundled up to keep warm, a threesome goes for a sleigh ride in Centreville. This home is still standing. (Dick Cripe Collection.)

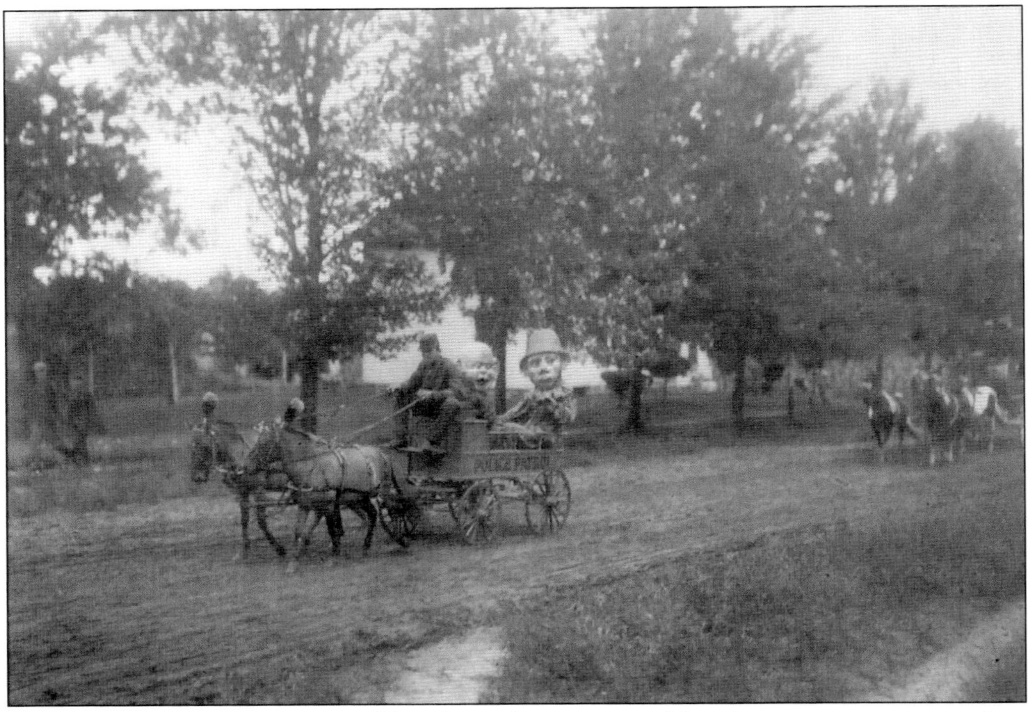

The circus comes to Constantine. This photo, showing one of the circus wagons on its way into town, was taken in 1898. (Governor Barry Historical Society Collection.)

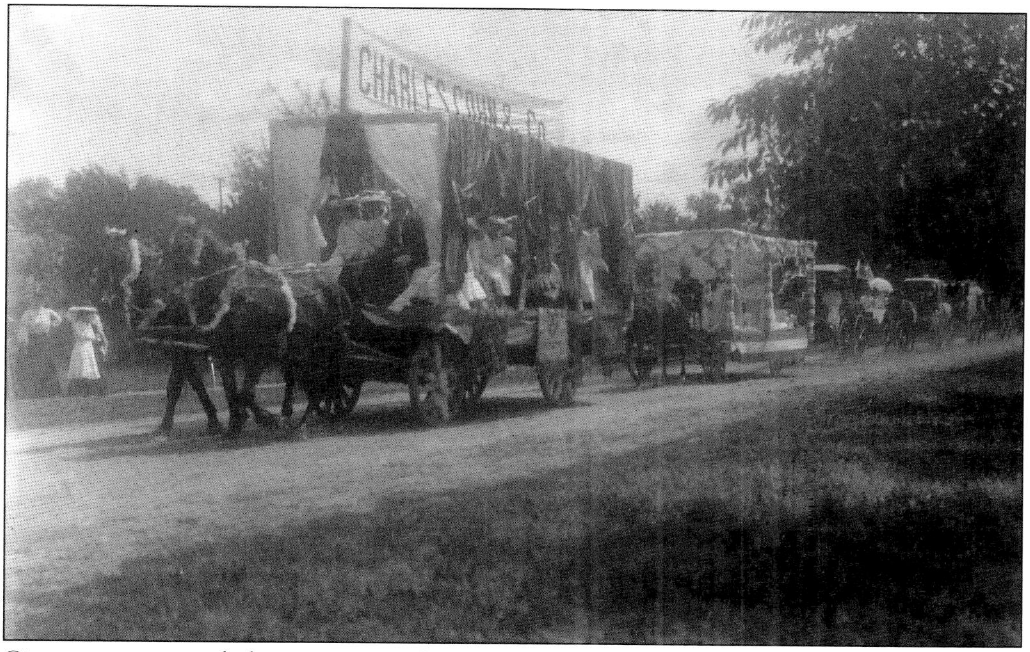

Circus wagons wind their way into Constantine in 1898 while people gather to look on. (Governor Barry Historical Society Collection.)

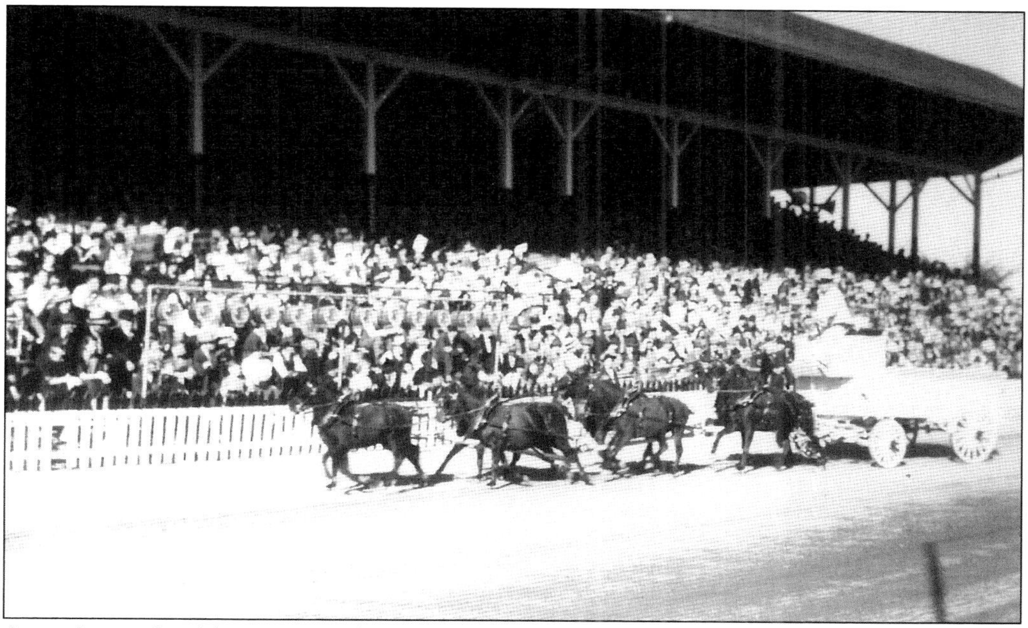

According to local historian Dick Cripe, the grandstand at the St. Joseph County Fairgrounds was built with materials from the 1933–1934 Century of Progress world's fair held in Chicago. Flat cars filled with lumber from the world's fair were purchased after the buildings there were torn down. The St. Joseph County Fair is over 150 years old and is still held each year. (Dick Cripe Collection.)

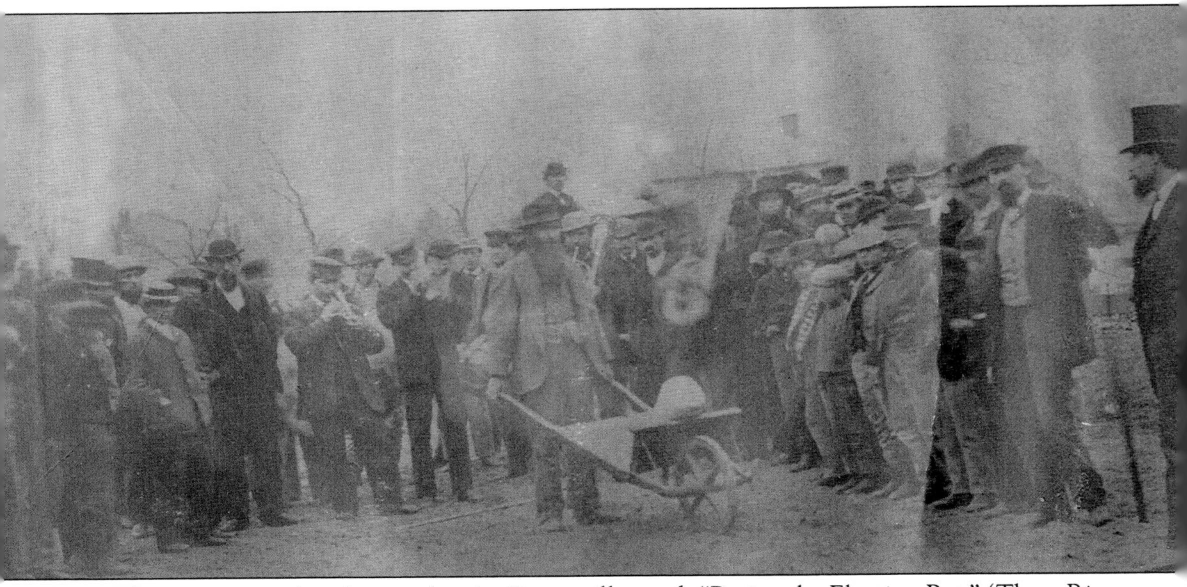

The caption on this photo, taken in Centreville, reads "Paying the Election Bet." (Three Rivers Library Collection.)

Three women in Three Rivers don Asian garb. From left are Gertrude Thoms, Mary Kelsey, and May Ikeler. (Three Rivers Library Collection.)

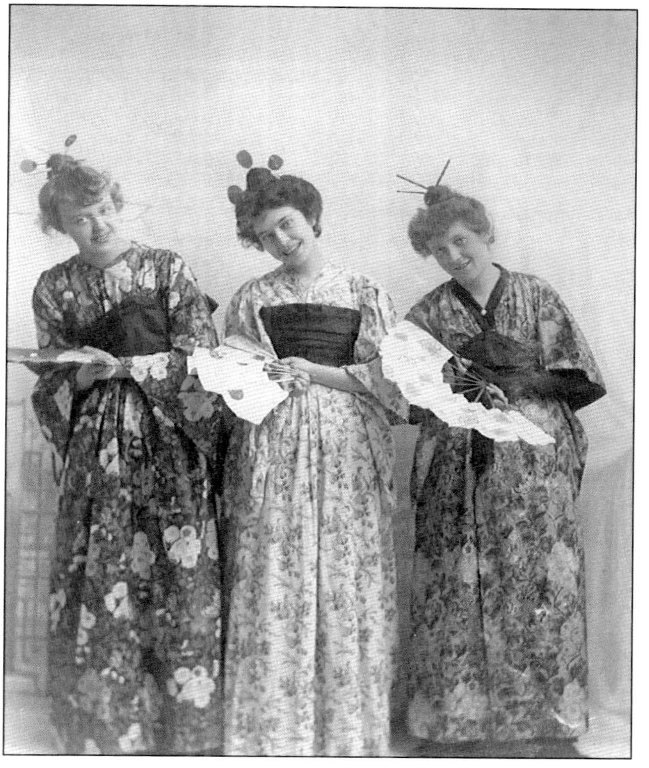

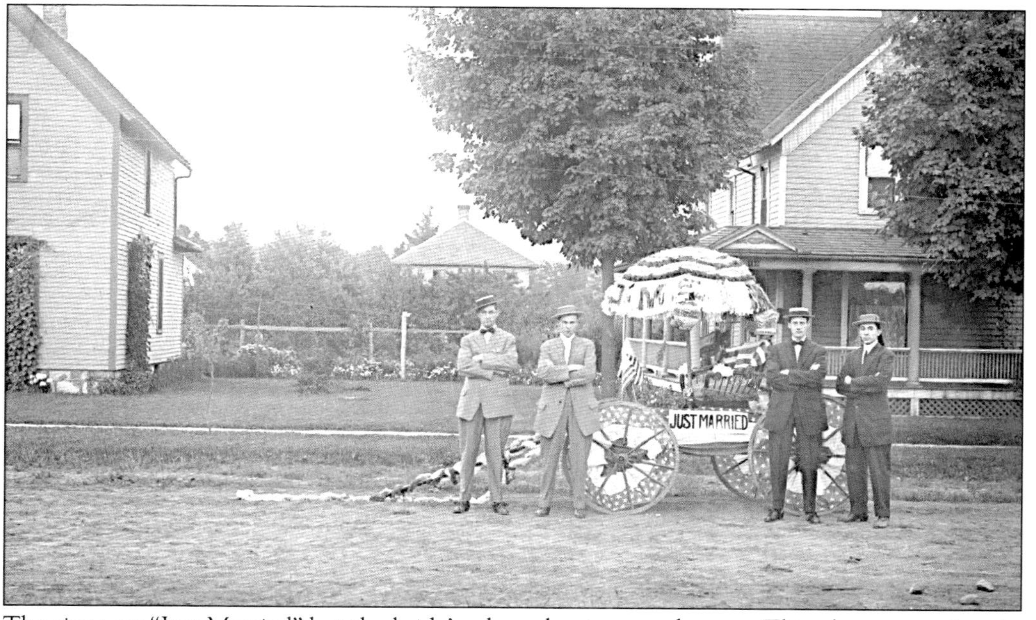

The sign says "Just Married" but the bride's whereabouts are unknown. This photo was taken in Three Rivers. (Sturgis Historical Society Collection.)

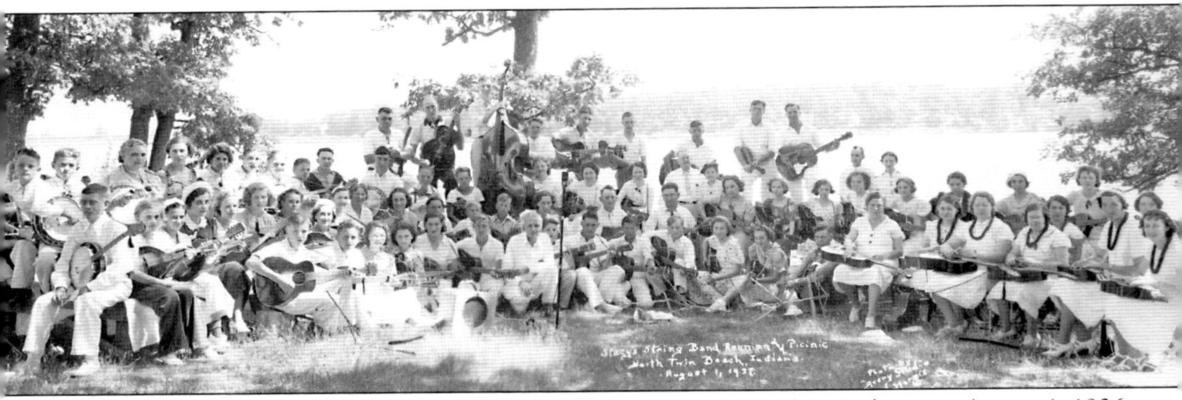

The Sturgis String Band is pictured playing at North Twin Beach in Indiana on August 1, 1936. (Sturgis Historical Society Collection.)

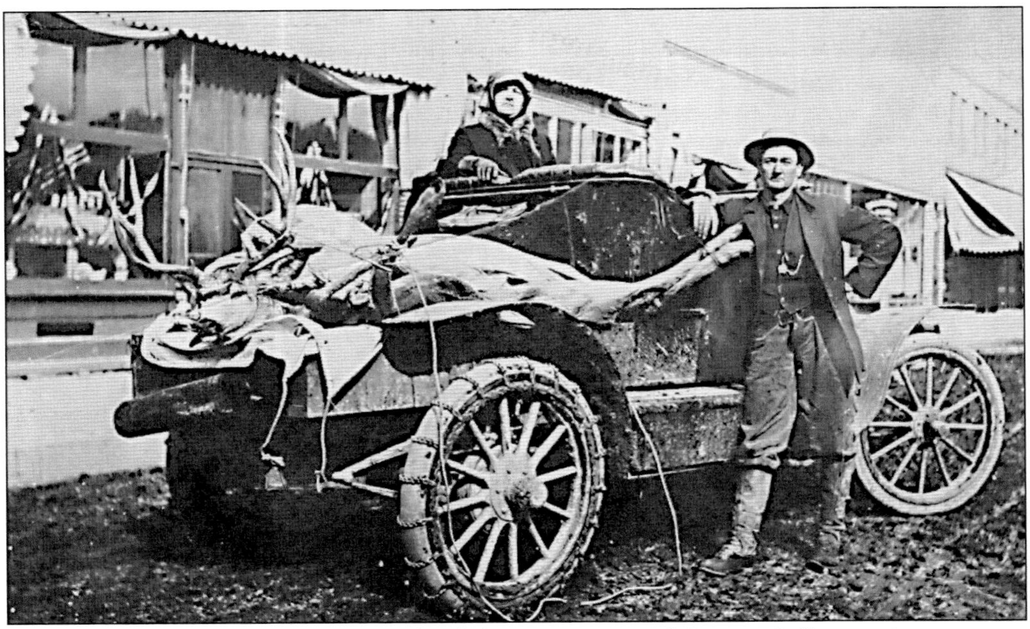

They got their deer. This photo is undated. (Sturgis Historical Society Collection.)

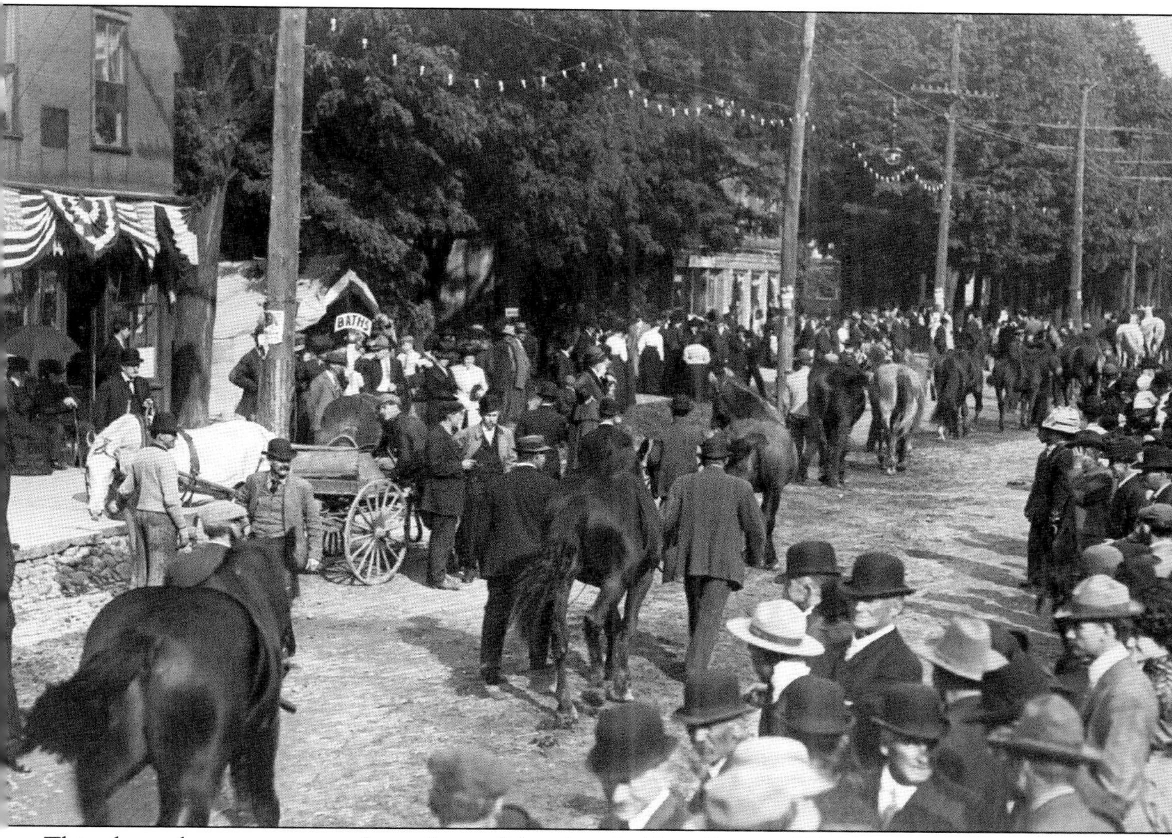

This photo documents one of two dam celebrations held in Sturgis. While many cities of the same size were still in the dark, Sturgis became known as the Electric City after a 150-kilowatt alternating current generator was installed in 1899. Demand grew and in 1905, it was decided that a dam would be constructed where the John M. Leland gristmill and sawmill had once stood on the St. Joseph River, north of Centreville. (Sturgis Historical Society Collection.)

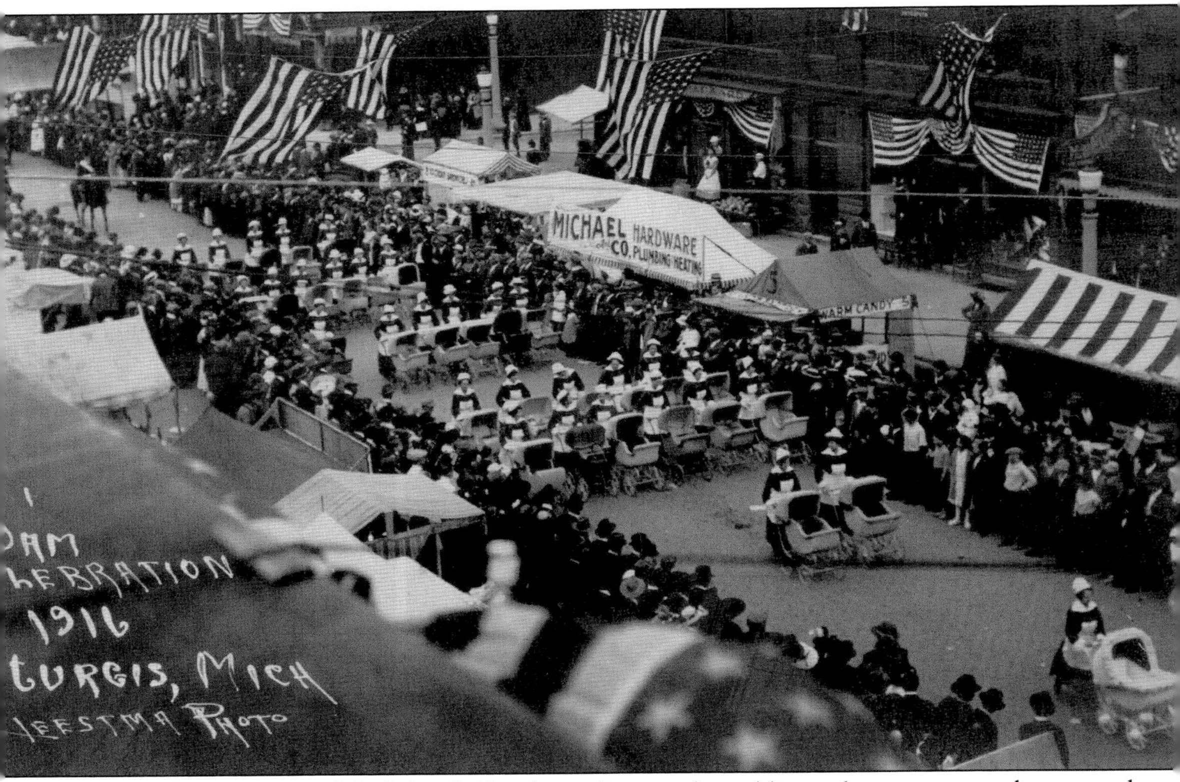

The dam was named for John S. Flanders, who was the public works manager, and generated so much local enthusiasm that two dam parades were held, one in 1911 and one in 1916. This photo is dated 1916. (Sturgis Historical Society Collection.)

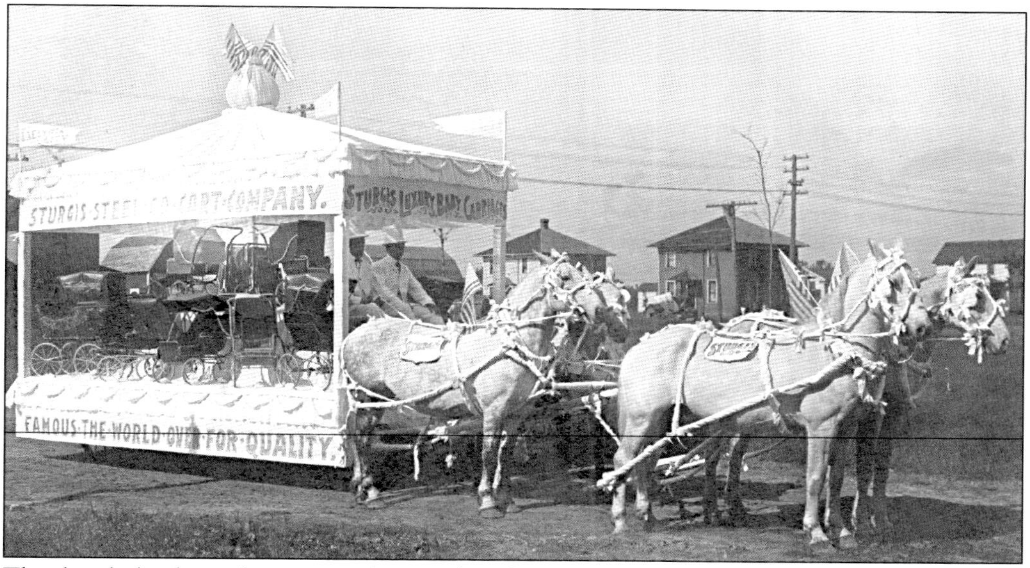

The dam helped spur business and assisted in the continuing prosperity of Sturgis. This photo shows one of the floats in the dam parade. According to historian Robert Hair, the float was a showcase for the variety of baby carriages manufactured by the Sturgis Steel Go-Cart Company, one of the town's largest employers in 1911, when this photo was taken. (Sturgis Historical Society Collection.)

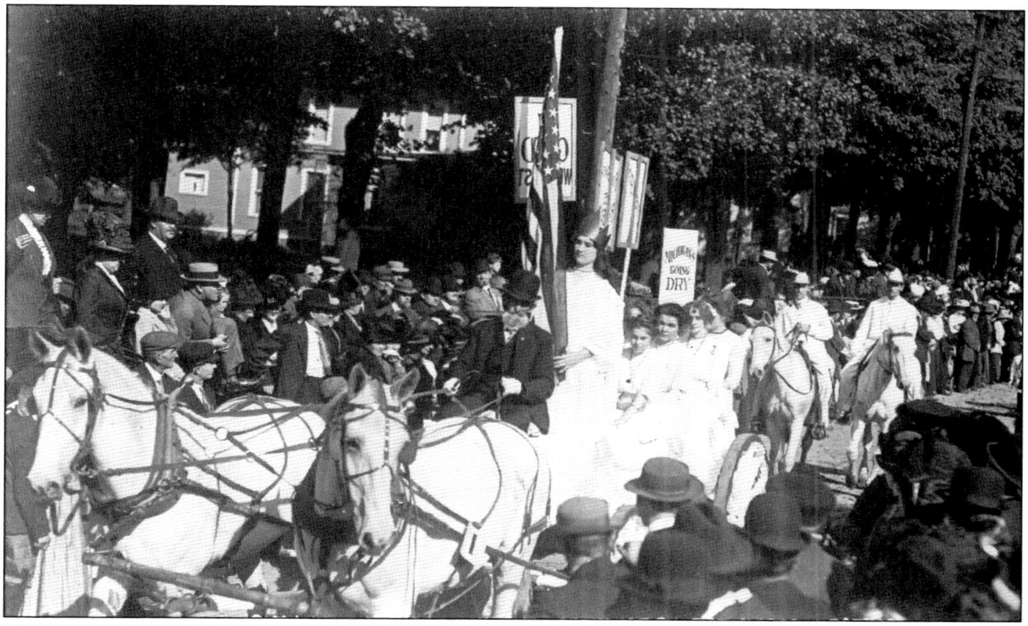

This is a photo of the dam parade. but there were many other types of parades in Sturgis—including one led by proponents of prohibition that wound its way through downtown on Chicago Road. According to historian and author Robert Hair, St. Joseph County voted itself dry on April 6, 1908, and the issue of whether to remain dry was contested at almost every election until the 18th Amendment, enforcing a national prohibition, became law on January 16, 1919. (Sturgis Historical Society Collection.)

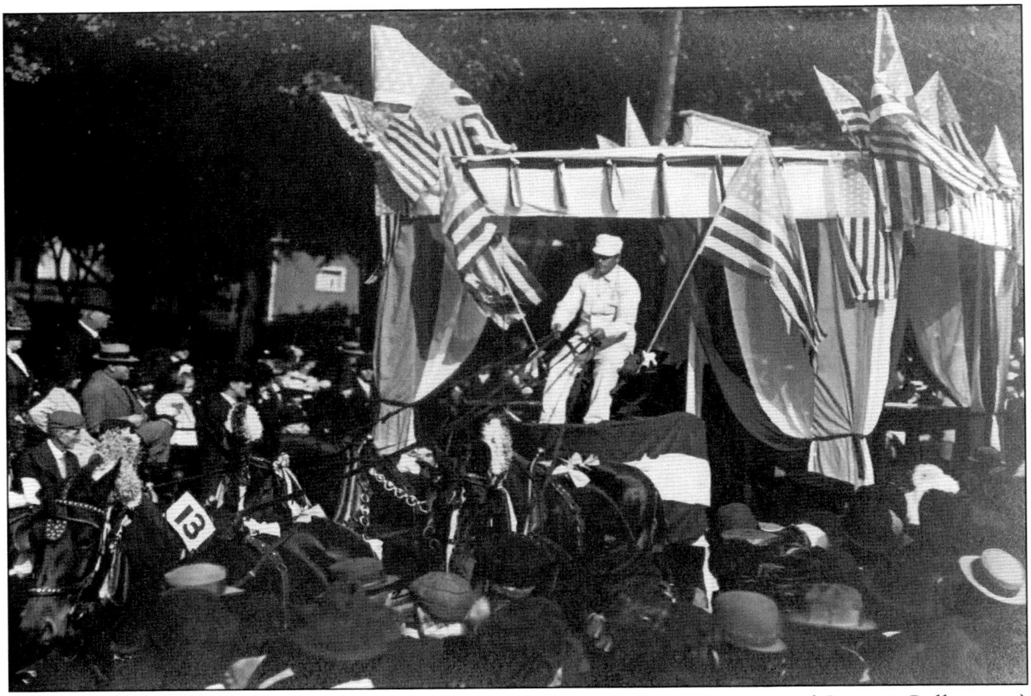

Flags are waving during the 1911 Dam Celebration in Sturgis. (Sturgis Historical Society Collection.)

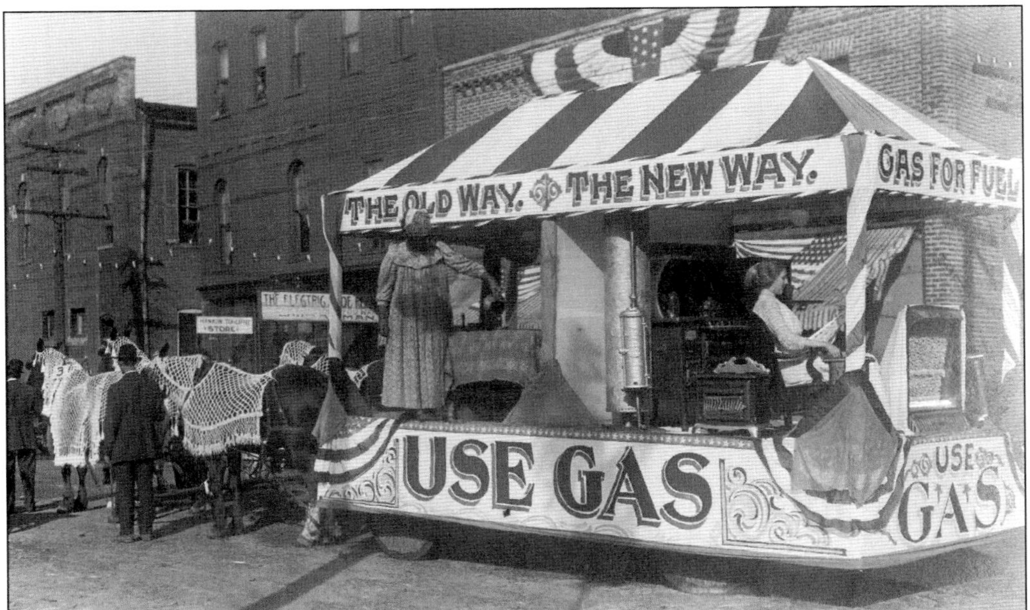

This float reflects an interesting perspective on fuel—"old" and "new." A note on the photo indicates that this Dam Celebration lasted for three days, from October 11th to the 13th, 1911. (Sturgis Historical Society Collection.)

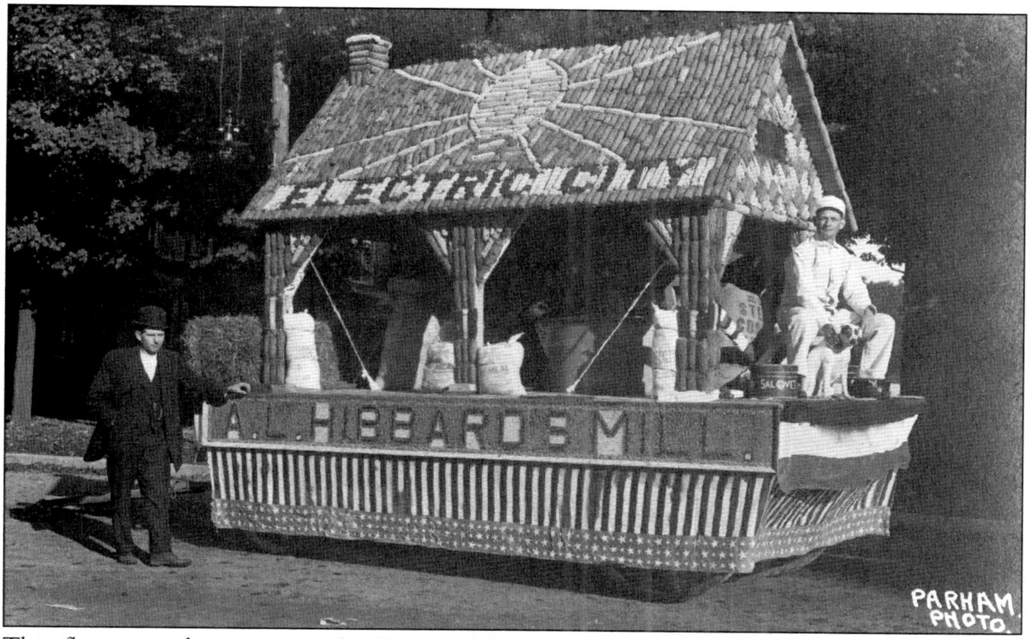

This float won first prize in the Dam Celebration. The image is dated October 12, 1911. According to historian Robert Hair, the Arthur L. Hibbard Feed Mill, which was located at 119 N. Nottawa Street, entered this float. Hair writes that it was composed mostly of different colored corn and was mounted on a motorized chassis. Hibbard, the man in the suit and hat standing on the left of the float, ran the feed mill from 1898 to 1912 and was also the city clerk from 1905 to 1908. He was city treasurer and one of the city's supervisors from 1931 to 1937. (Sturgis Historical Society Collection.)

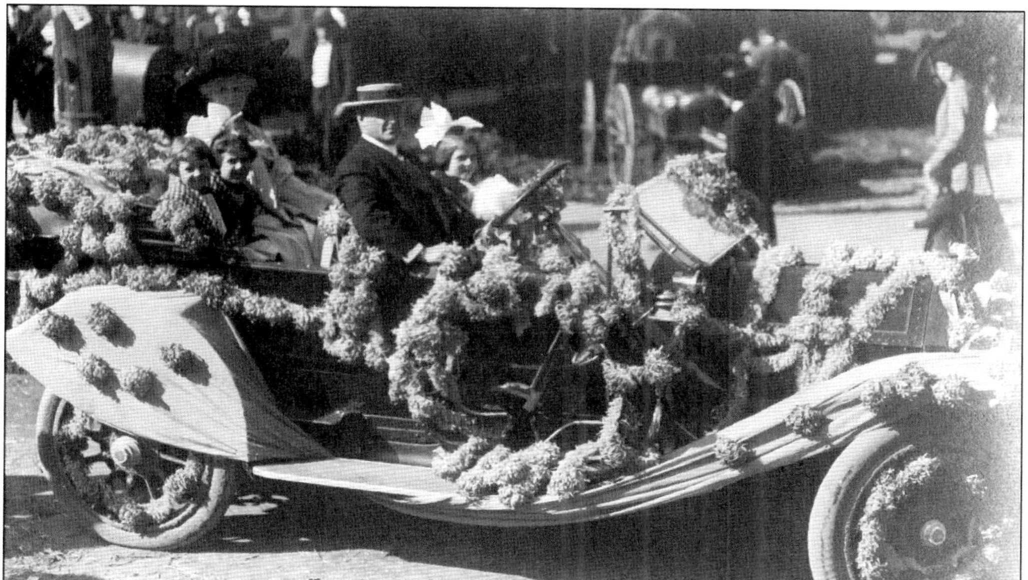
There's no identification on this old postcard, but these certainly look like bigwigs in another display of floral extravagance in the Dam Celebration. (Sturgis Historical Society Collection.)

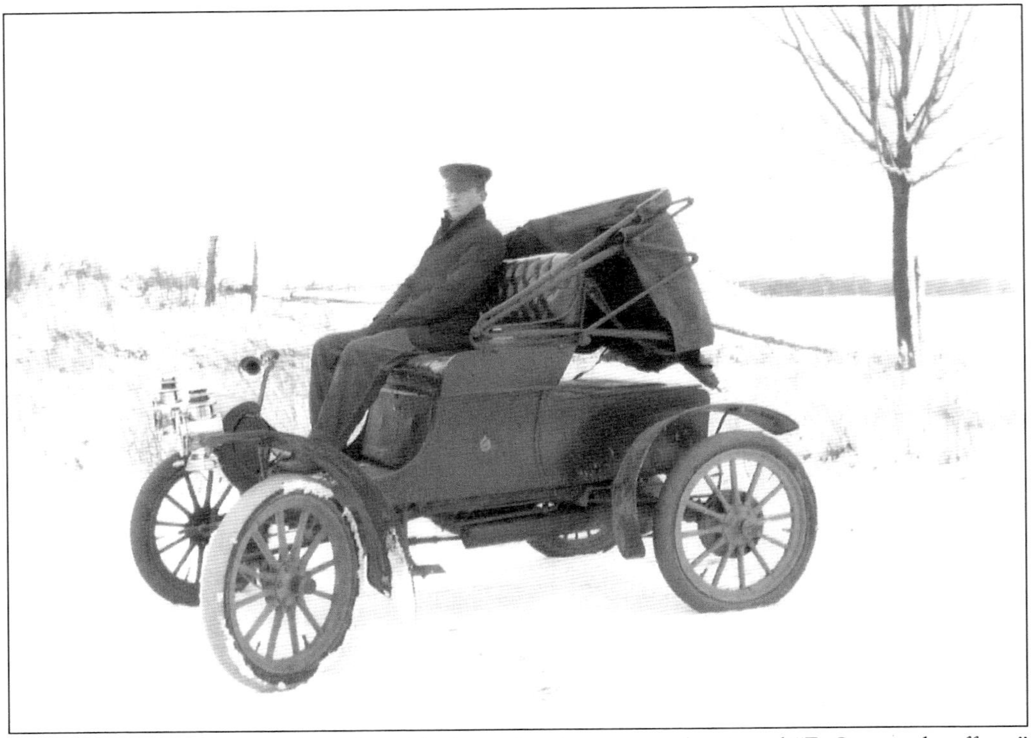

The writing is hard to read on this old photo, but it seems to be signed "E. Sucor, chauffeur." (Sue Silliman House Museum Collection.)

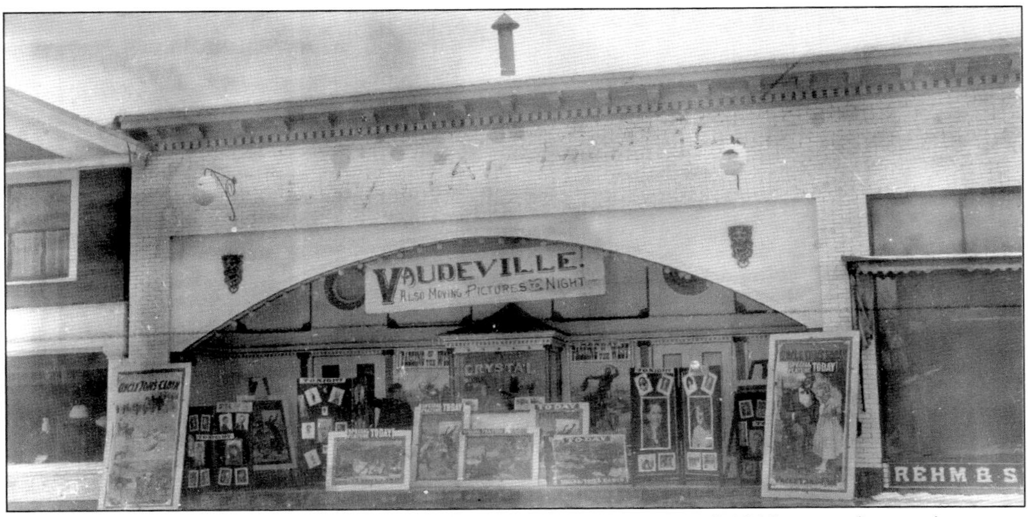

The first motion picture theater most likely came to Sturgis around 1900, according to historian Robert Hair's book on Sturgis. That's when the popularity of nickelodeons was gaining momentum. Some of the theaters in the early part of the 20th century were the White Star (which featured both movies and vaudeville acts), the Crystal, the Mars, and the Strand. Until then, vaudeville was a more popular form of entertainment. (Sturgis Historical Society Collection.)

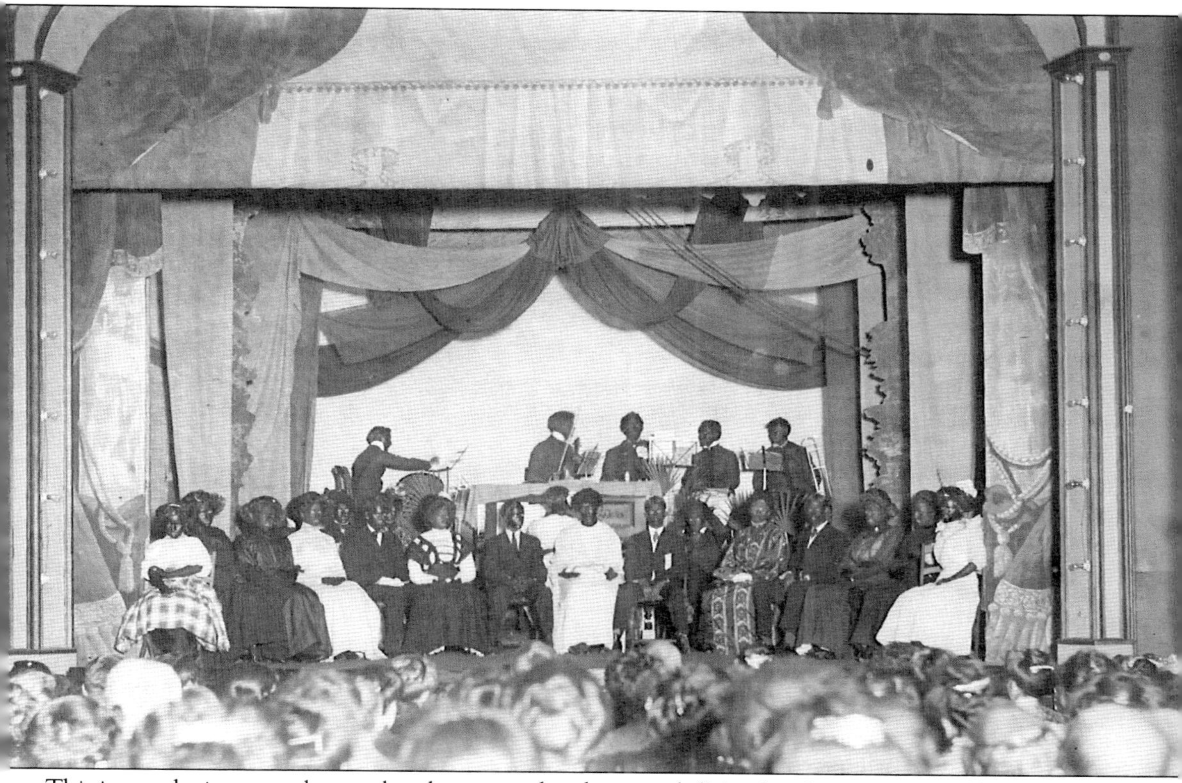

This image depicts an unknown band on an undated postcard. (Mendon Country Inn Collection.)

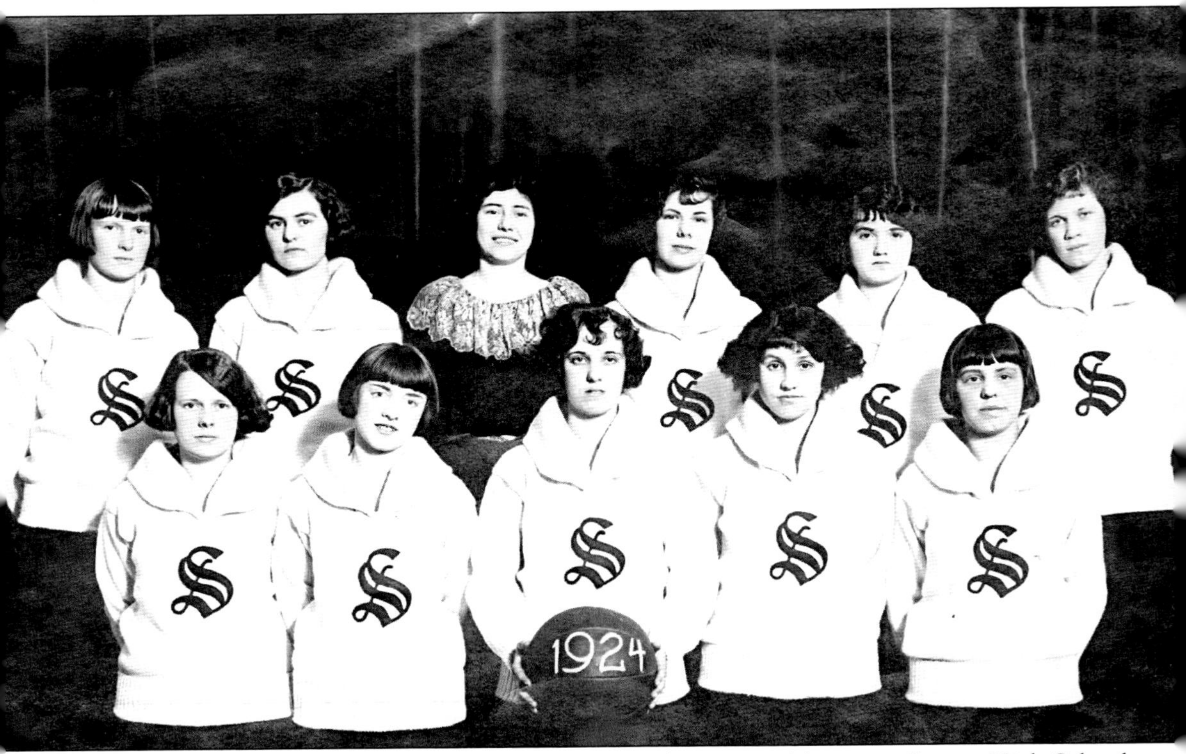

Women's basketball isn't something new. This is the 1924 girls' team at Sturgis High School. (Sturgis Historical Society Collection.)

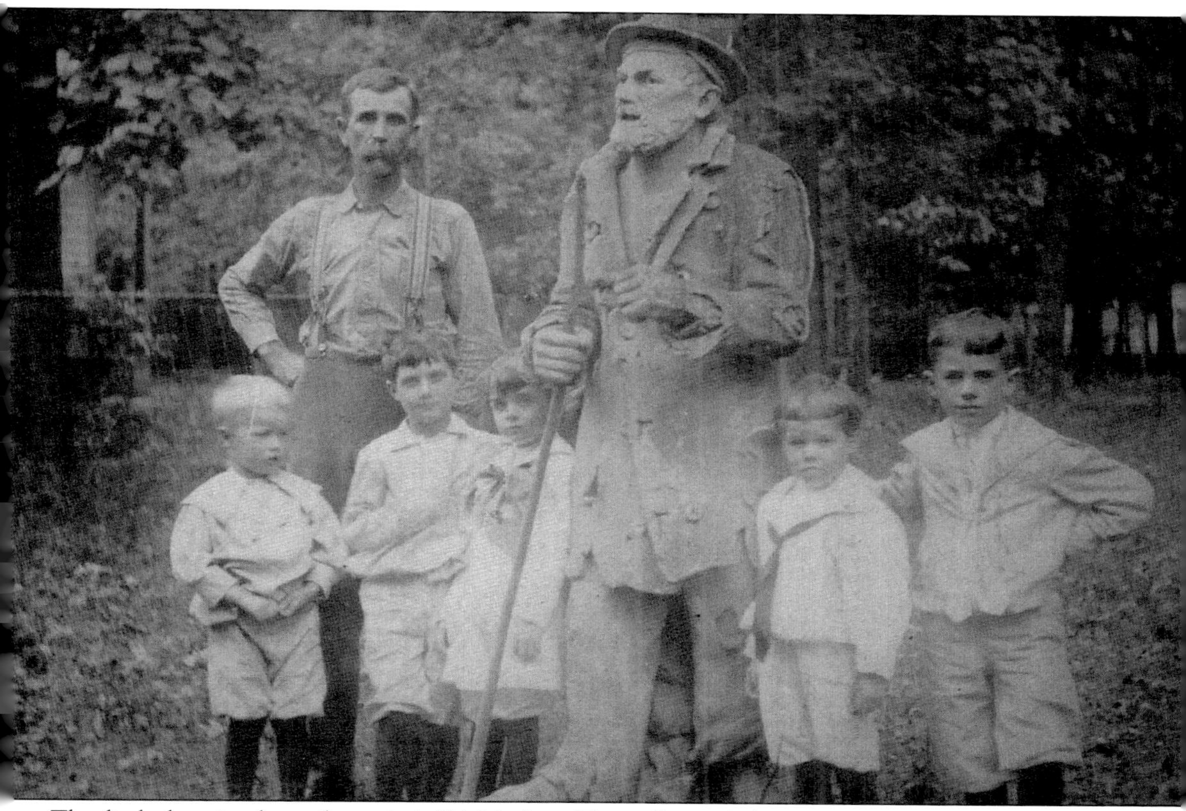

The little boy in the sailor suit is Ed Mosher. The tall man's last name is Hovey (his first name is unknown) and he is, according to Dick Cripe, the man who brought the stone tramp to Centreville. The stone tramp was originally commissioned by a Battle Creek tavern owner named pump Arnold, to spite the city's mayor. Arnold was angry becausethe mayor, as the story goes, disguised himself as a tramp, and caught the tavern owner selling alcohol illegally. When Hovey moved away from Centreville to Manistique some 30 years ago, he took the stone tramp with him. (Dick Cripe Collection.)

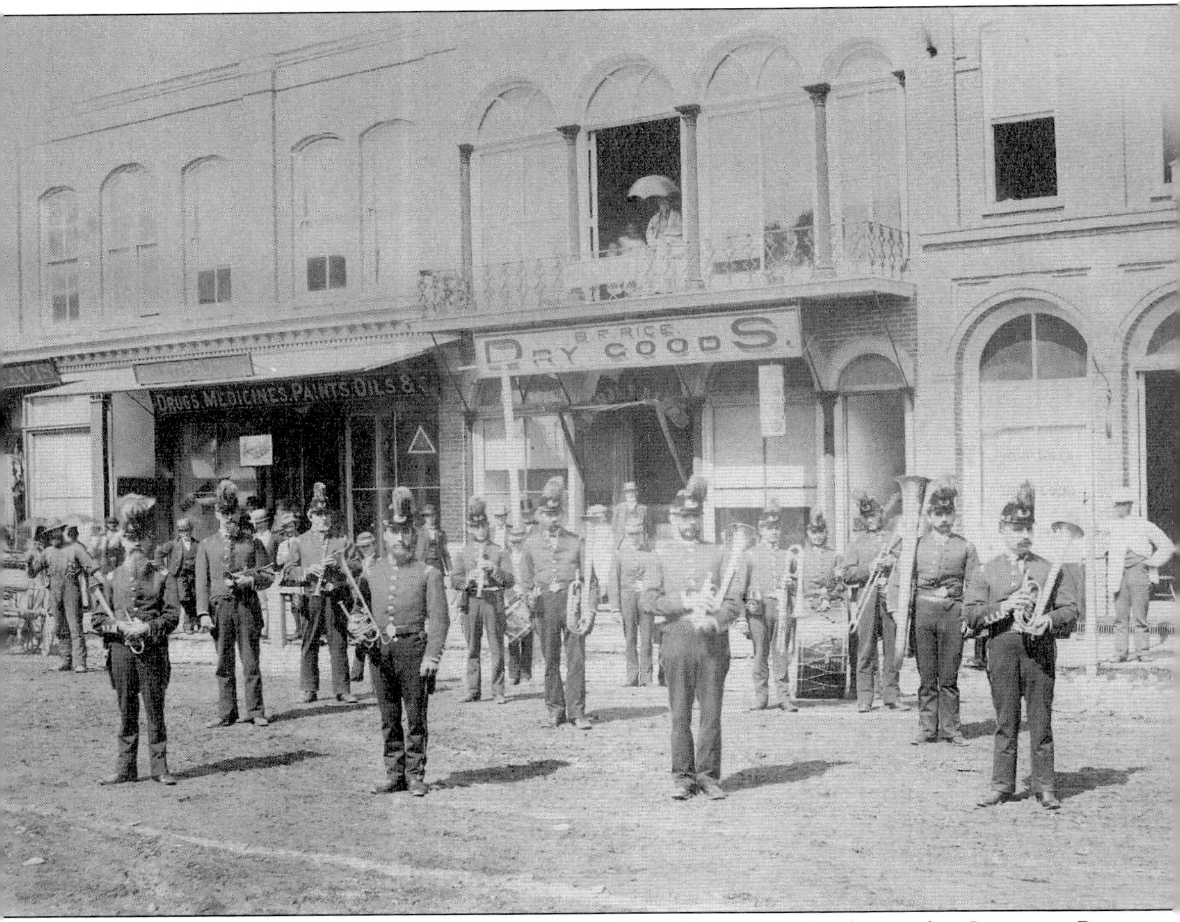

A band performs in downtown Constantine. This photo is on display at the Governor Barry House on Washington Street in Constantine. Band members include Frank Crossette, Walter Smith, Dan Arnold, Carl Cotherman, Dewane Arnold, Guss Arnold, G.B. Simmons, Julius Treluff, George Wers, J. Well, H. Drake, and Charles Arnold. Several names are missing and one is illegible. According to Dr. M.E. Vercler, mineral springs became popular in St. Joseph County after oil was first discovered in Pennsylvania in 1869. This led to widespread digging for oil wells. Though the oil discoveries were practically nonexistent in the county, the beneficial mineral waters became a draw. (Governor Barry Historical Society Collection.)

Five

Times of Stress

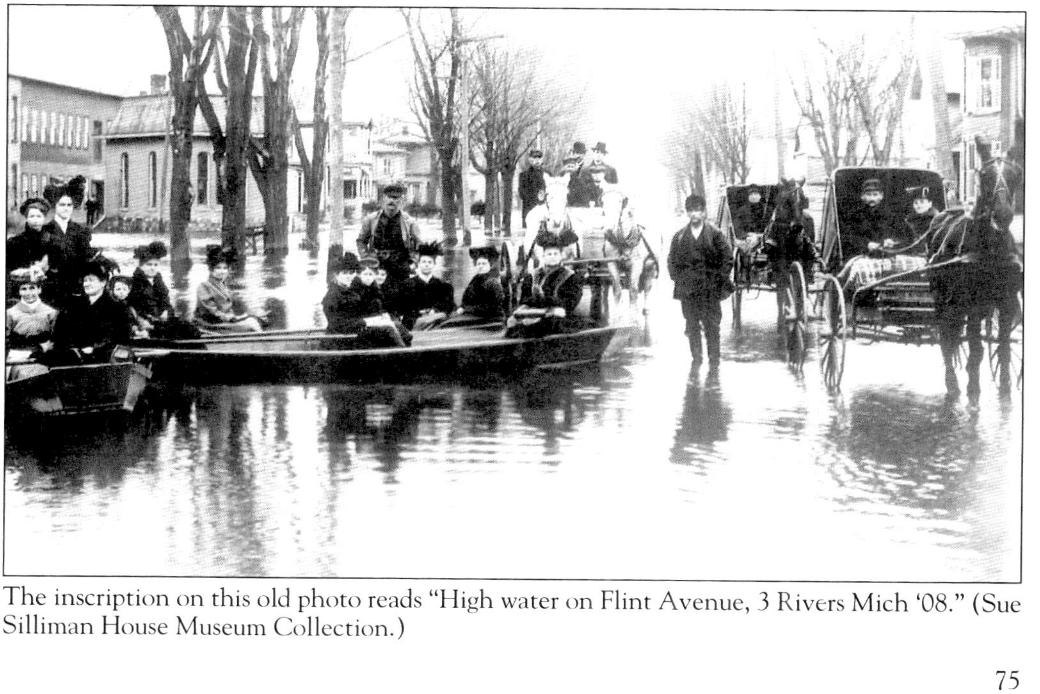

The inscription on this old photo reads "High water on Flint Avenue, 3 Rivers Mich '08." (Sue Silliman House Museum Collection.)

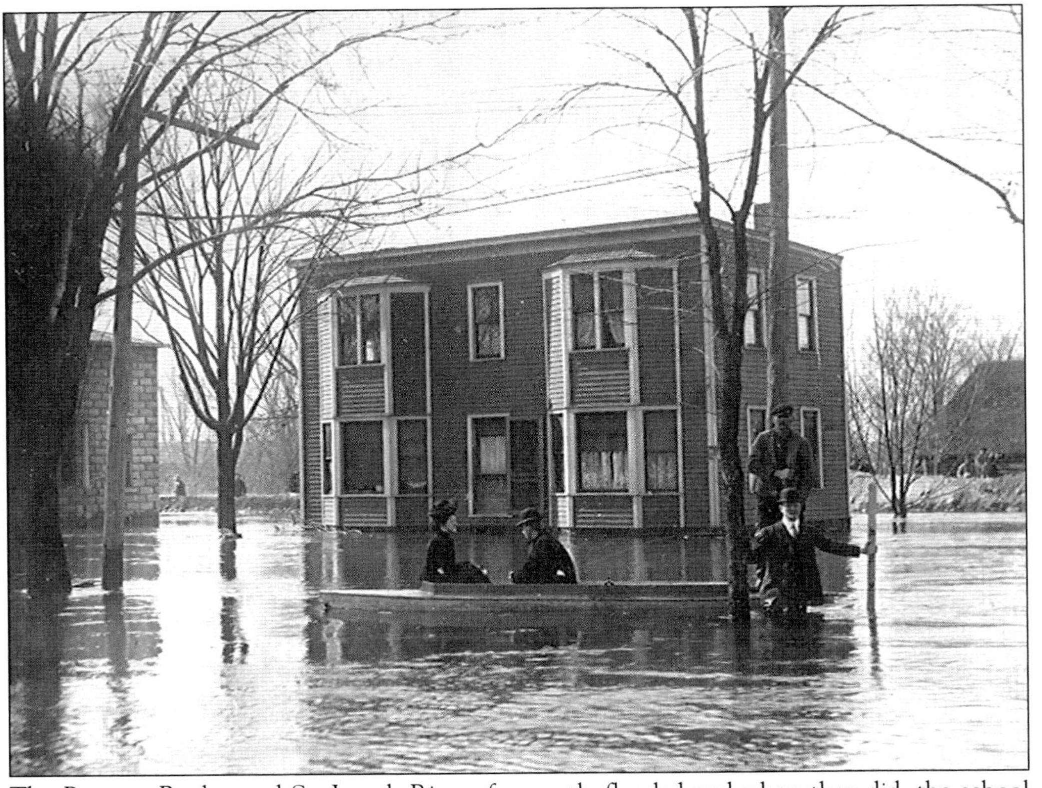

The Portage, Rocky, and St. Joseph Rivers frequently flooded and when they did, the school board paid to have students ferried to school. According to the book *Three Rivers: The Early Years*, published in 1986 by the City of Three Rivers Sesquicentennial Committee, a local telegraph operator had to hire a boat to get to his hotel room. (Three Rivers Library Collection.)

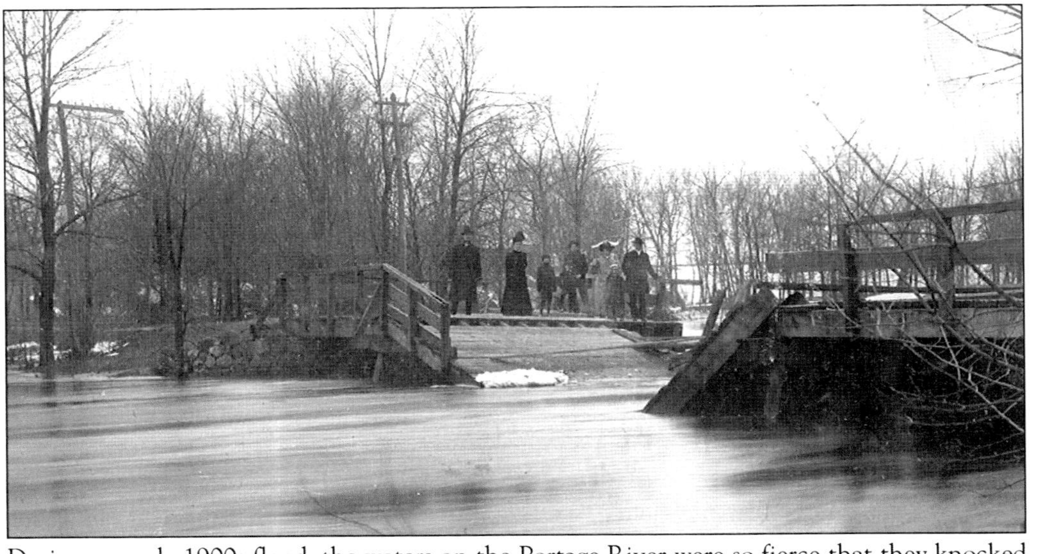

During an early 1900s flood, the waters on the Portage River were so fierce that they knocked out the Hoffman Street Bridge at the Hoffman Mill. (Three Rivers Library Collection.)

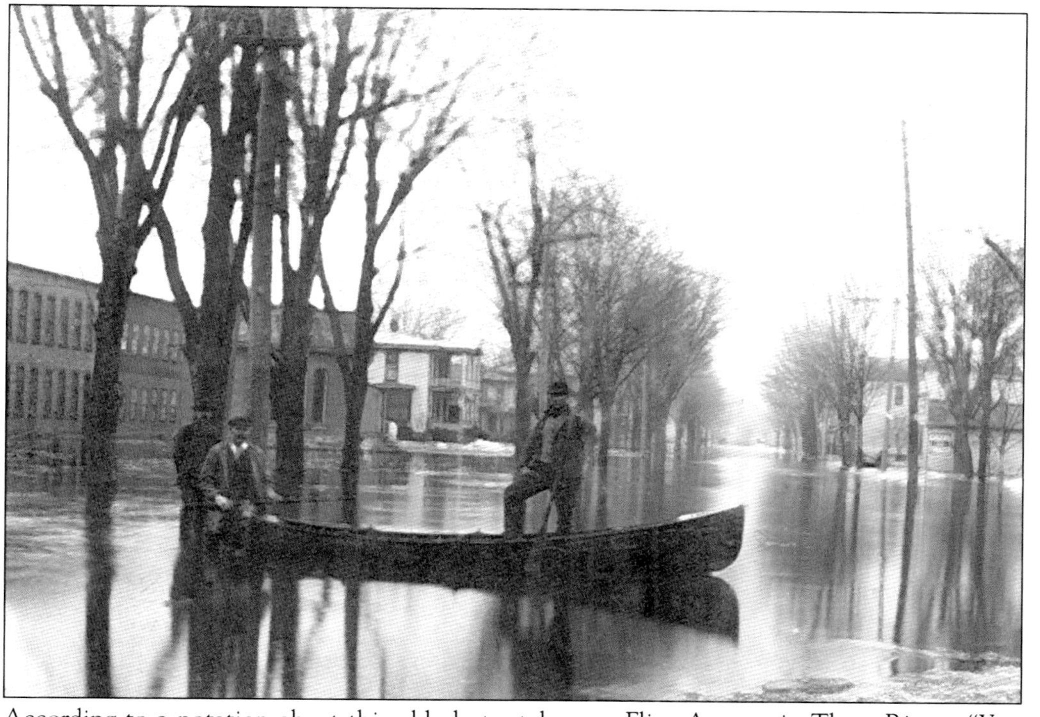

According to a notation about this old photo, taken on Flint Avenue in Three Rivers, "You could row a boat right down the avenue. Sometimes it would get as deep as three feet." (Three Rivers Public Library Collection.)

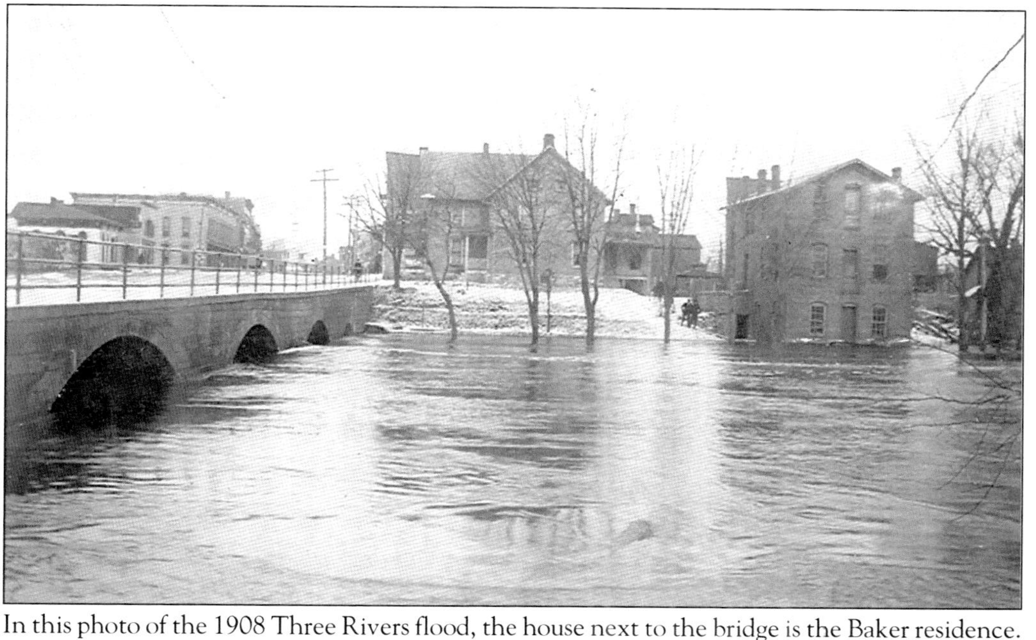

In this photo of the 1908 Three Rivers flood, the house next to the bridge is the Baker residence. Though the documentation is hard to decipher, it appears that the one next to it belonged to the Sullivans. (Three Rivers Library Collection.)

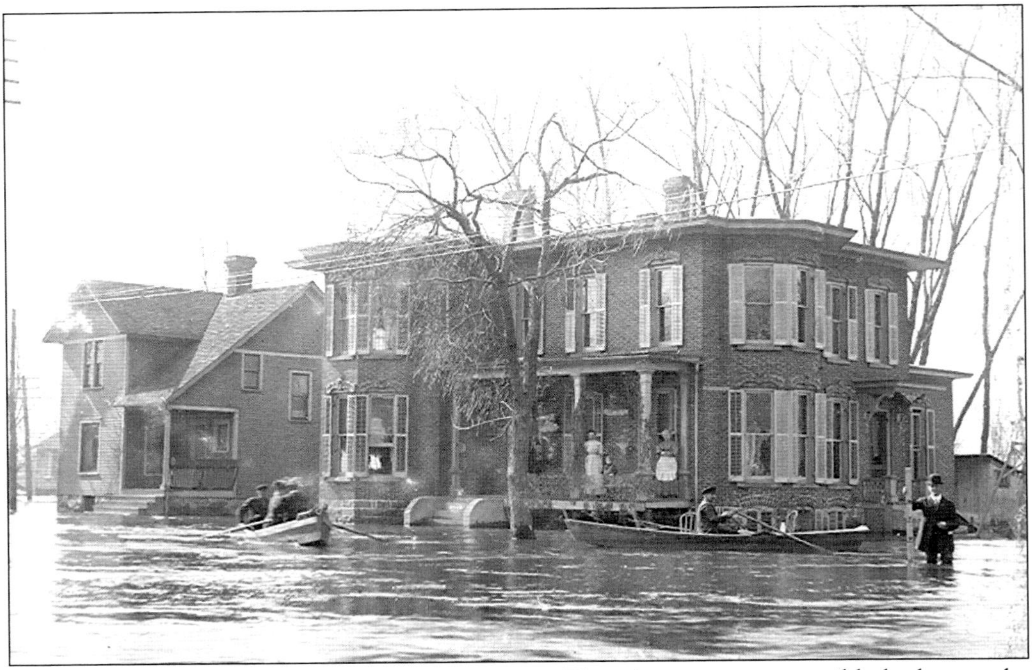

During the 1908 flood, the Tennyson property on Flint Avenue was accessible by boat or by wading in water that was almost waist-high. (Three Rivers Library Collection.)

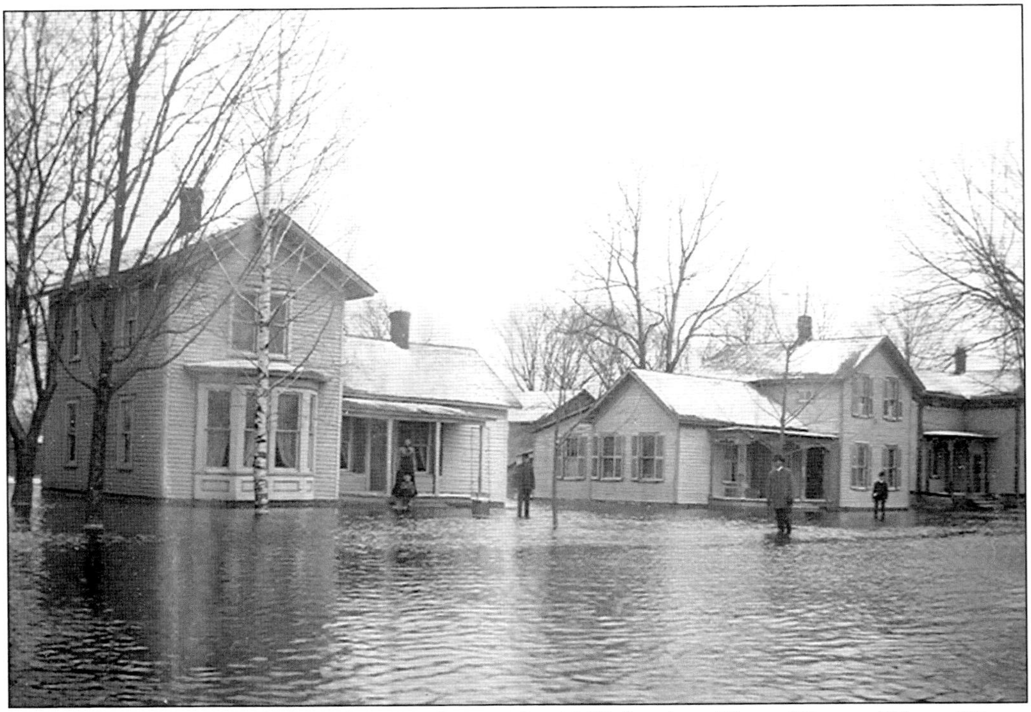

This is another view of Flint Avenue during the 1908 flood in Three Rivers. (Three Rivers Library Collection.)

In 1895, Three Rivers had 16 wagon bridges and two railroad bridges. Here, men cross the Flint Avenue Bridge (built in 1904) as water laps its sides during the flood. (Three Rivers Library Collection.)

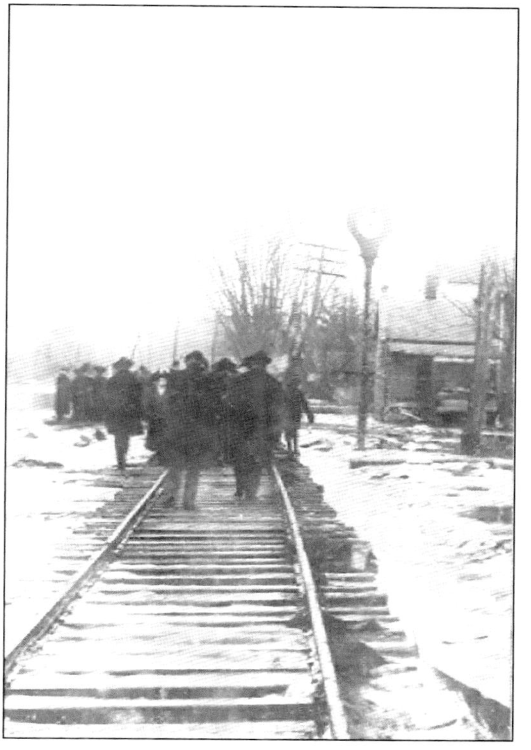

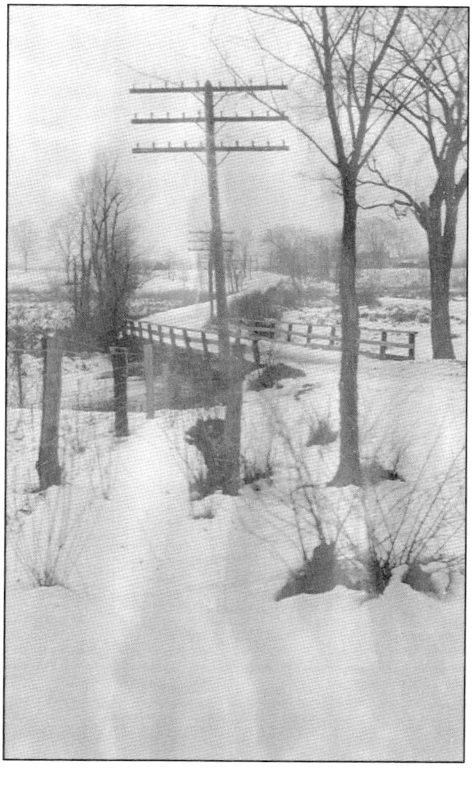

A sleet storm in 1905 covered everything in the Three Rivers area with a layer of ice. (Three Rivers Library Collection.)

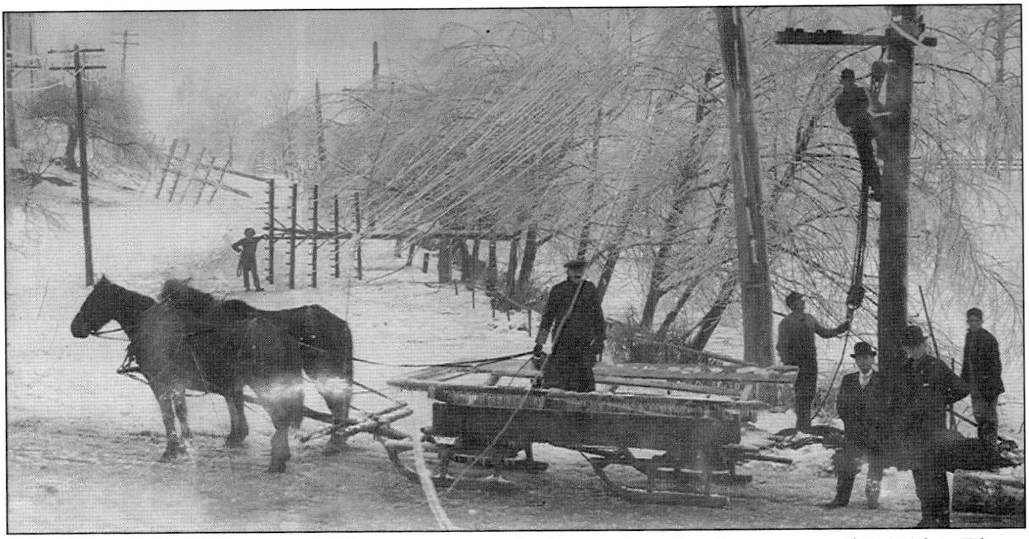

Horses pull a sleigh as men work on repairing the lines after the sleet storm of 1905 hit Three Rivers. (Bill Dehn Collection.)

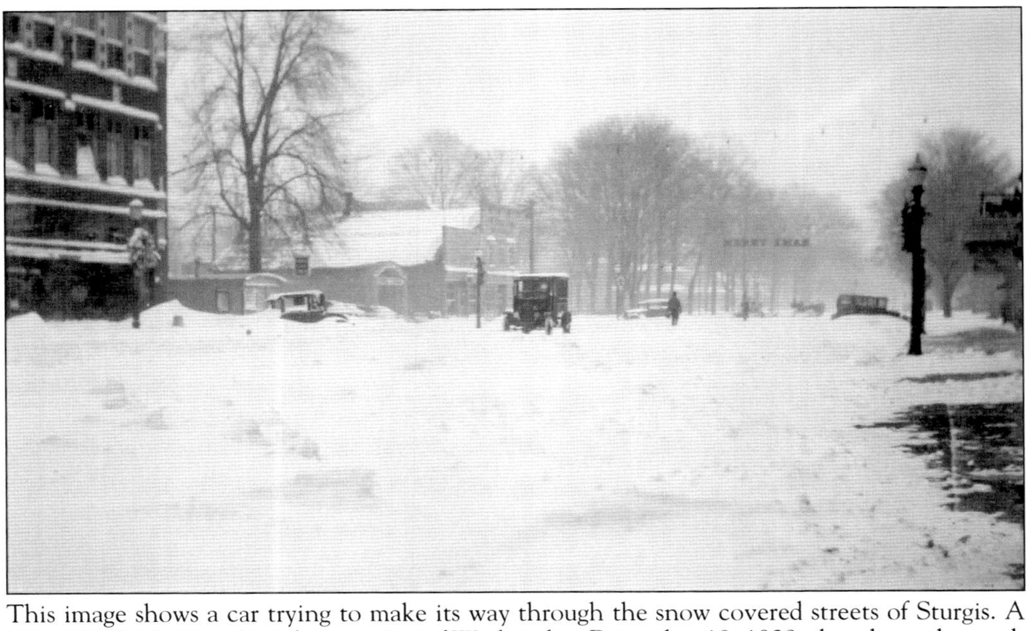

This image shows a car trying to make its way through the snow covered streets of Sturgis. A blizzard, which started on the morning of Wednesday, December 19, 1929, shut down the roads leading to and from Sturgis. (Sturgis Historical Society Collection.)

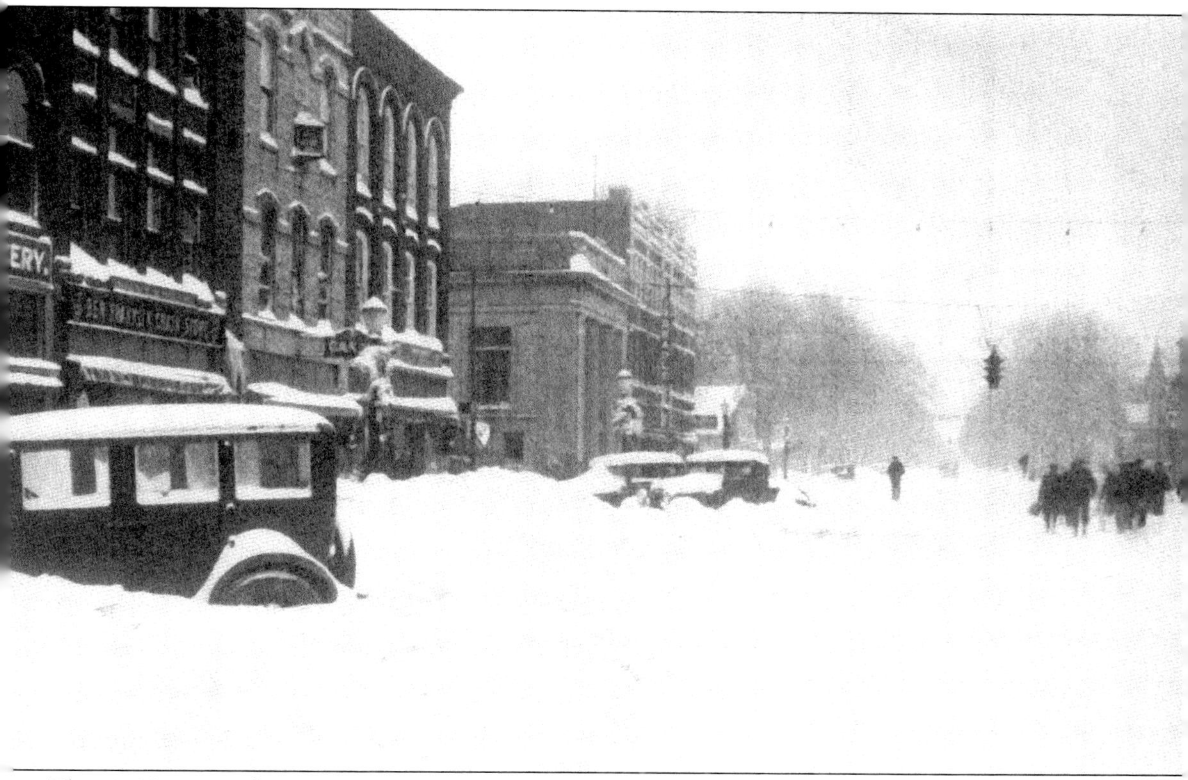

This 1929 image shows snowdrifts covering the cars on Chicago Road in downtown Sturgis during a blizzard. According to historian Robert Hair, Louis Meitus of Chicago was in Sturgis the day of the blizzard with a group of 15 Oakland and Pontiac car dealers. He was originally going to try to hit a golf ball in the heavy snow, but decided to go skiing down Chicago Road instead. (Sturgis Historical Society Collection.)

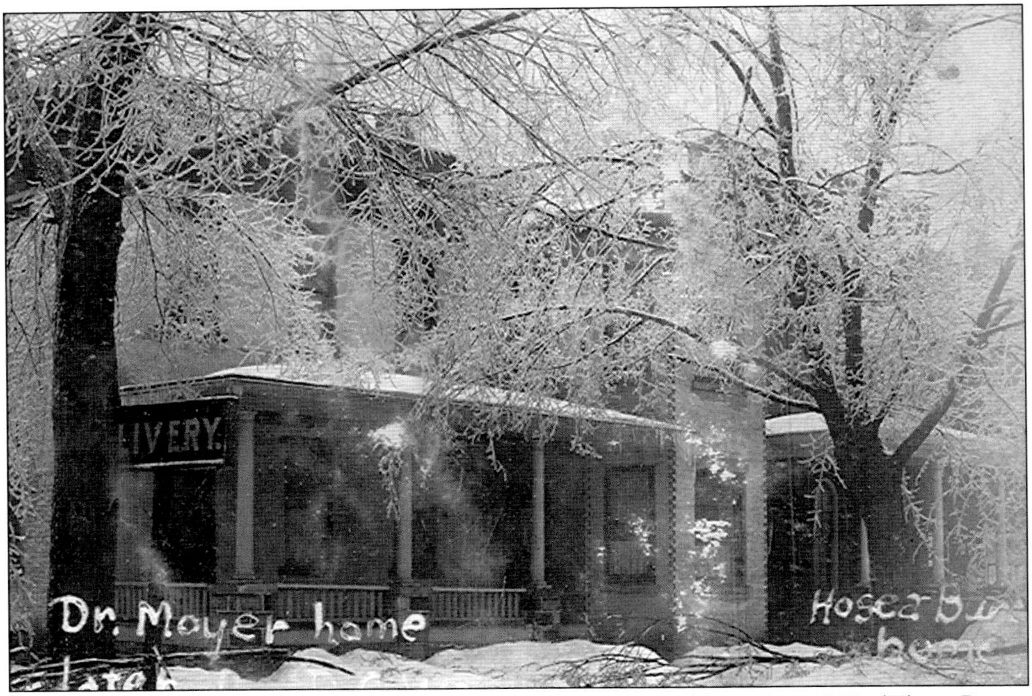

This image shows Dr. Moyer's home in Three Rivers during a blizzard in 1908. (Three Rivers Library Collection.)

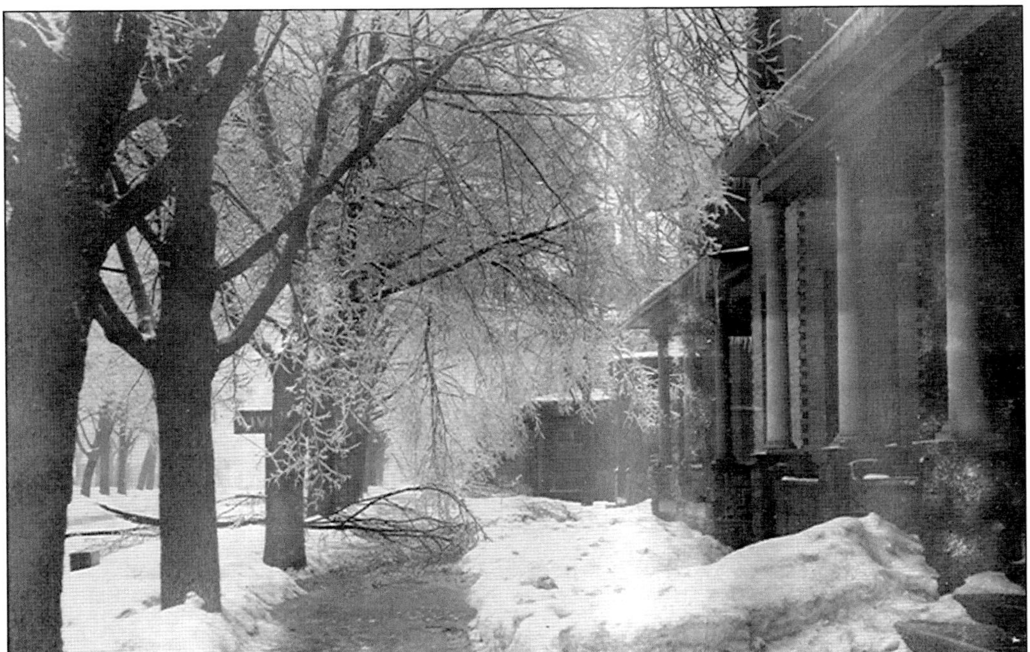

Snow blankets a residential neighborhood in Three Rivers during a blizzard in 1908. (Three Rivers Library Collection.)

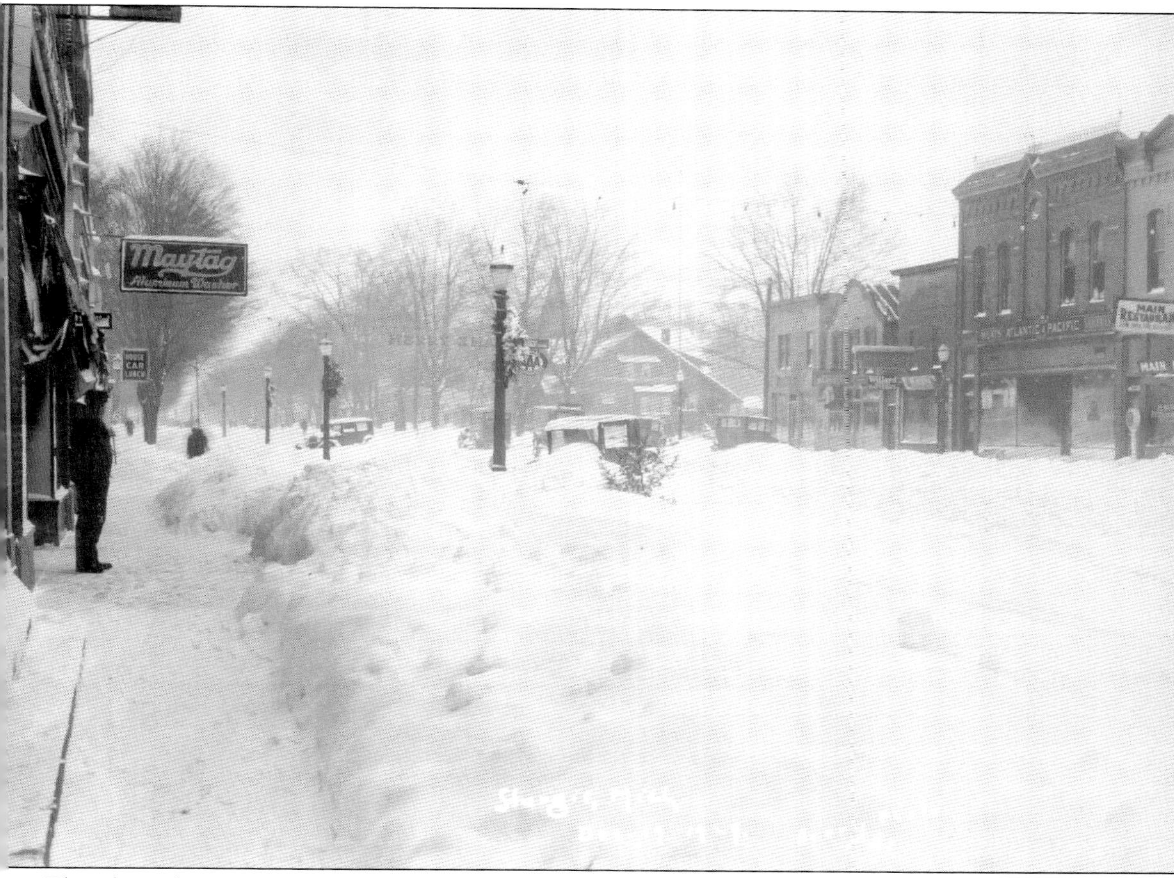

This photo shows a man standing on the sidewalk near the Maytag dealer looking out at the snow-covered street during the 1929 blizzard in Sturgis. (Sturgis Historical Society Collection.)

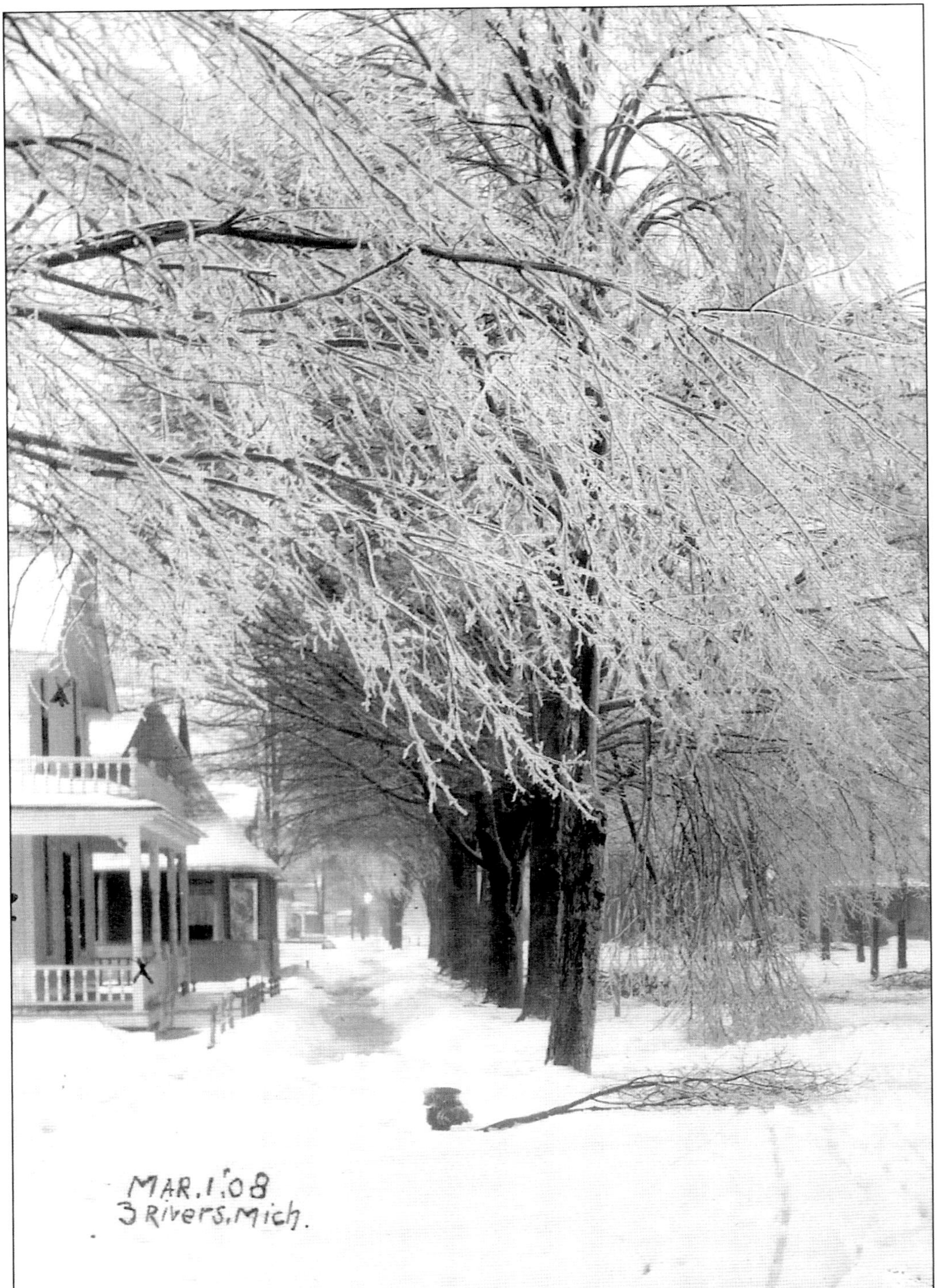

A late sleet and snow storm toppled tree limbs in Three Rivers, as seen in this photo taken on March 1, 1908. (Sue Silliman House Museum Collection.)

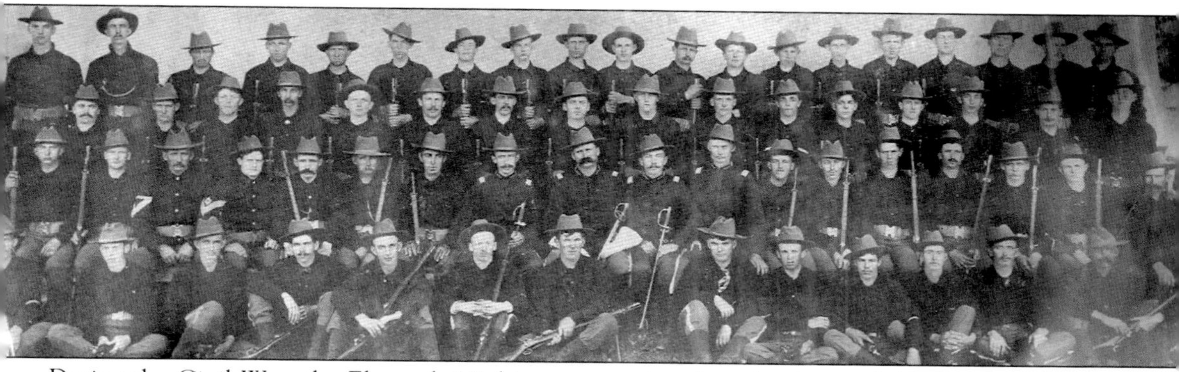

During the Civil War, the Eleventh Michigan was assigned to the Army of the Cumberland during the Tennessee Campaign. According to the Sturgis Historical Society, they fought gallantly in the battles of Stone River, Chickamauga, and Missionary Ridge. The Eleventh Michigan lost 286 men: 51 were killed in action, 37 died of wounds, and 198 died of disease. (Three Rivers Library Collection.)

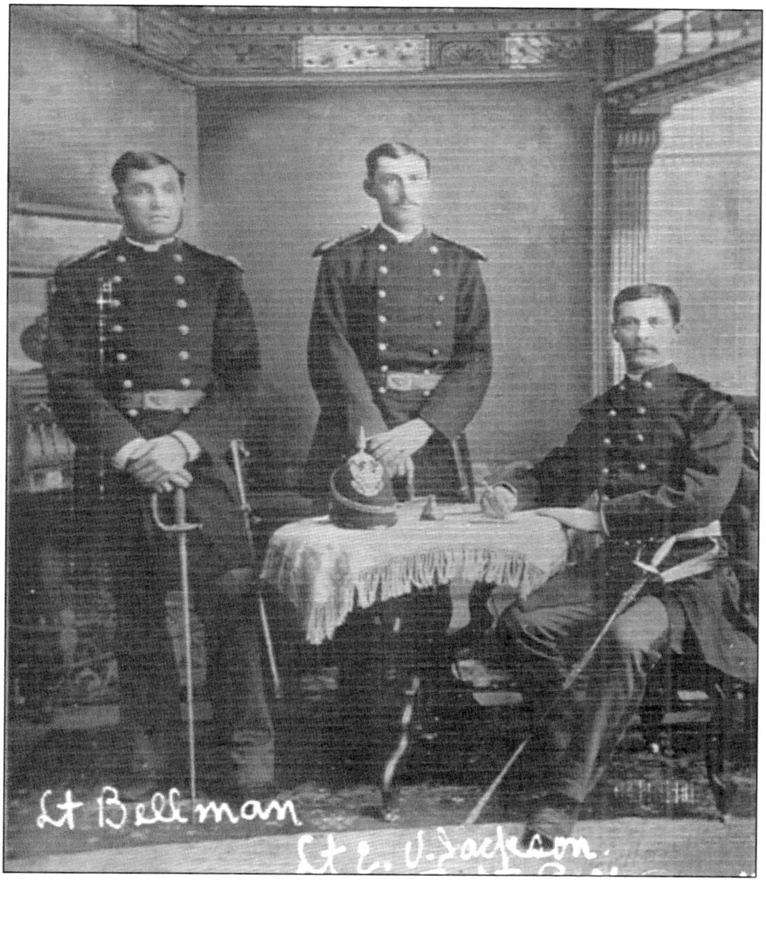

The Eleventh Michigan Infantry, consisting of 1,329 soldiers and officers, was mustered into service on September 24, 1862 in White Pigeon and Constantine. Colonel William May of White Pigeon and Lieutenant Colonel Stoughton of Sturgis were its commanding officers. The only officer in this photo whose name is legible is pictured on the left and is identified as Lieutenant Bellman. In all, St. Joseph County sent 2,836 men, consisting of 10 infantry regiments and three artillery units, to fight for the union. (Three Rivers Library Collection.)

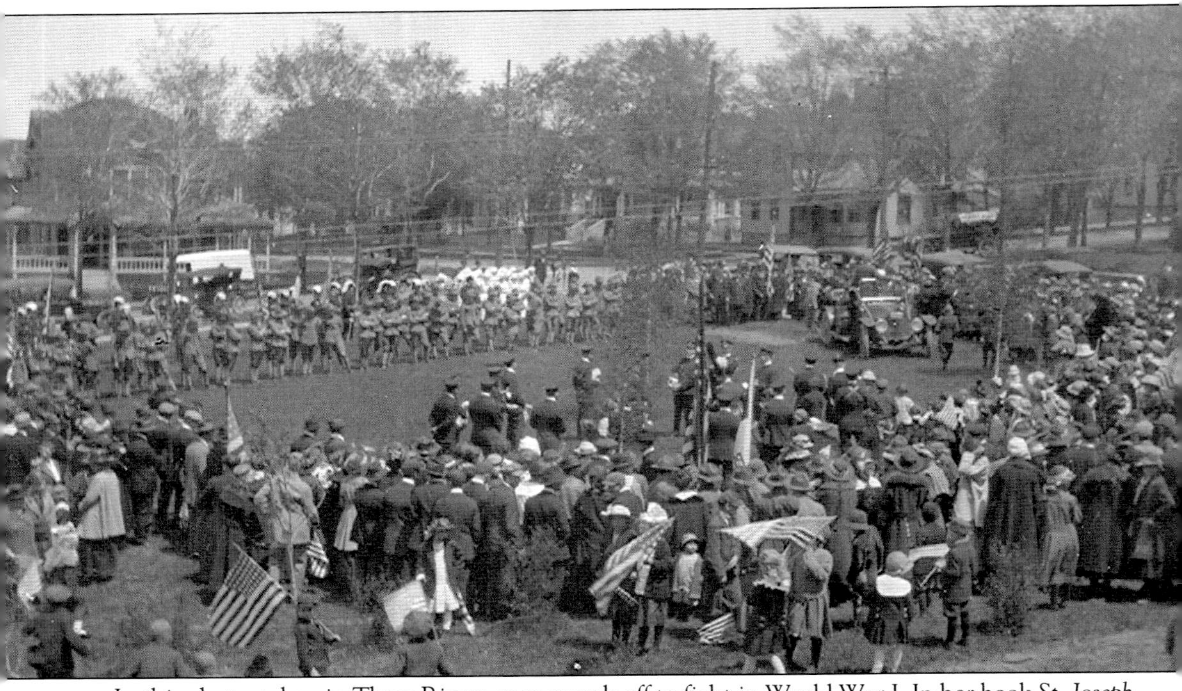

In this photo, taken in Three Rivers, men march off to fight in World War I. In her book *St. Joseph in Homespun: A Centennial Souvenir*, published in 1931, Sue Silliman wrote the following passage:

> *Not the glories but the horrors of the World's War and the splendid spirit of endurance which characterized the St. Joseph county men, are shown in a letter written by Arthur Stears and published in the Daily Commercial of December 31, 1918. He writes: 'I am writing this from the Base Hospital in France. I feel that I have done my bit in this Great War for I have lost my left leg. I was transferred from the 85th to the 3rd. Was in Co. F 38th. This was four times filled in with new men and fifty-four added to Co. F and I was one of the new men. The 38th was called the "Rock of the Marne" for courageously holding back the Germans under great odds in the battle of July. I am proud to belong to the 38th.*
>
> *'I have gone through many trying experiences and lots of suffering and have seen terrible sights—towns and homes destroyed. I was wounded and captured on the Argonne front Oct. 18 at two in the morning. I had been sent out as a runner to see who was on the right flank and I ran into the Germans, thinking them French. They shot at me and wounded me in my left leg. I crawled away but they found me and took me from one place to another, finally on Oct. 24 to the hospital at Longway. The Germans found blood poison had set in and did not operate. Would have been better off in an American hospital. After the Germans evacuated, the French cared for me until the Americans came. I hope my next move is to the U.S.A.'*

(Three Rivers Library Collection.)

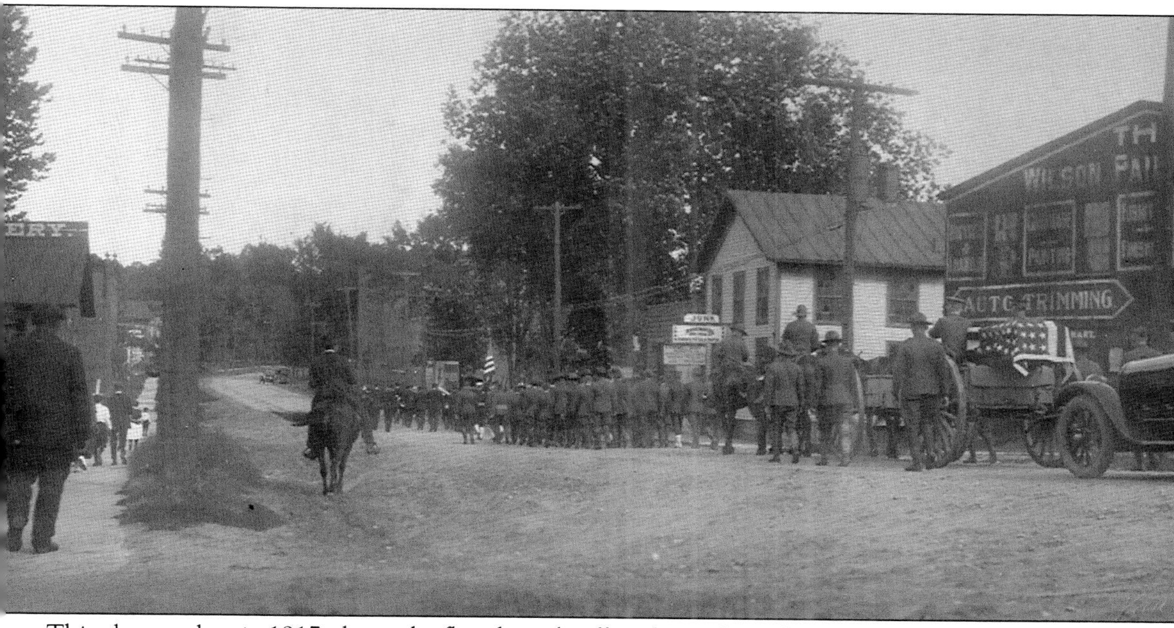

This photo, taken in 1917, shows the flag-draped coffin of a war hero during a funeral procession. (Three Rivers Library Collection.)

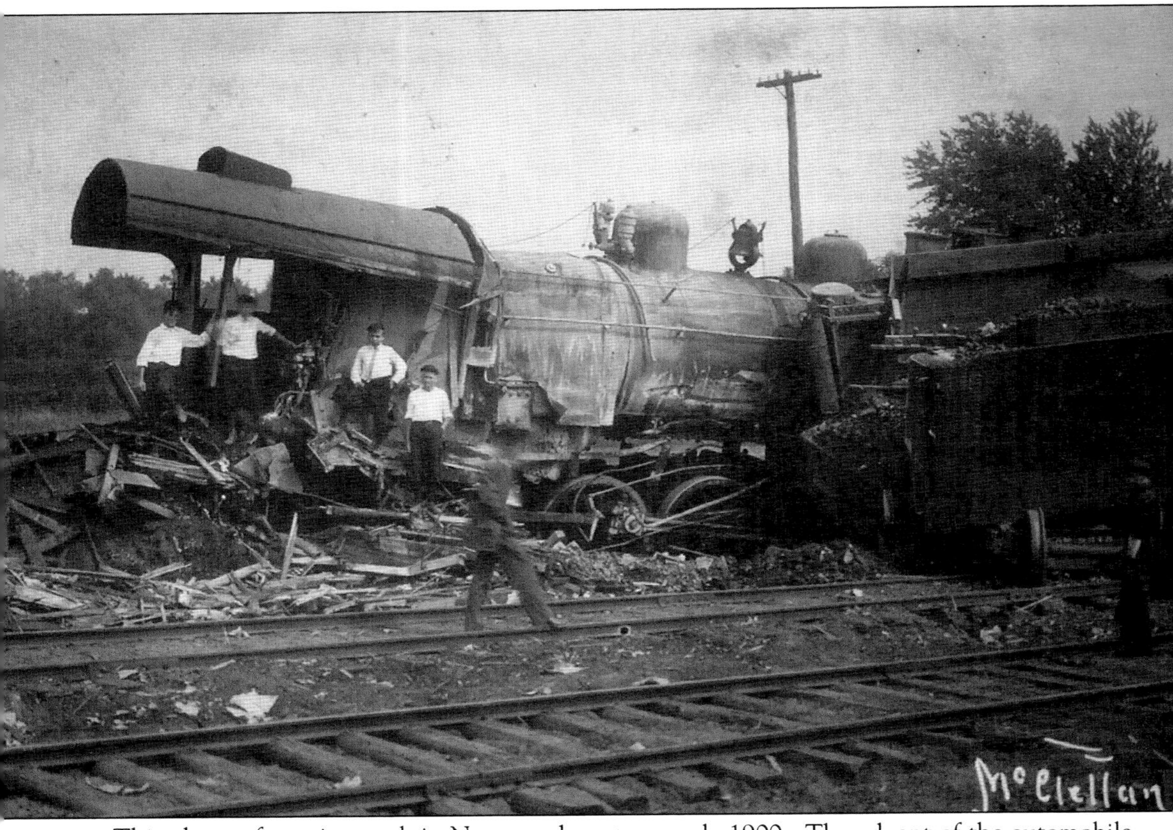

This photo of a train wreck in Nottawa dates to c. early 1900s. The advent of the automobile and better roads caused the train station in Nottawa to close. (Dick Cripe Collection.)

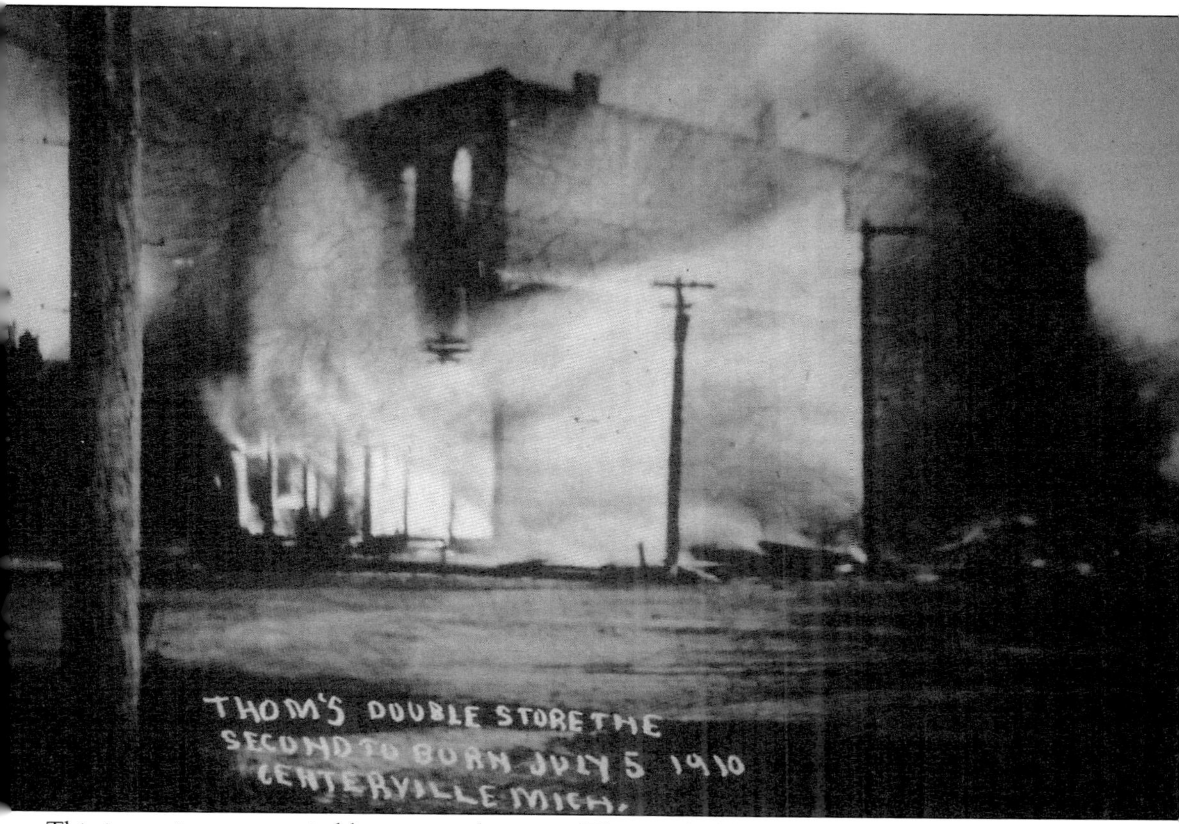

This image is accompanied by writing that says, "Thom's double store the second burn July 5 1910 Centreville Michigan." (Dick Cripe Collection.)

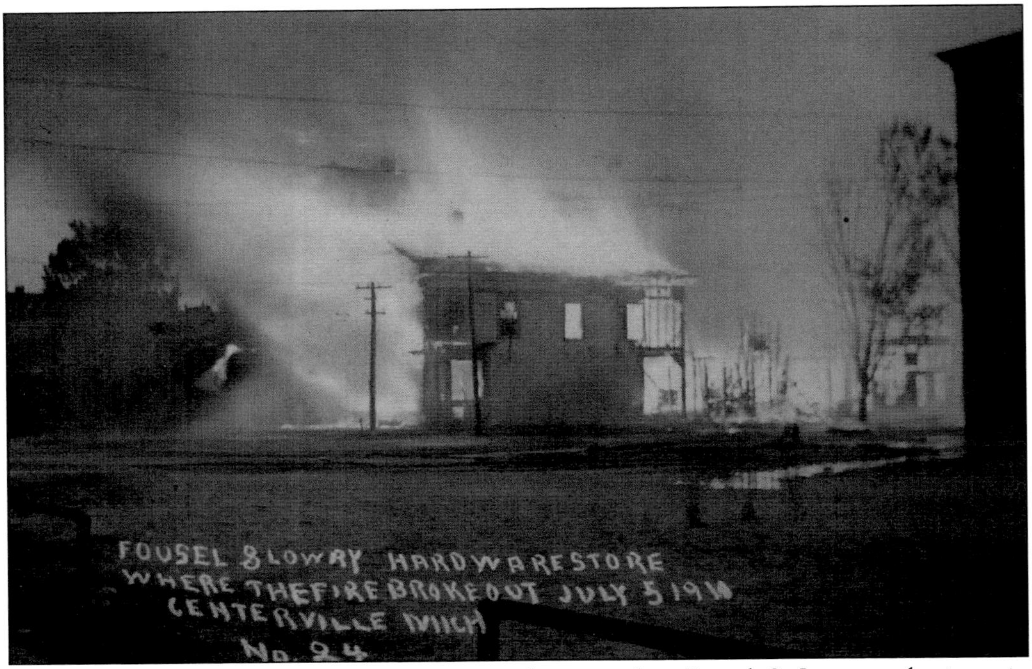

During the early morning of July 5, 1910, a fire started at Fousel & Lowry, a business in downtown Centreville. According to historian Dick Cripe, the fire hydrants had rusted shut, so a call to Three Rivers was made and the townspeople there put equipment on the Michigan Central and railroaded it to Centreville. At that time, train tracks ran between all the small towns in St. Joseph County. (Dick Cripe Collection.)

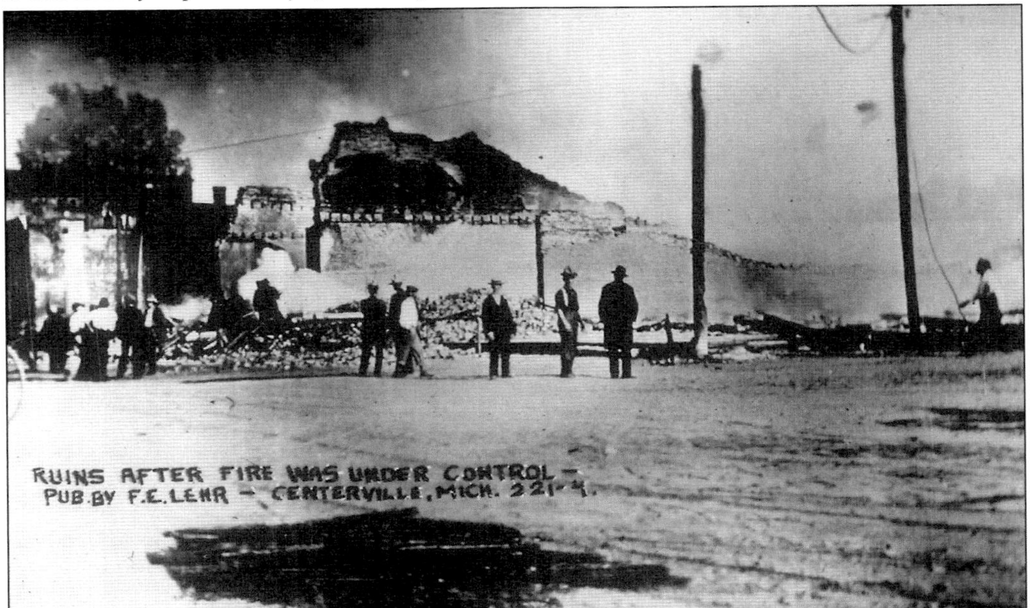

The information that accompanies this photo reads: "Ruins after fire was under control, Centreville, Michigan." (Dick Cripe Collection.)

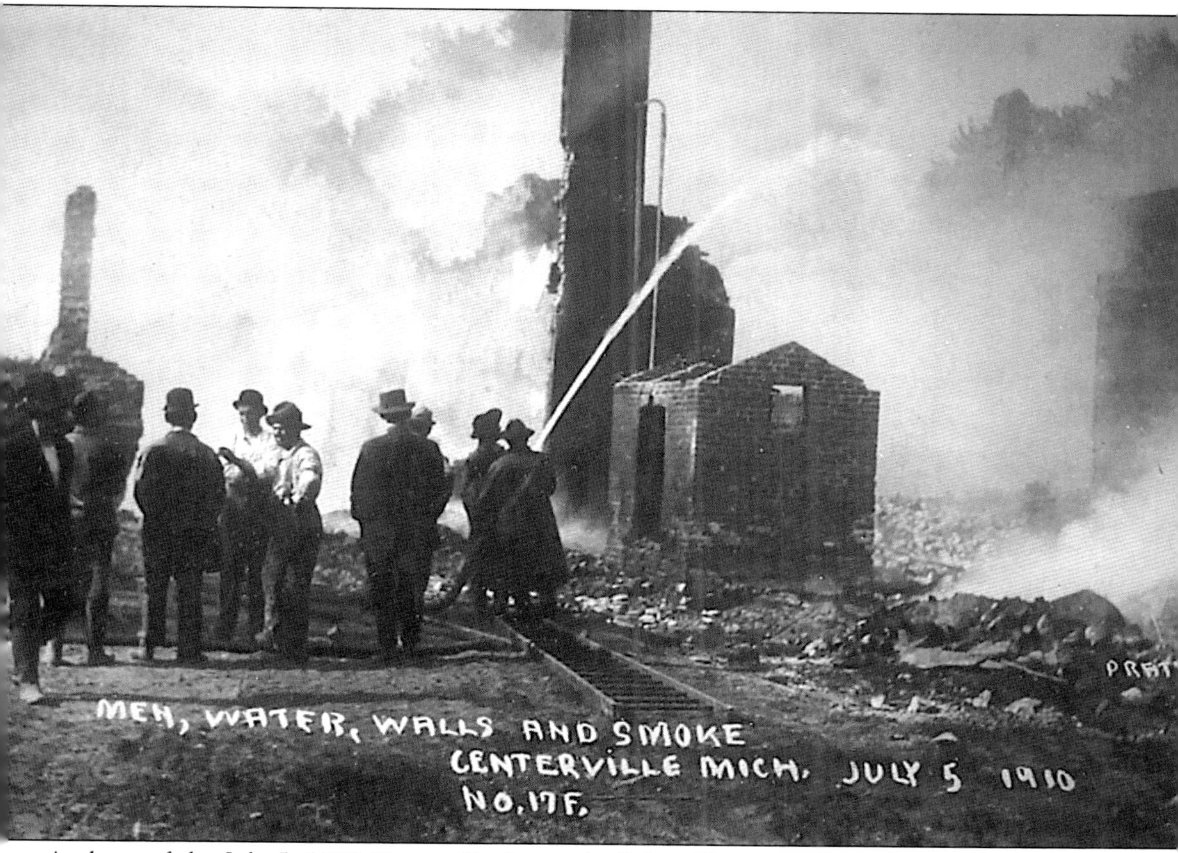

A photo of the July 5, 1910 Centreville fire reads: "Men, Water, Walls and Smoke." (Dick Cripe Collection.)

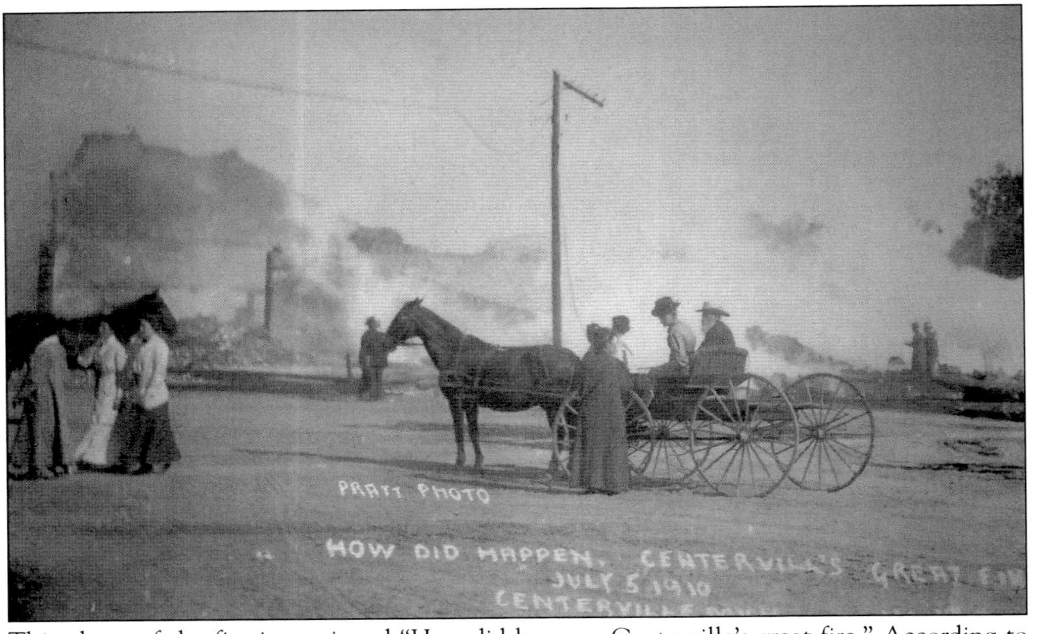

This photo of the fire is captioned "How did happen, Centreville's great fire." According to Dick Cripe, one of the women in the photo is Grace Gee, a longtime Centreville resident, who pumped her cistern dry to help fight the fire. (Dick Cripe Collection.)

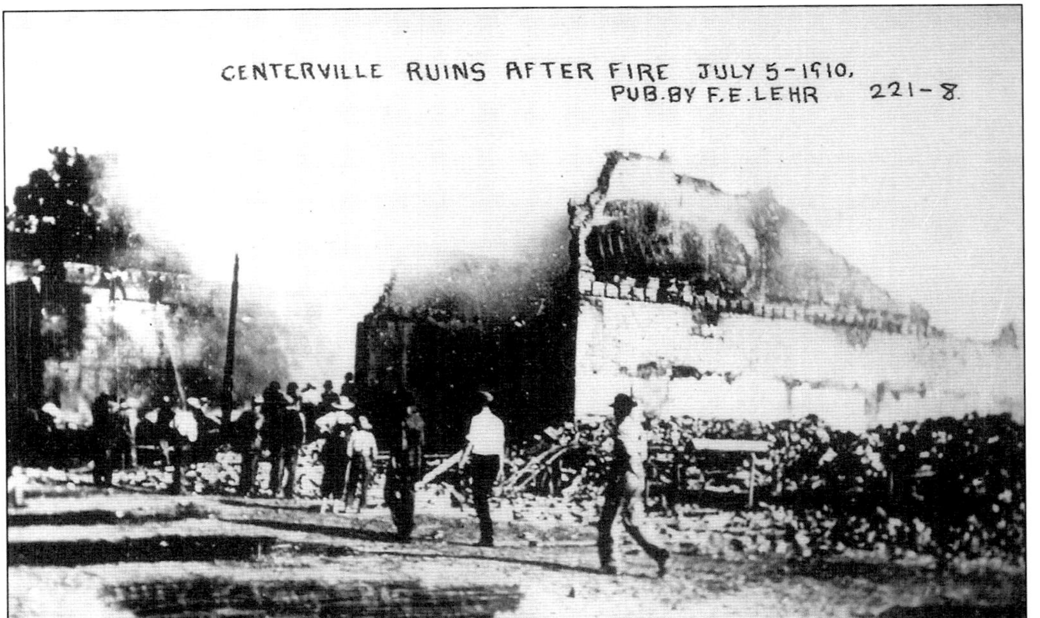

This photo shows people rushing to view the remains of the fire and is captioned "Centerville after the fire." As an aside, Centreville was originally spelled the British way with "re," but was changed to Centerville because of constant misspellings of the original name, only to later be officially changed back to Centreville. (Dick Cripe Collection.)

Six

BYWAYS AND HIGHWAYS OF THE PAST

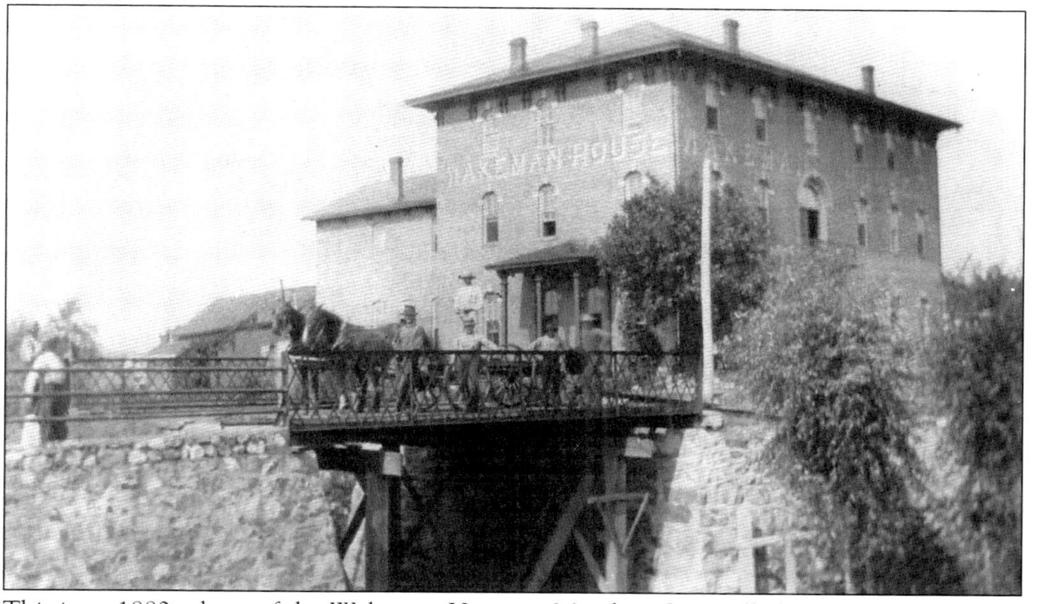

This is an 1880s photo of the Wakeman House in Mendon. Originally known as the Western Hotel, when it was first built in the 1840s, Adams Wakeman rebuilt the inn, which at one time was a stagecoach stop, in 1873. Wakeman used bricks made of St. Joseph River clay and fired on the property to reconstruct the large and rambling home. Now known as the Mendon Country Inn, the building retains its original design including eight-foot windows, high ceilings, fanlights, and a winding walnut spiral staircase that leads from the lobby to the second floor. The bridge in this photo no longer exists. (Mendon Country Inn Collection.)

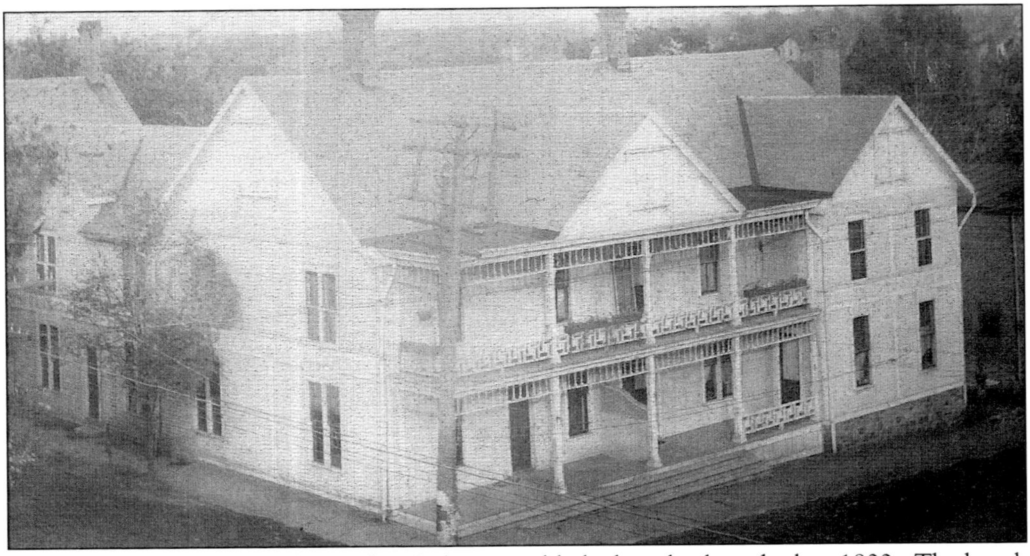

This photo of the St. Joseph Hotel in Colon most likely dates back to the late 1800s. The hotel, which is now gone, stood in the downtown area and had a livery stable in the rear. (Community Historical Society.)

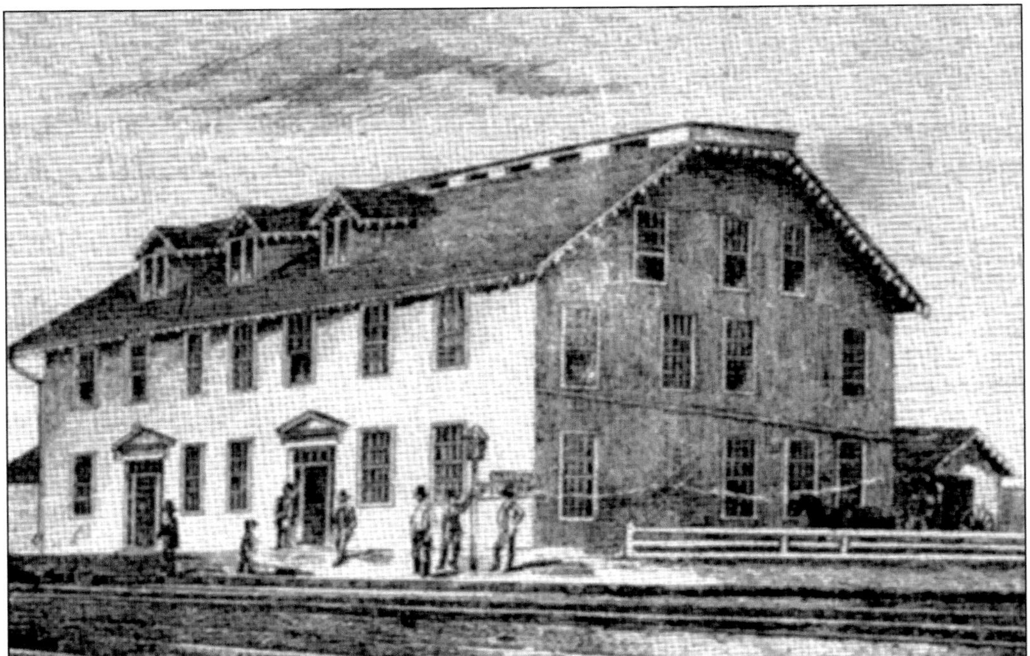

This ambrotype (a positive picture made by a photographic negative on glass), made by I. Caul, shows a drawing of the White Pigeon Eating House & Hotel in White Pigeon. In the 1830s, White Pigeon had three hotels due to both the heavy traffic on Chicago Road, which connected Detroit to Chicago, and the town's role as a railroad stop. According to a notation on the photo, Dr. Wm. N. Elliott was the proprietor. The image was taken from a recent reproduction of a land survey book first published in 1857. (Mendon Country Inn Collection.)

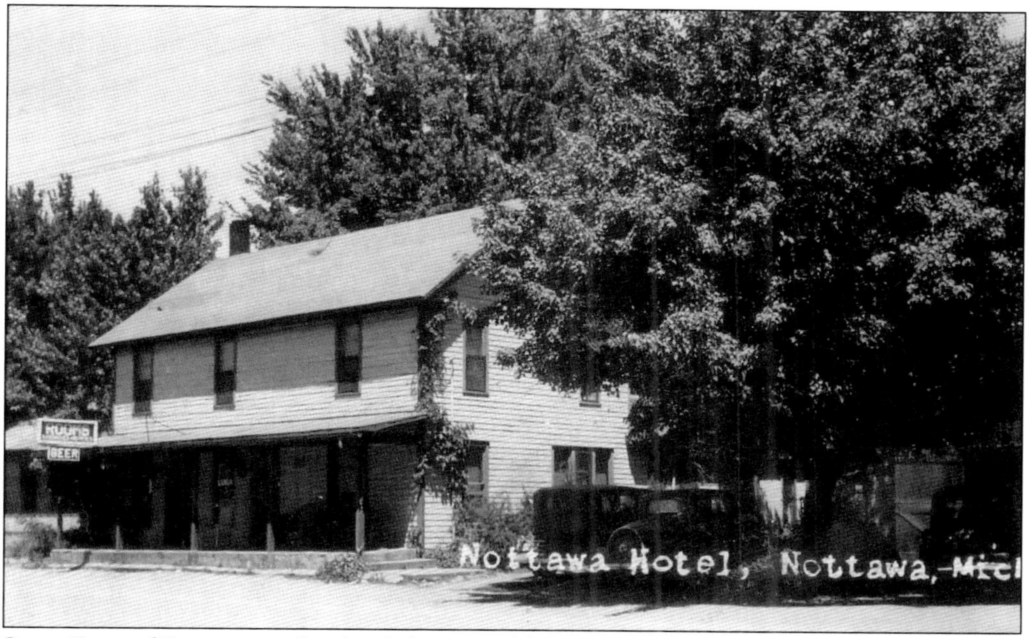

Steve Zazra of Sturgis says that his father stayed here at the Nottawa Hotel in the 1930s when he worked on the mint farms owned by the Todd family. At one time, mint was one of the most important crops in St. Joseph County. The population of small towns like Nottawa swelled after 1869 when the company opened because of the large influx of workers hired by the mint company. After a blight, the A.M. Todd Company moved to Kalamazoo, Michigan, and is still the world's largest supplier of natural peppermint and spearmint oils. Mrs. W.L. Rice owned the Nottawa Hotel at one time and its phone number was 184-F4. The building now serves as a private home. (Steve Zazra Collection.)

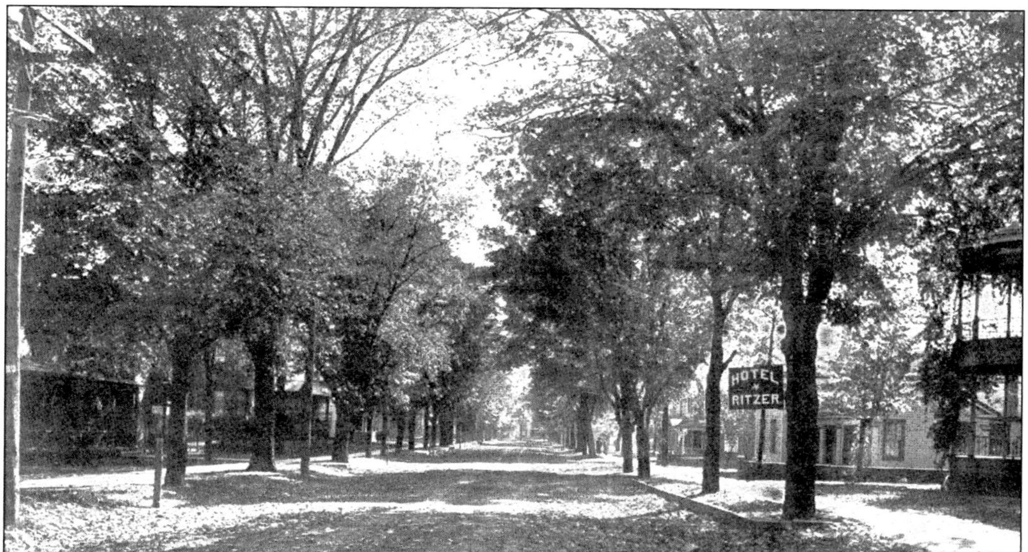

This photo shows a quiet city street with an old hotel sign. This undated photo shows the old Hotel Ritzer in Sturgis. (Sturgis Historical Society Collection.)

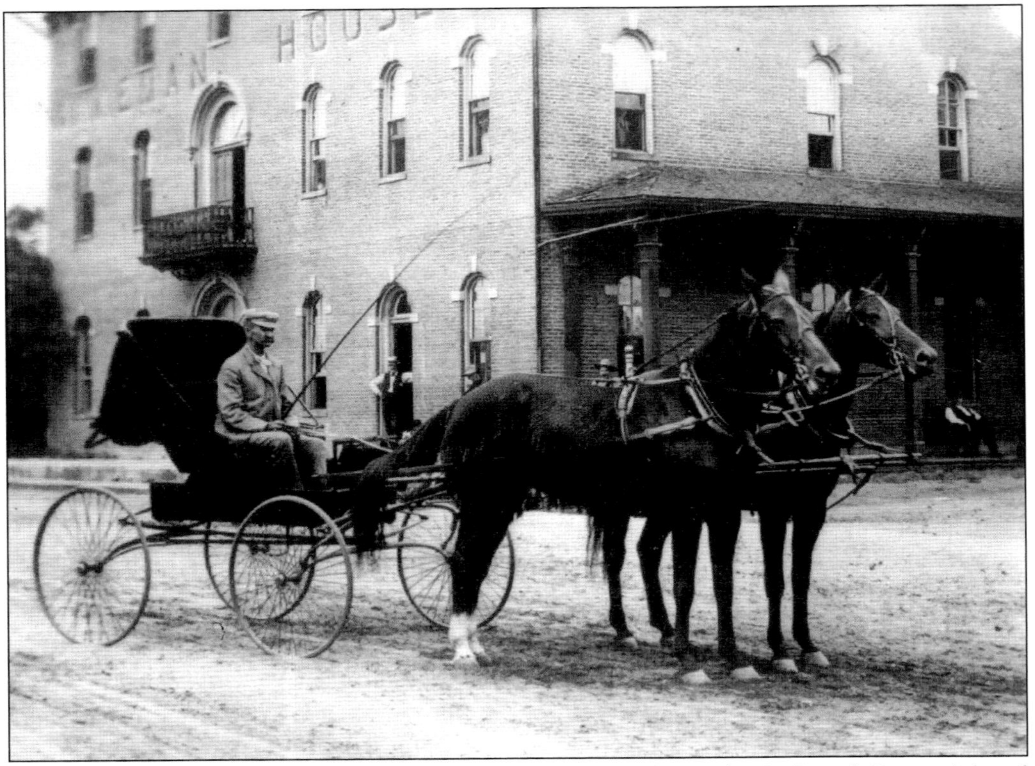

A man sits in his buggy outside the Wakeman House located near the St. Joseph River. A hotel has stood on this spot since at least 1843. At that time it was known as the Western Hotel and was a stage coach stop. (Mendon Country House Collection.)

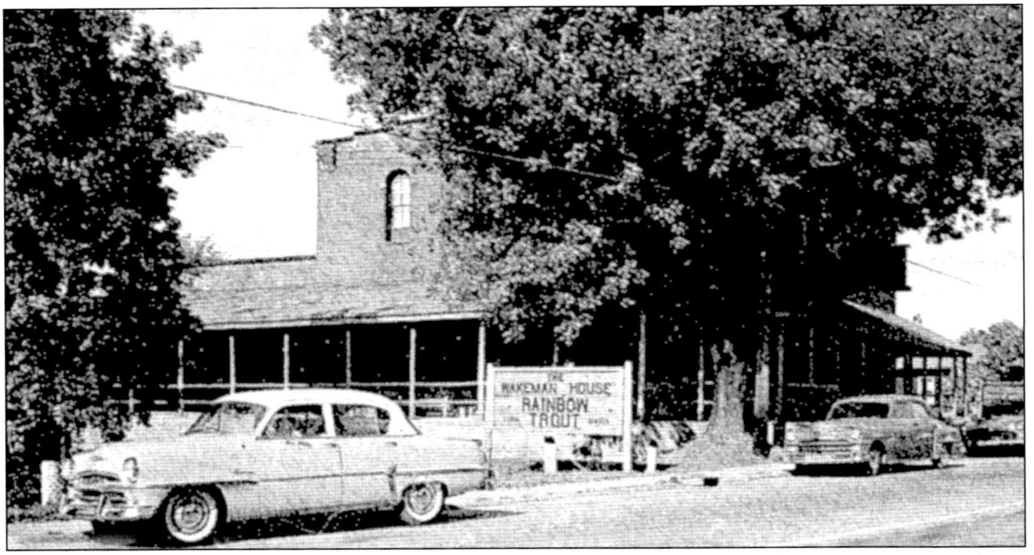

The exterior of the Mendon House hasn't changed during the more than 130 years it's been in business, although the third floor was removed. This postcard was published in the 1950s. (Mendon Country House Collection.)

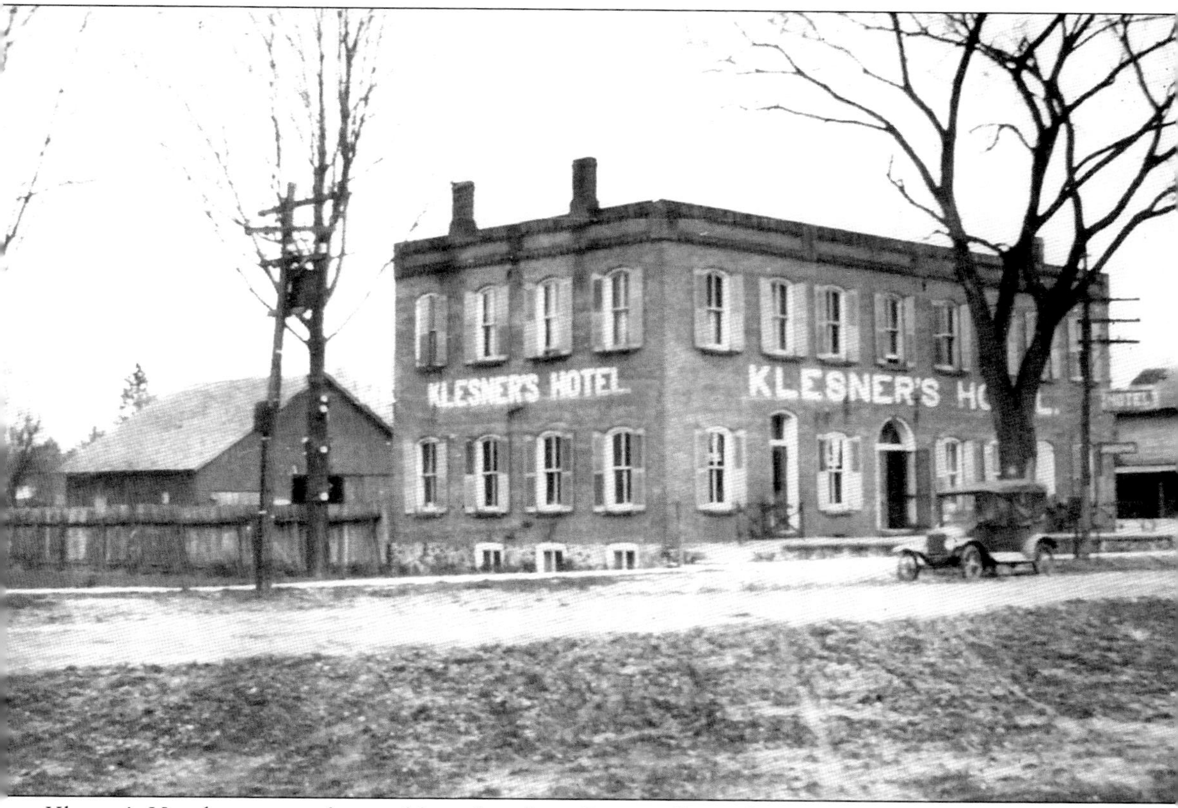

Klesner's Hotel was one of several large hotels in Centreville in the early 1900s. Though there is a car parked out front, horses were still popular modes of transportation at the time this photo was taken. Note the livery barn in the back of the hotel. (Dick Cripe Collection.)

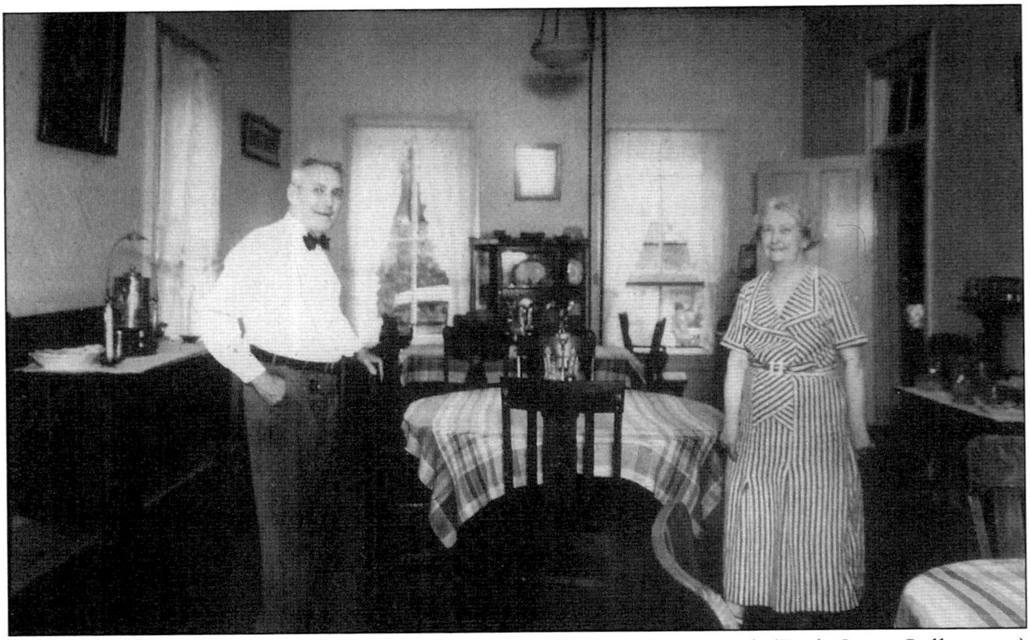

This is a photo of the Klesners standing in the dining room of their hotel. (Dick Cripe Collection.)

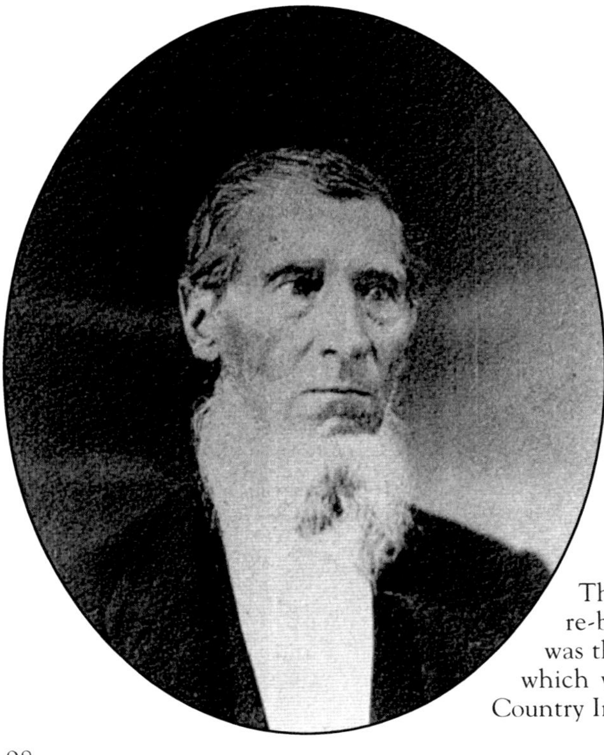

This is Adams Wakeman, the man who re-built the Wakeman House in 1873. He was the largest landowner in the township, which was renamed in his honor. (Mendon Country Inn Collection.)

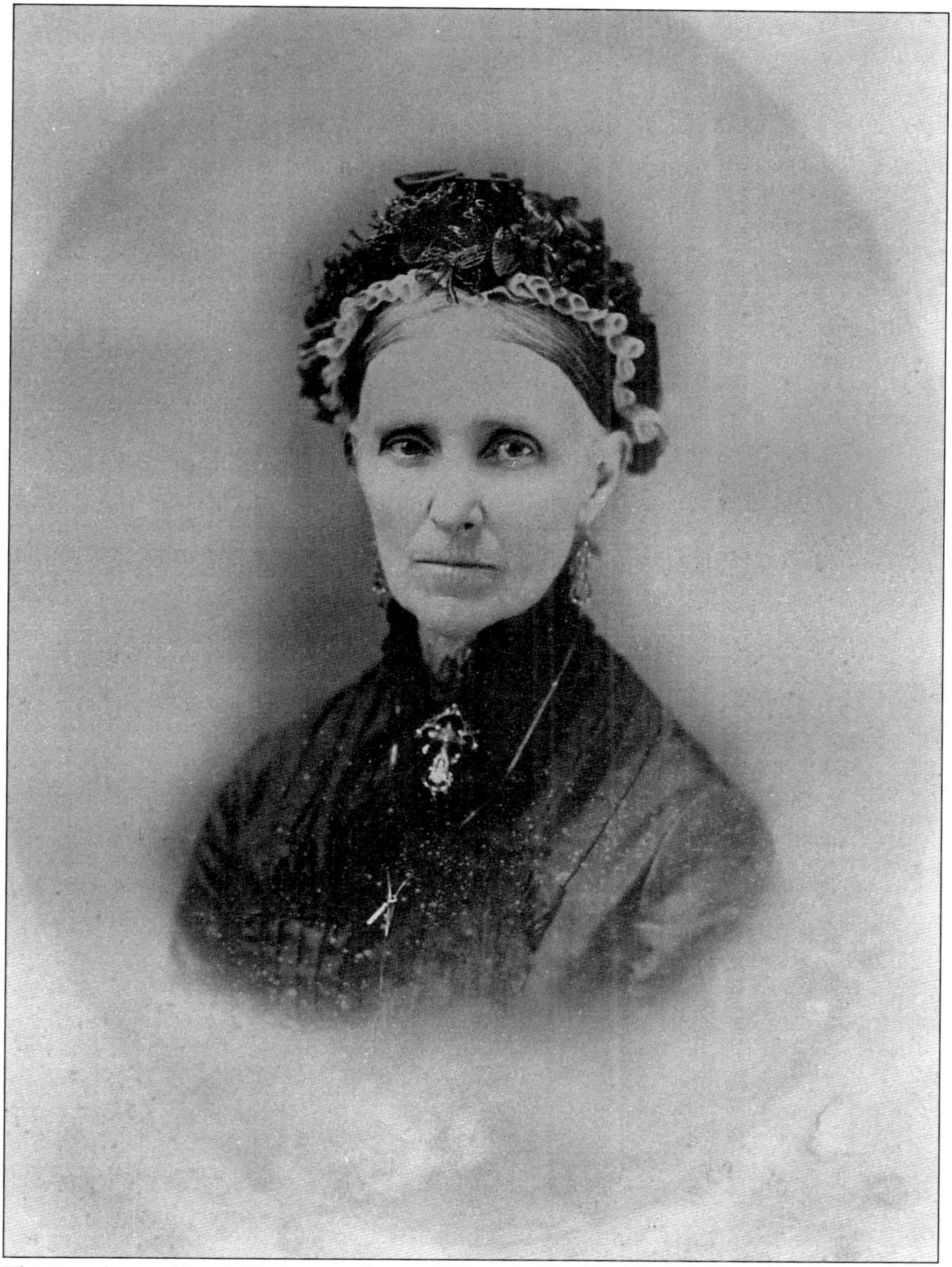

This is a photo of Sarah Wakeman, Adams Wakeman's wife. She had the reputation of being a spiritualist. (Mendon Country Inn Collection.)

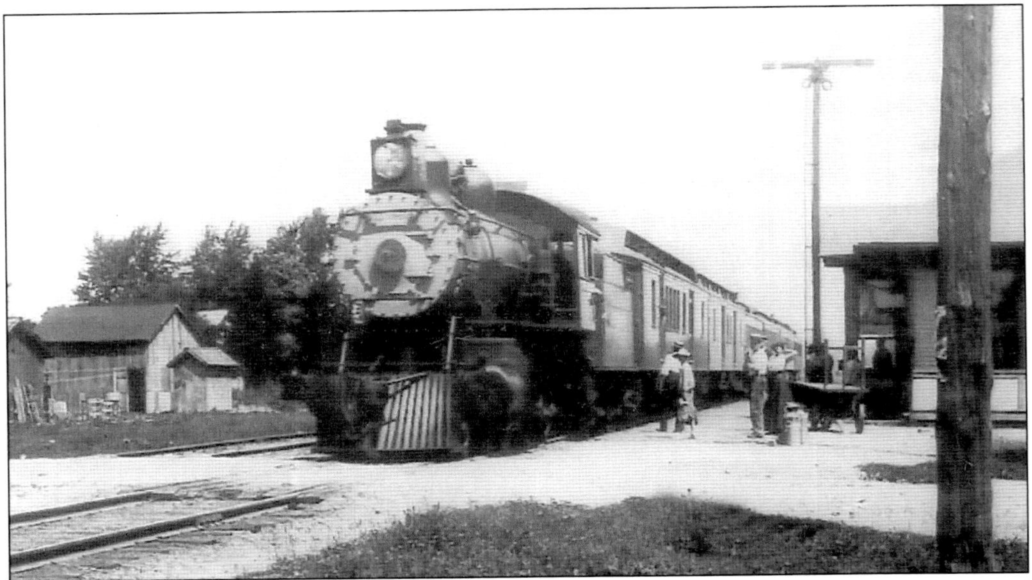

A train waits to pull out of the Nottawa train station *c.* 1800s. There were several railroad companies that traveled to St. Joseph County, including the Grand Rapids & Indiana and the Pumpkin Vine Railroad. (Steve Zazra Collection.)

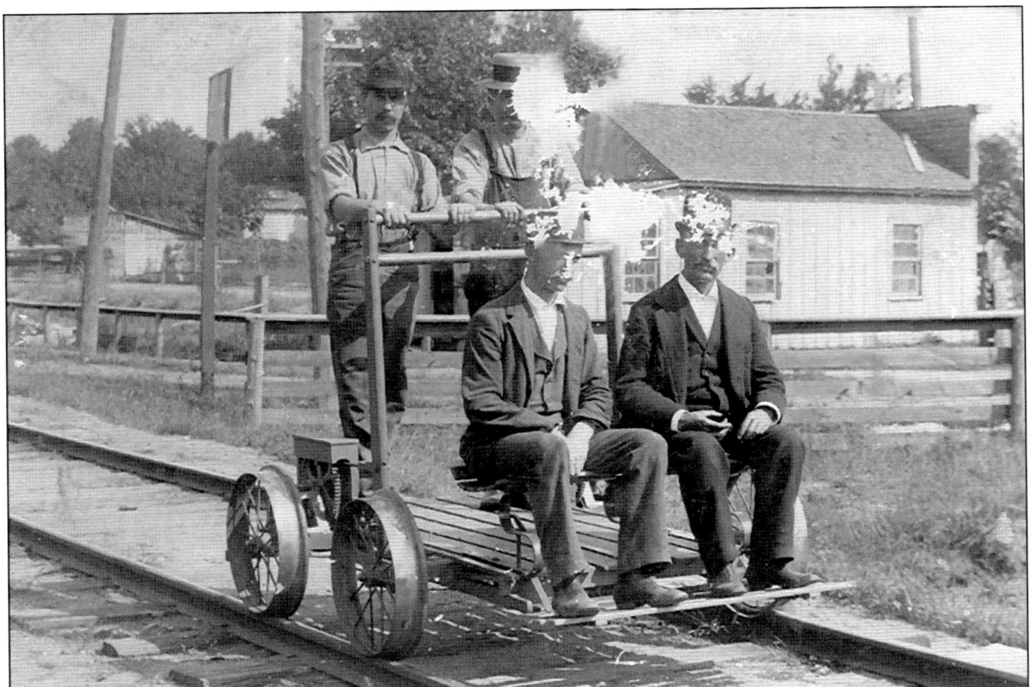

Four men take a ride on a Sheffield Handcar in Three Rivers, Michigan. (Three Rivers Library Collection.)

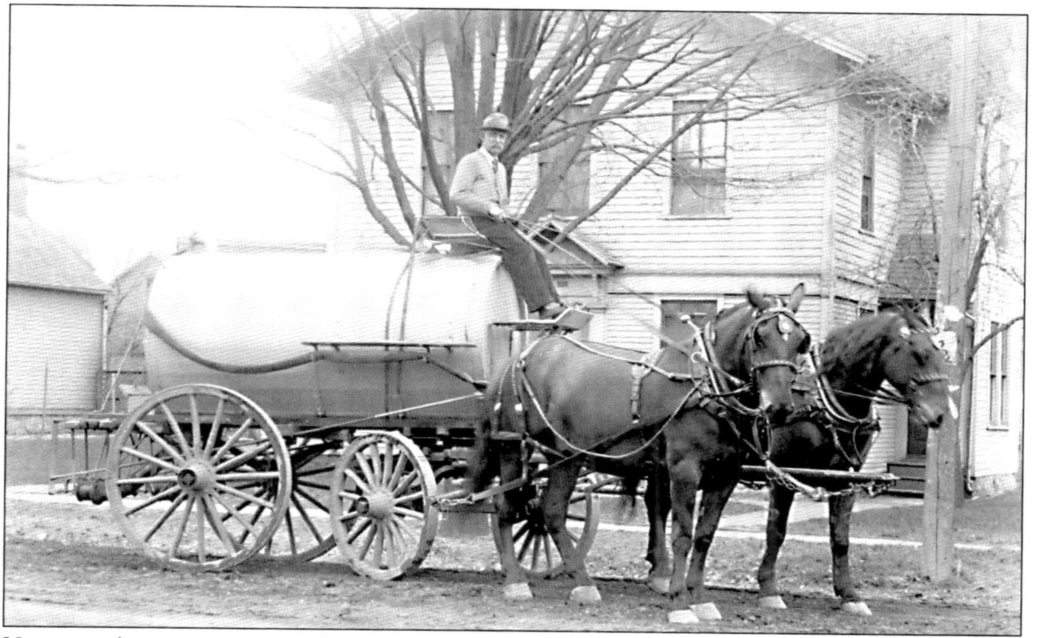

Horses and wagons continued to be a viable mode of transportation well into the 1910s. This undated photo is from the Sturgis Historical Society Collection and was probably taken in the early 1900s in Sturgis.

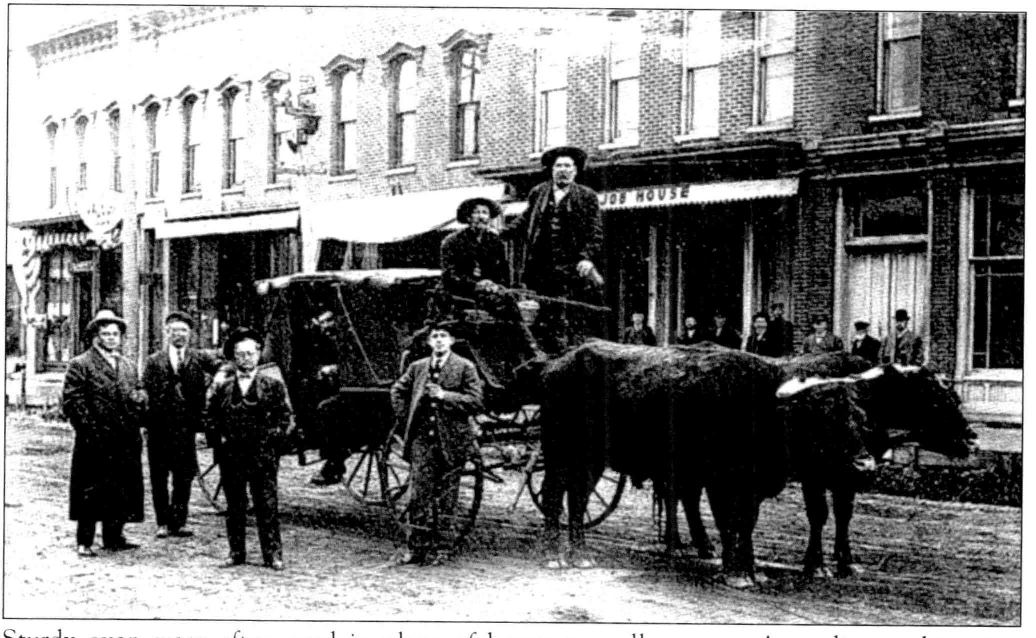

Sturdy oxen were often used in place of horses to pull wagons. According to historian Priscilla Massie, using oxen had a side benefit—they could also be eaten. (Three Rivers Library Collection.)

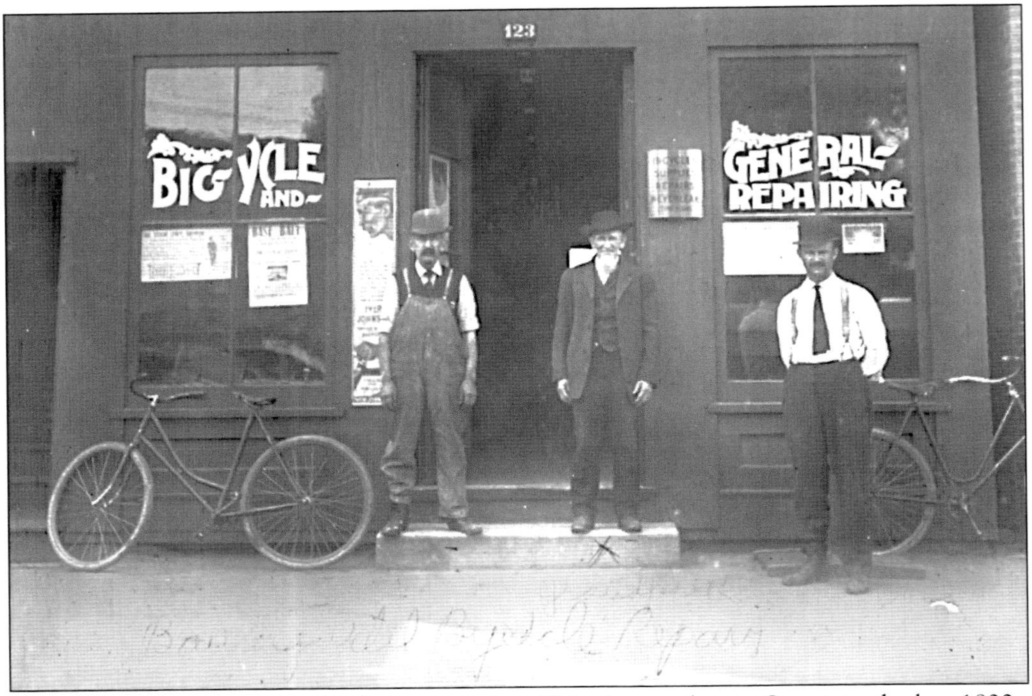

Bicycles were a common mode of transportation. This photo, taken in Sturgis in the late 1800s, shows one shop that sold and repaired bicycles. (Sturgis Historical Society Collection.

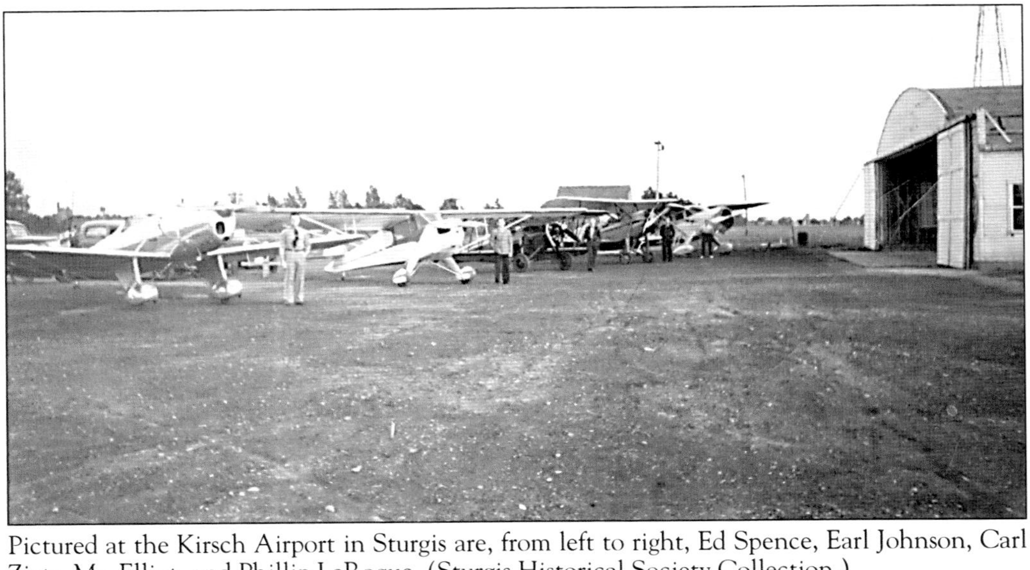

Pictured at the Kirsch Airport in Sturgis are, from left to right, Ed Spence, Earl Johnson, Carl Zietz, Mr. Elliot, and Phillip LaRoque. (Sturgis Historical Society Collection.)

Seven

Country Life

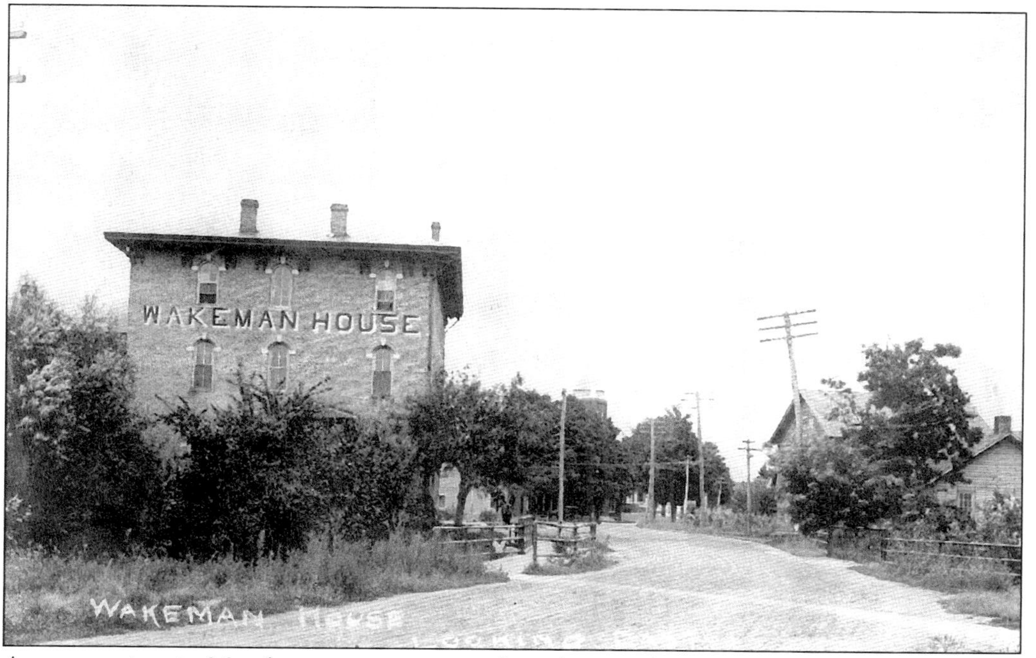

A country inn in Mendon was a stopping place for travelers and stagecoaches in the late 1800s. This photo, taken looking east, shows that the roads were still unpaved. In the distance, a dome from one of the town's churches can be seen above the tree tops. (Mendon Country Inn Collection.)

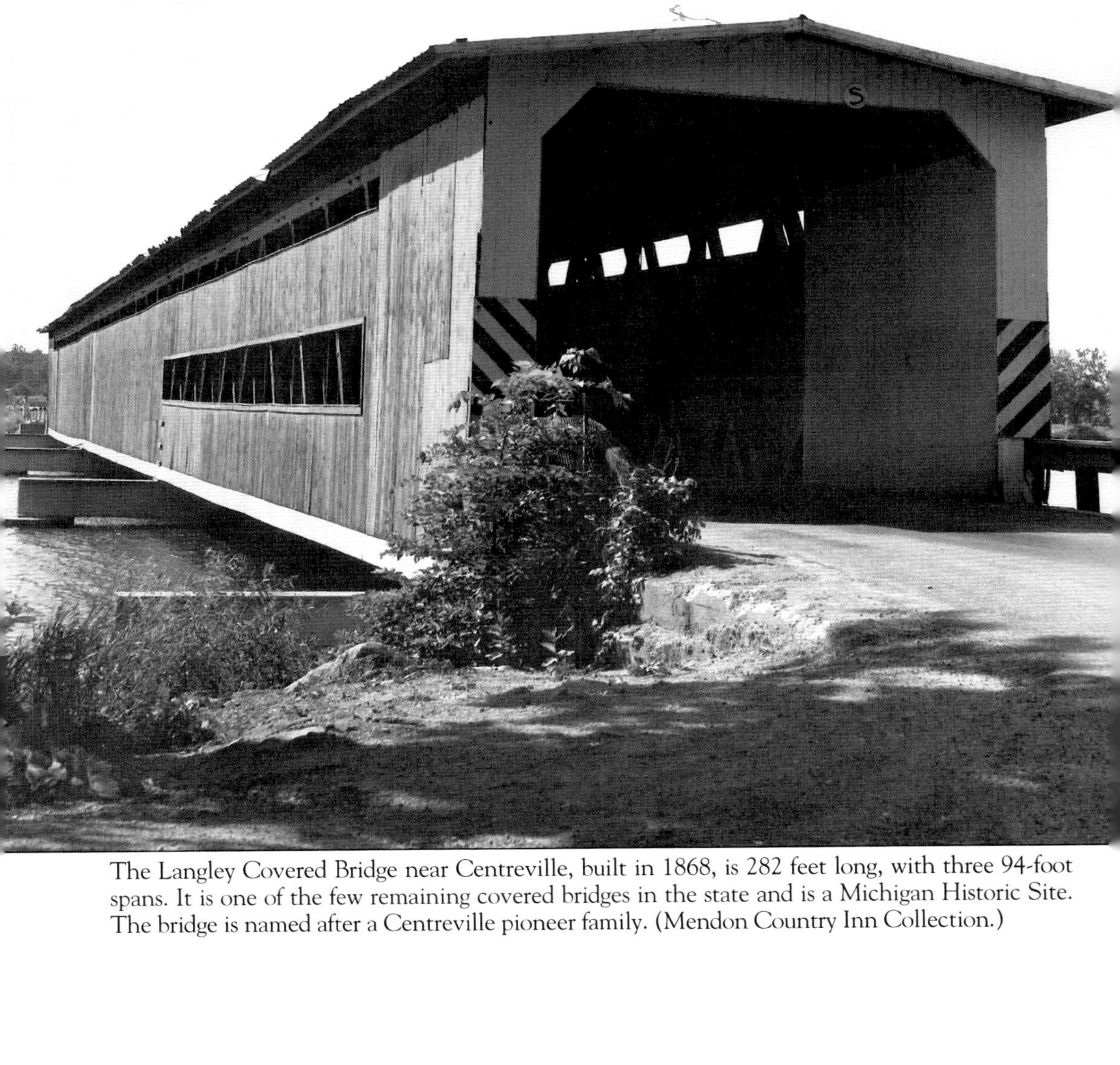

The Langley Covered Bridge near Centreville, built in 1868, is 282 feet long, with three 94-foot spans. It is one of the few remaining covered bridges in the state and is a Michigan Historic Site. The bridge is named after a Centreville pioneer family. (Mendon Country Inn Collection.)

A country road crosses an old bridge over one of the many rivers and creeks that earn St. Joseph County the honor of having the most navigable waterways in the state. (Three Rivers Library Collection.)

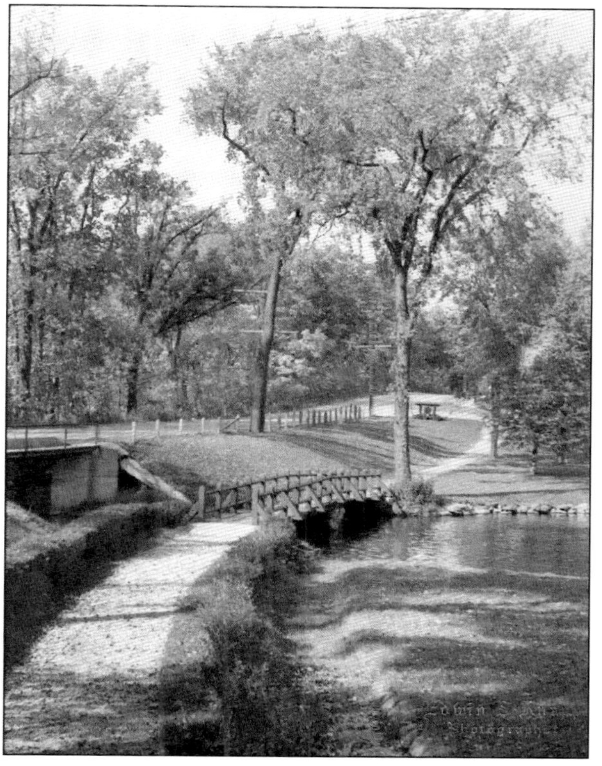

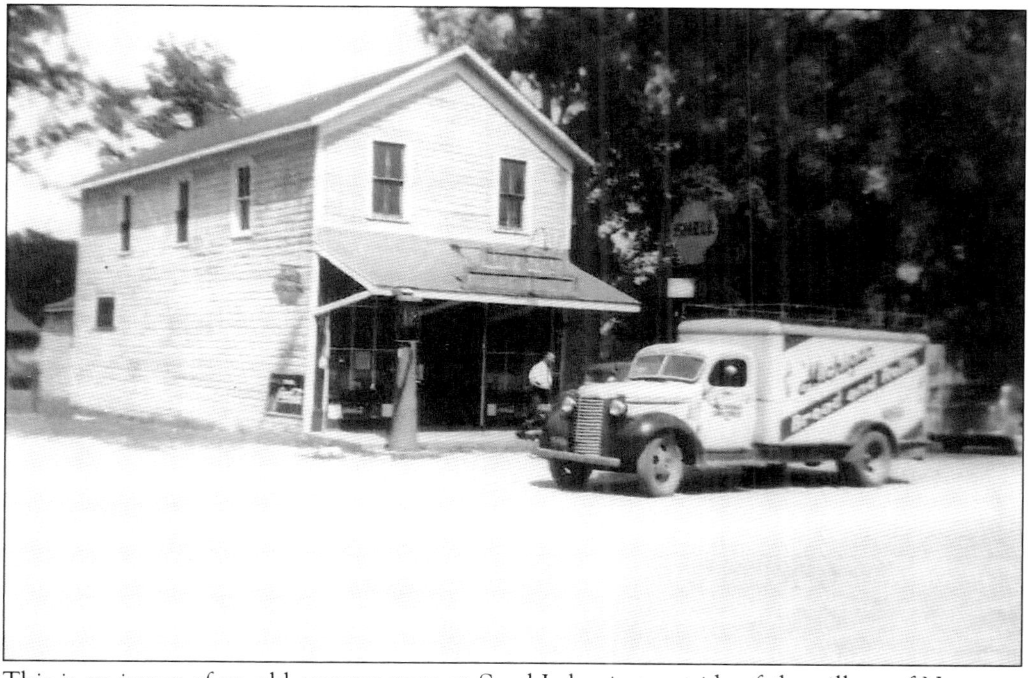

This is an image of an old country store at Sand Lake, just outside of the village of Nottawa. (Steve Zarza Collection.)

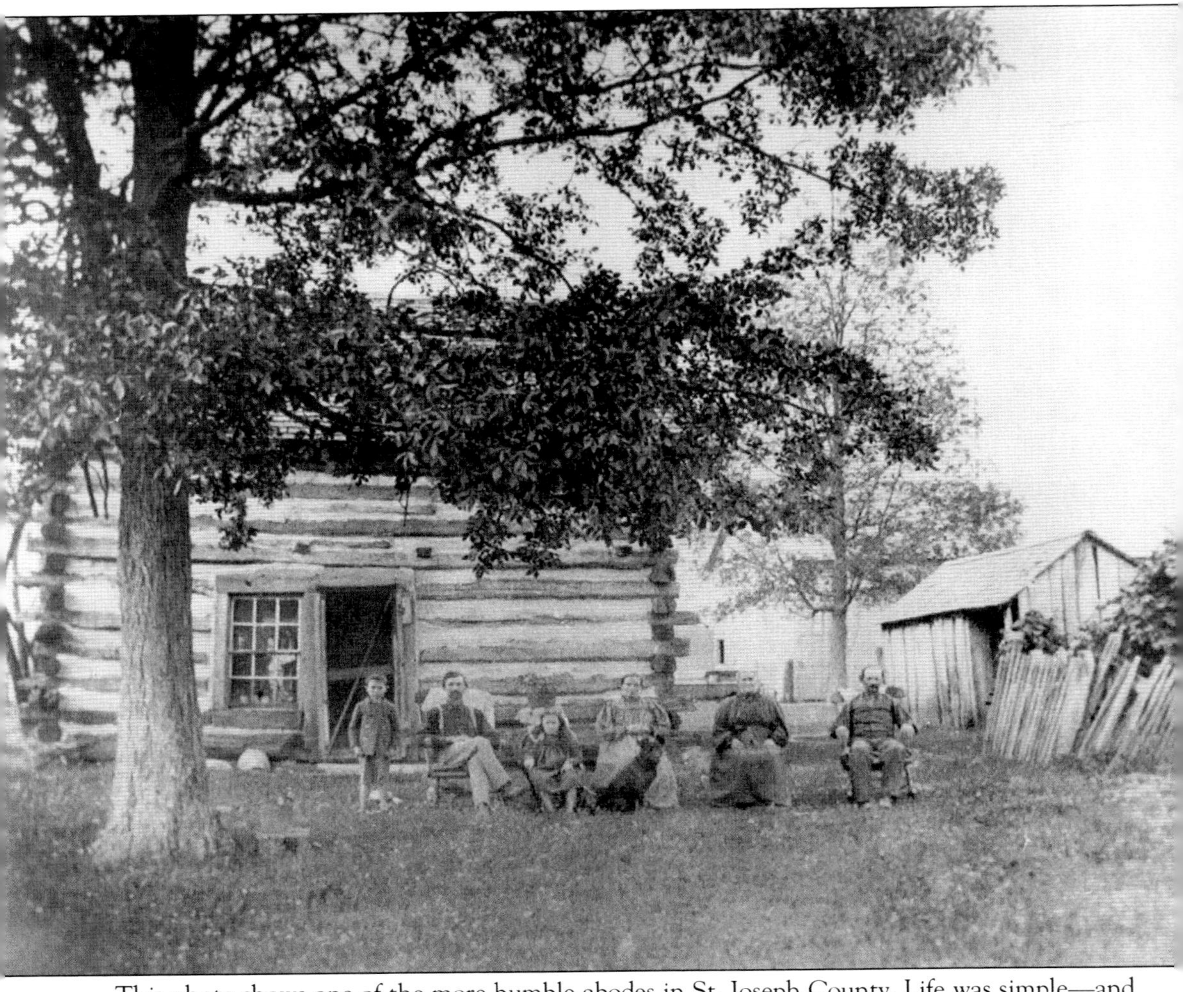

This photo shows one of the more humble abodes in St. Joseph County. Life was simple—and hard, for some. In this undated photo, a St. Joseph County family sits in front of their cabin. Early settler cabins sometimes consisted of just one room—one side was used for cooking and congregating, while the other was for sleeping. (Three Rivers Library Collection.)

Eight

Enterprises and Enterprisers

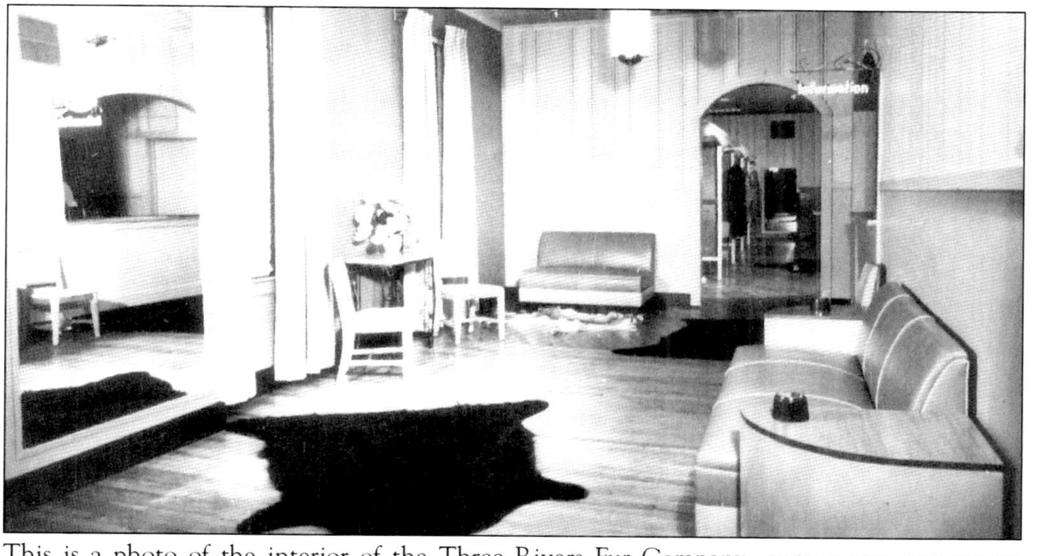

This is a photo of the interior of the Three Rivers Fur Company, once a very prosperous business in Three Rivers. Originally known as the Three Rivers Robe Tannery, started by a man named O.T. Avery, the company became known as the Three Rivers Fur Company in 1935, according to the book *Three Rivers: The Early Years*, published by the City of Three Rivers Sesquicentennial Committee in 1986. Trappers could earn large amounts of money for hides. The Three Rivers Robe Tannery advertised that you could bring in a hide, have it tanned, and then watch it made into a robe or coat. It was especially good if you needed a warm fur robe to wrap up in while riding in an open sleigh or in the back of a wagon. (Sue Silliman House Museum Collection.)

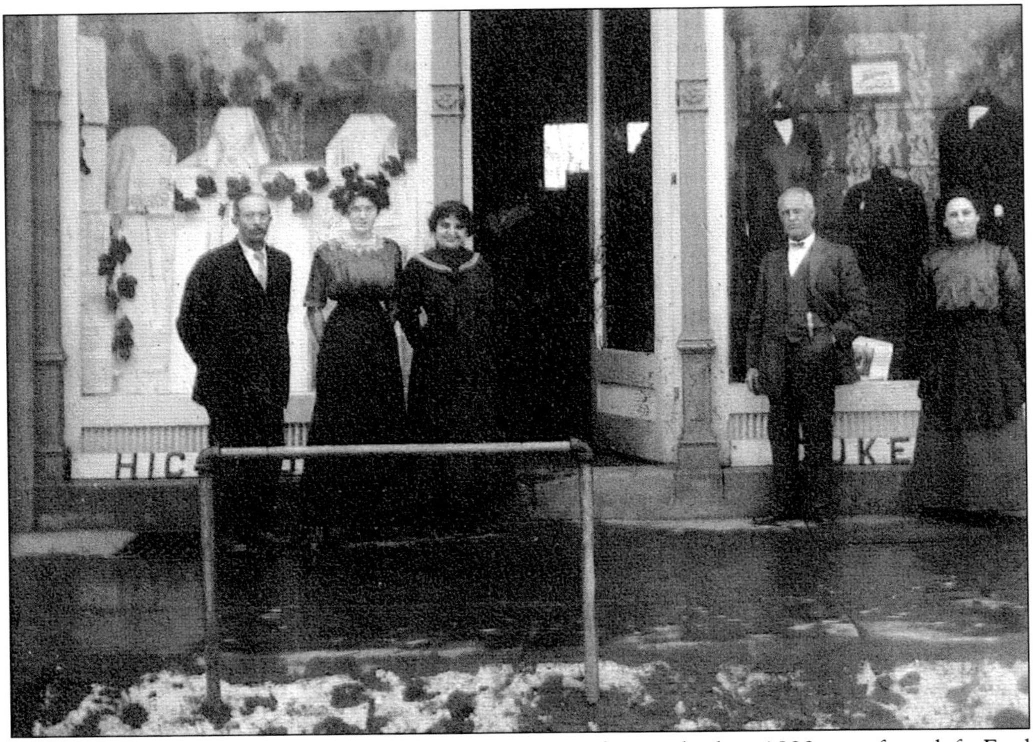

Pictured in this photo of a business in downtown Mendon in the late 1800s are, from left, Fred Flanders, Winnie Laird, Donna Marantette, Mike Dukette, and Myrt Zigler. (Mendon Country Inn Collection.)

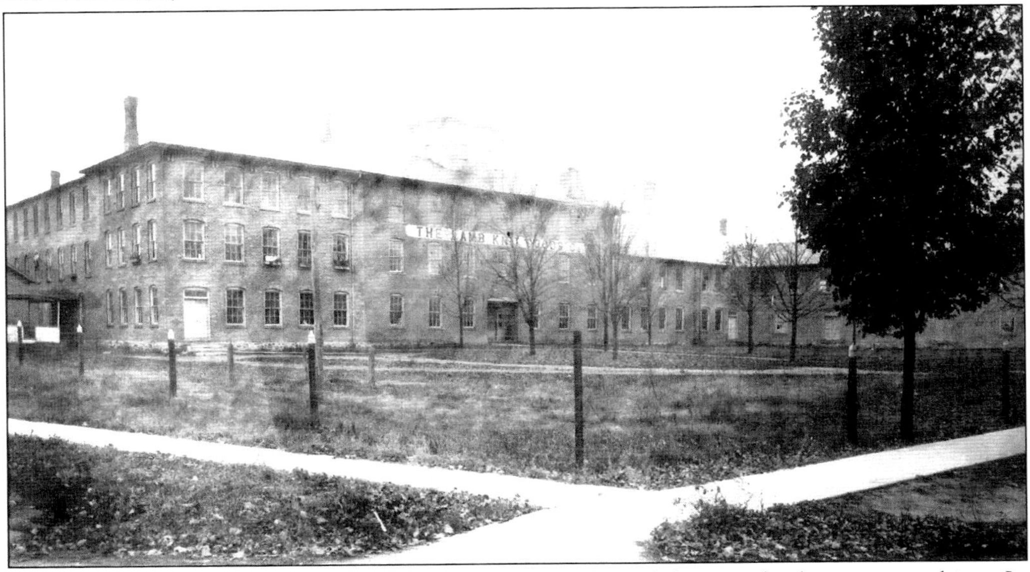

Lamb Knit Goods in Colon was owned by the inventor of the circular knitting machine. In 1903 alone, the company produced 58,457 dozen pairs of knit gloves and mittens. The company closed in the 1960s but the building still stands. Prior to housing the knitting company, the building was used by a junior college. (Community Historical Society Collection.)

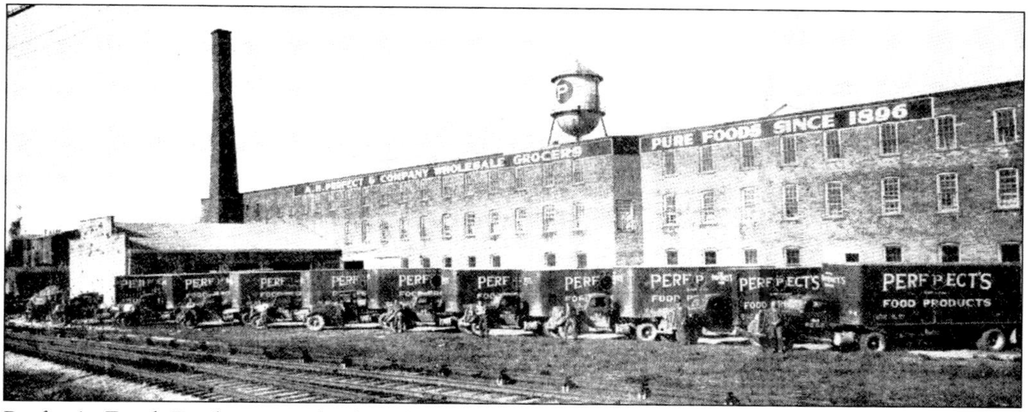

Perfect's Food Products trucks lined up outside of the company's factory. Perfect's started business in Sturgis in 1896. (Sturgis Historical Society Collection.)

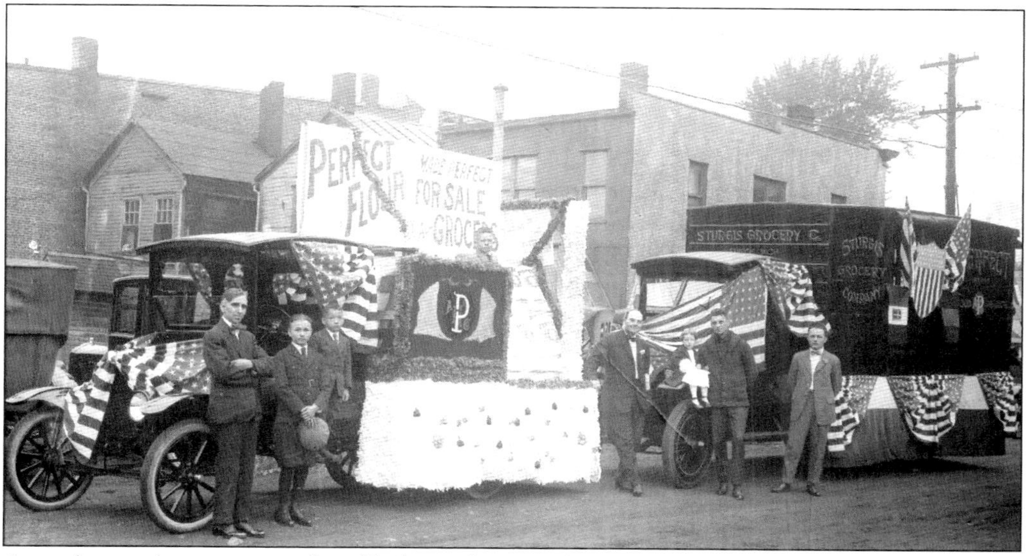

According to the writing on this old photo, these trucks from A.H. Perfect & Co., which supplied groceries to IGA grocery stores, are decorated for a 1920 parade. The Perfect warehouse at the time this photo was taken stood across the street from the fire station at 119 N. Nottawa in Sturgis. From left to right are W. Davis, Davis's son, Lyle Wyer, Mosil Wyer, J.S. Winters, Arlene Wyer, Otto Kronenberg, and A.A. Wyer, manager. (Sturgis Historical Society Collection.)

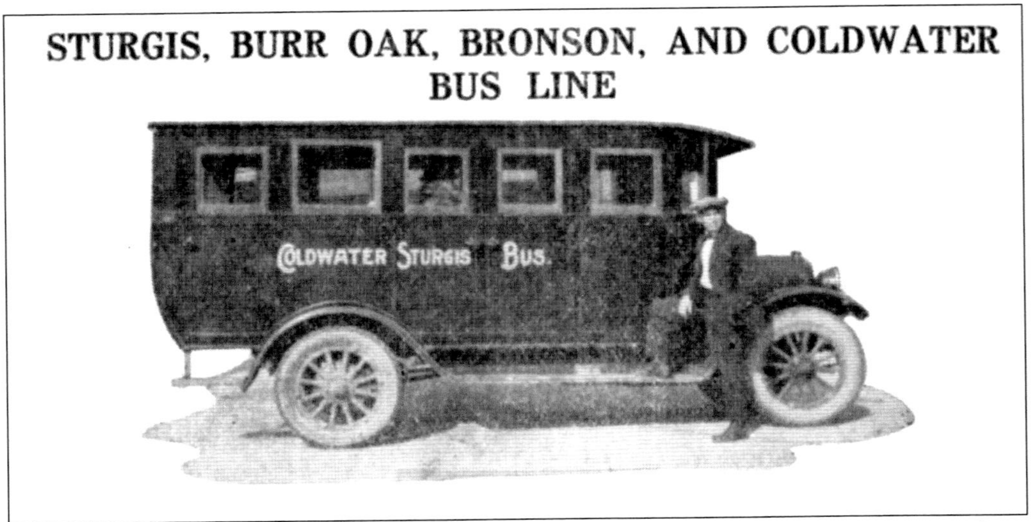

According to historian Robert Hair, there were five bus lines serving Sturgis as of 1925. These lines connected Sturgis with Kalamazoo, Elkhart, Indiana, Three Rivers, and Kendallville, as well as Burr Oak, Bronson, and Coldwater. The local bus stop for all the lines was the Elliott Hotel, which stood on the northwest corner of Chicago Road and North Street. In all, the five bus lines transported about 200 passengers per day. (Sturgis Historical Society Collection.)

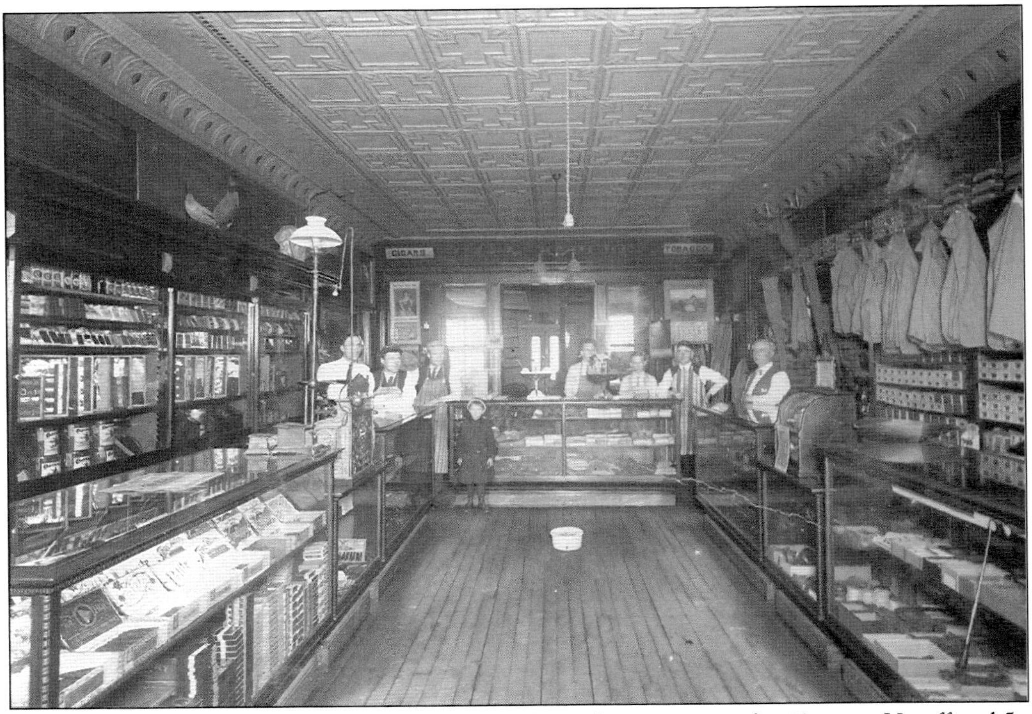

Carl Klocke, who moved to Three Rivers in 1882, ran his cigar store for 40 years. He offered 5¢ cigars with names like Blue Ribbon, Petite, and Hazel, and a 10¢ cigar called the R&K. Besides cigars, Klocke also sold guns, fishing gear, and baseball equipment. The Carl Klocke Cigar Store was located at 140 St. Joseph Street. (Three Rivers Library Collection.)

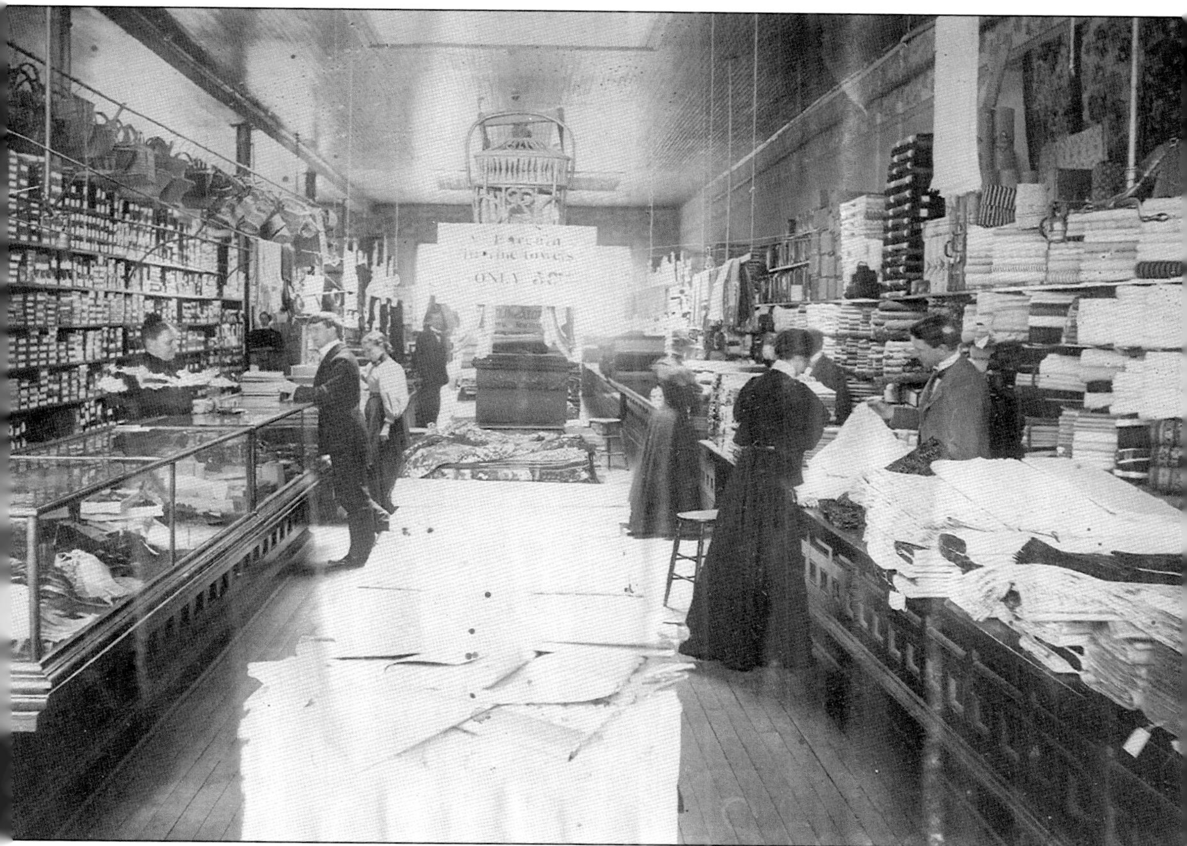

Located on St. Joseph Street in Three Rivers, Starr's Dry Goods Store, owned by Charles Starr, was located in a two-story building, and sold clothes, curtains, dresses, odorless feathers, and carpet sweepers. According to the book *Three Rivers: The Early Years*, the store, which opened in 1881, was considered to be one of the largest and finest in the area. The building later housed a Home Furnishing Store and Funeral Parlor, owned by F.W. Balch, considered one of the leading furniture dealers, along with O.L. Haring, a funeral director. Though embalming took place in the back of the store, at that time it was traditional to hold wakes and funerals in the family home. Haring opened the first funeral home in Three Rivers in 1917. (Three Rivers Library Collection.)

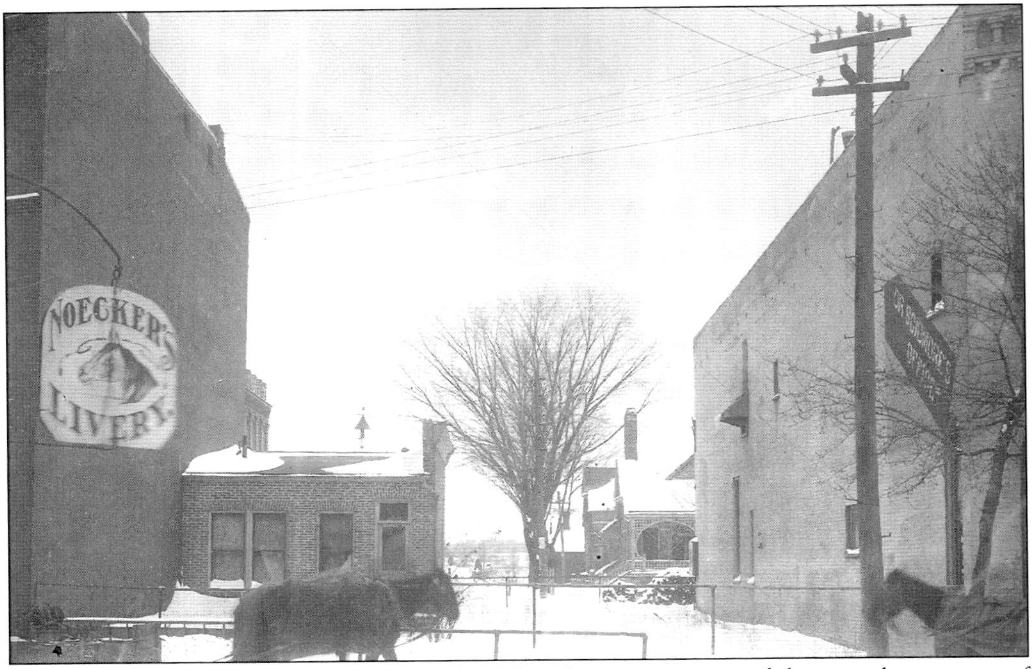

Liveries were an important part of everyday life as horses were one of the prevalent means of transportation. Much as we call for taxis to pick us up at a certain time and place today, horses could often be ordered in the same way. (Three Rivers Library Collection.)

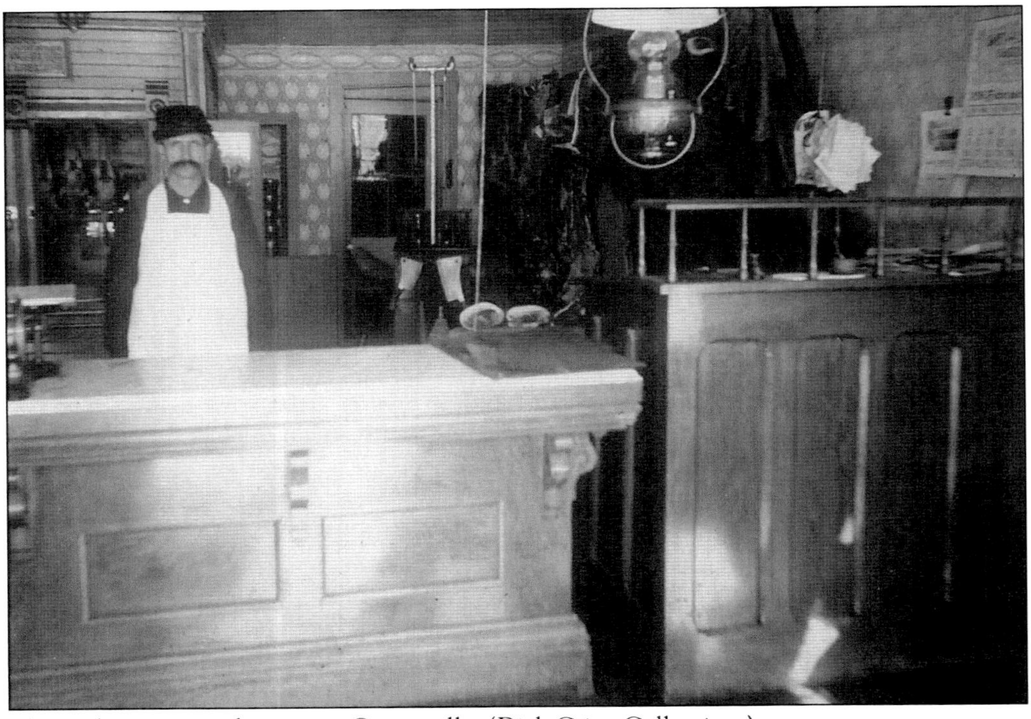

This is the interior of a store in Centreville. (Dick Cripe Collection.)

Margaret Thomas was the daughter of the mill's manger. Dressed in her Dr. Denton's, as shown in this photo, she became the trademark of the mill, appearing in numerous advertisements. (Information and photo contributed by Dick Cripe.)

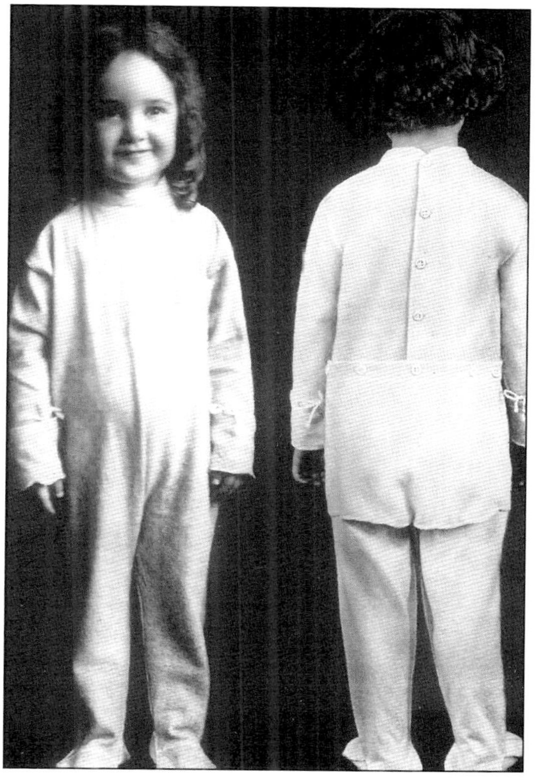

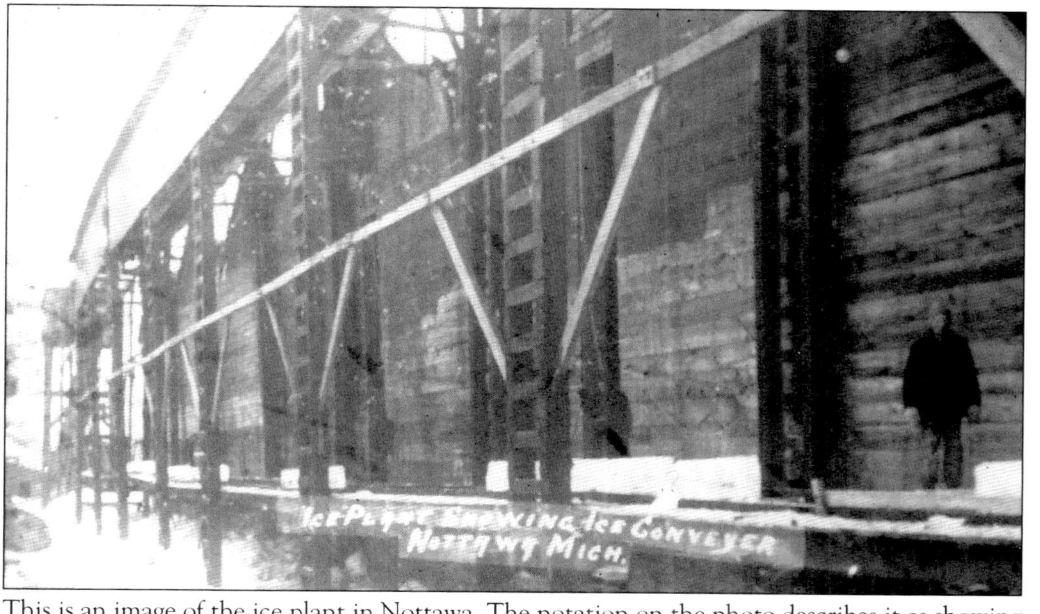

This is an image of the ice plant in Nottawa. The notation on the photo describes it as showing the ice conveyor. Before refrigeration, ice was cut from the lakes in St. Joseph County and stored in big warehouses, where it was covered with straw to keep it from melting During the warm months it was sold to customers who used it to keep their foods cold. (Dick Cripe Collection.)

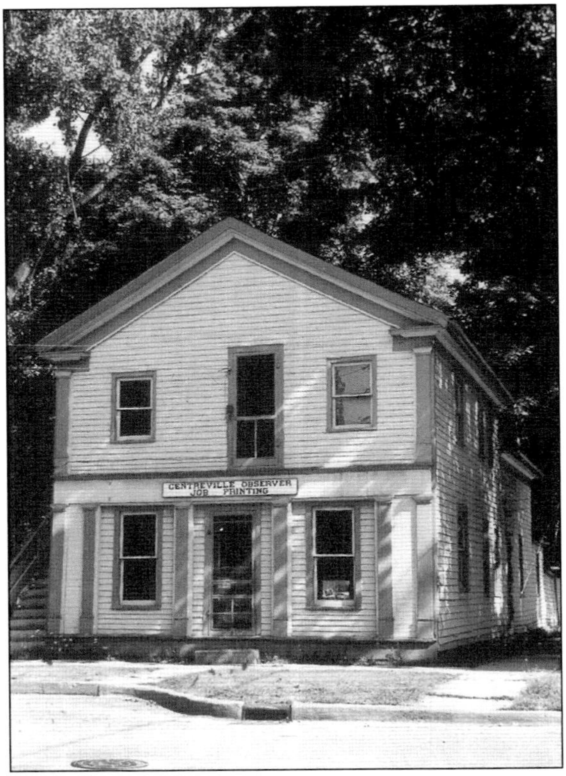

This old photo shows the offices of the *Centreville Observer*, the town's newspaper. (Dick Cripe Collection.)

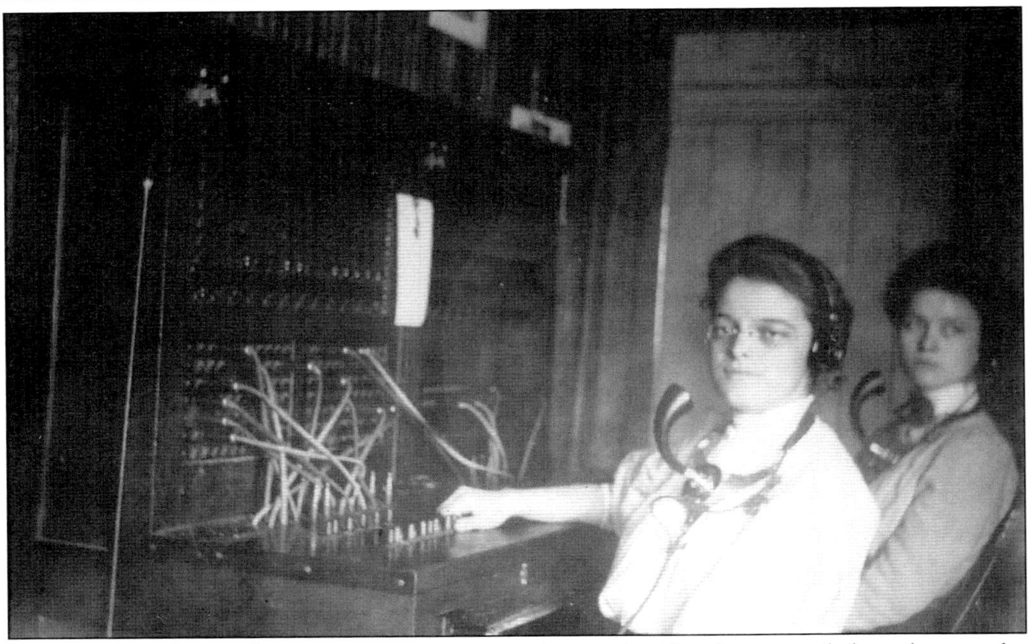

Centreville had two phone companies, one on the north side of town and the other on the south. Calls from one end of town to another were billed as long distance. The photo here shows operators at the company on the south side of town. (Dick Cripe Collection.)

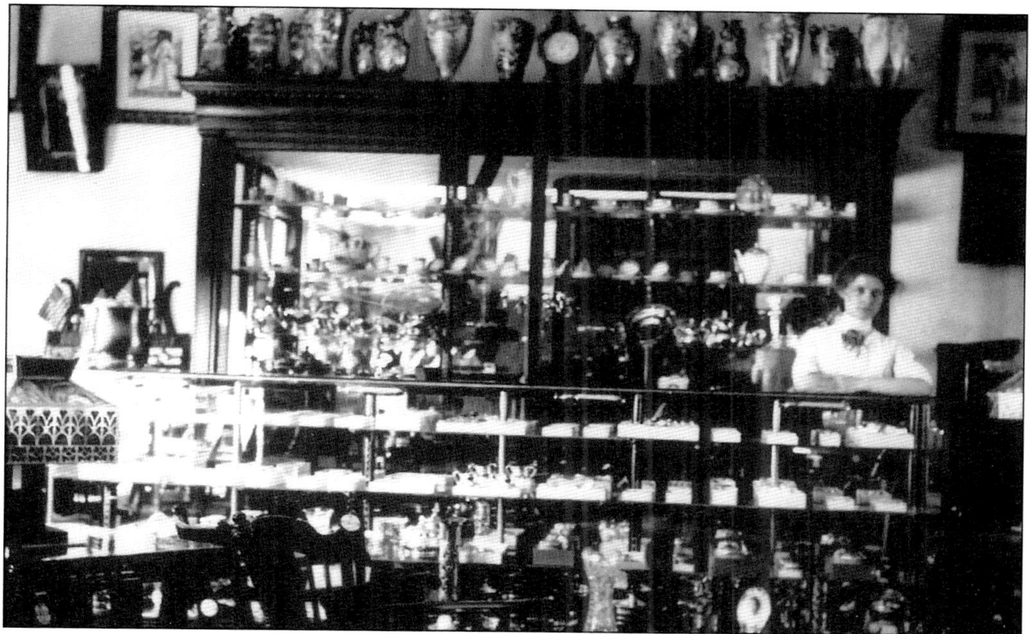

This is a photo of the S&H Green Stamp Redemption Center in Centreville. When people shopped at grocery stores, they "earned" stamps, and when they accumulated enough stamps, they redeemed them for items at stores like this one. One of the founders of the company summered in Centreville. (Dick Cripe Collection.)

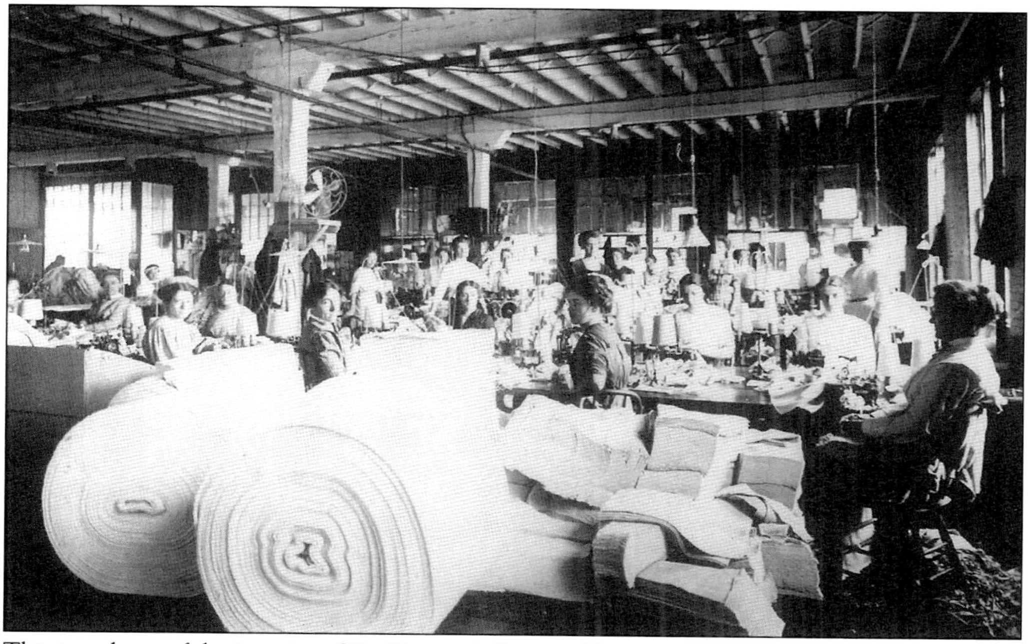

This is a photo of the interior of Dr. Denton's Denton Knitting Mill in Centreville. Denton was not actually a doctor, but the material in the gray Dentons (as they were called) had a strand of wool in with the cotton, and the oil in that wool was supposedly good for children's skin. At one time, according to local historian Dick Cripe, the mill employed over 300 people.

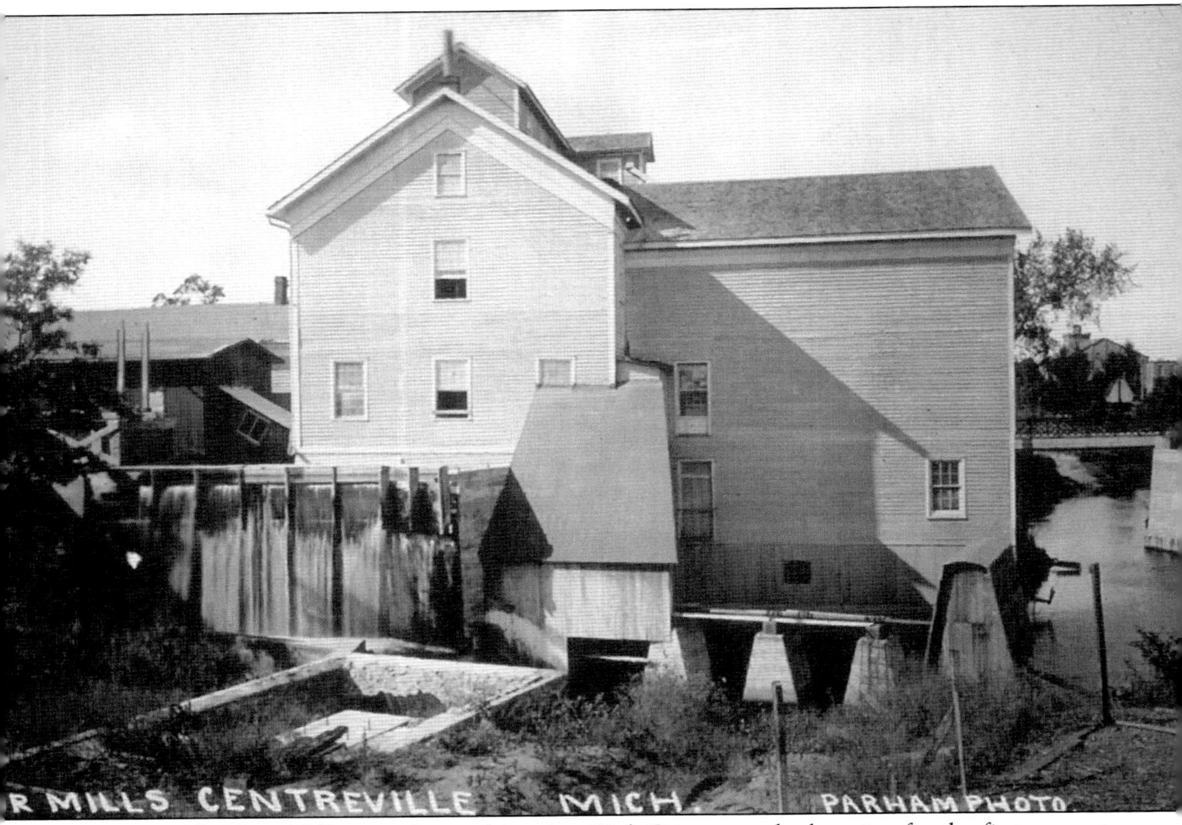

Reynold's Flour Mill, according to historian Dick Cripe, was the location for the first generator put in place for the Centreville Electric Company. At the time, generators needed water to function and were often located on rivers. The electric company only had two shifts so the generator ran from 6 a.m. until midnight. (Dick Cripe Collection.)

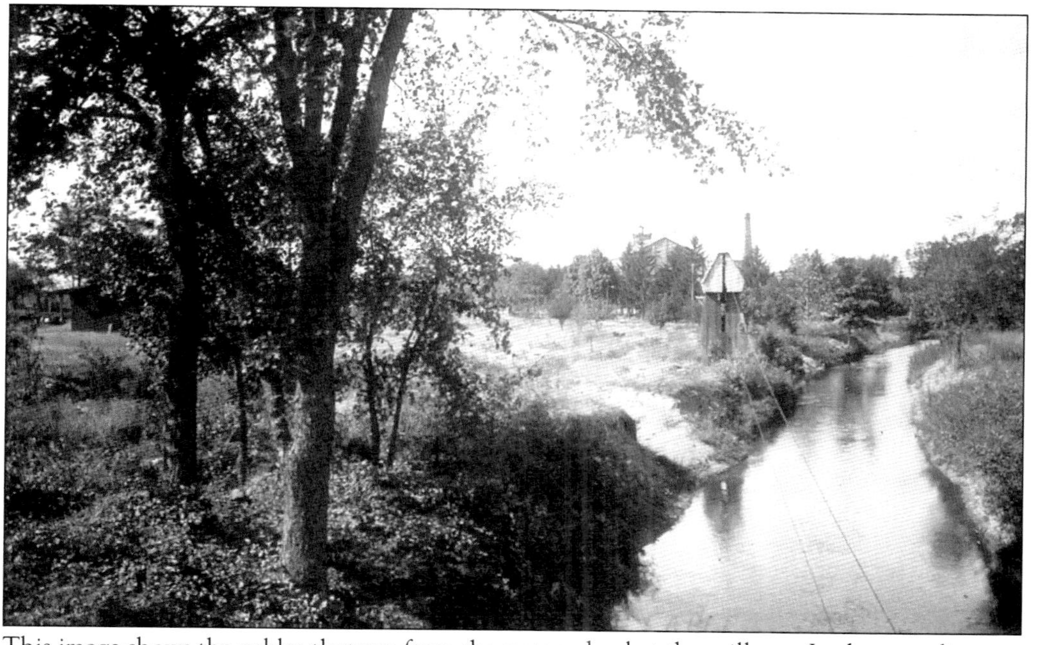

This image shows the cables that ran from the water wheel at the millrace. In the very distance is Reynold's Flour Mill. The water wheel harnessed electricity which powered the mill. (Dick Cripe Collection.)

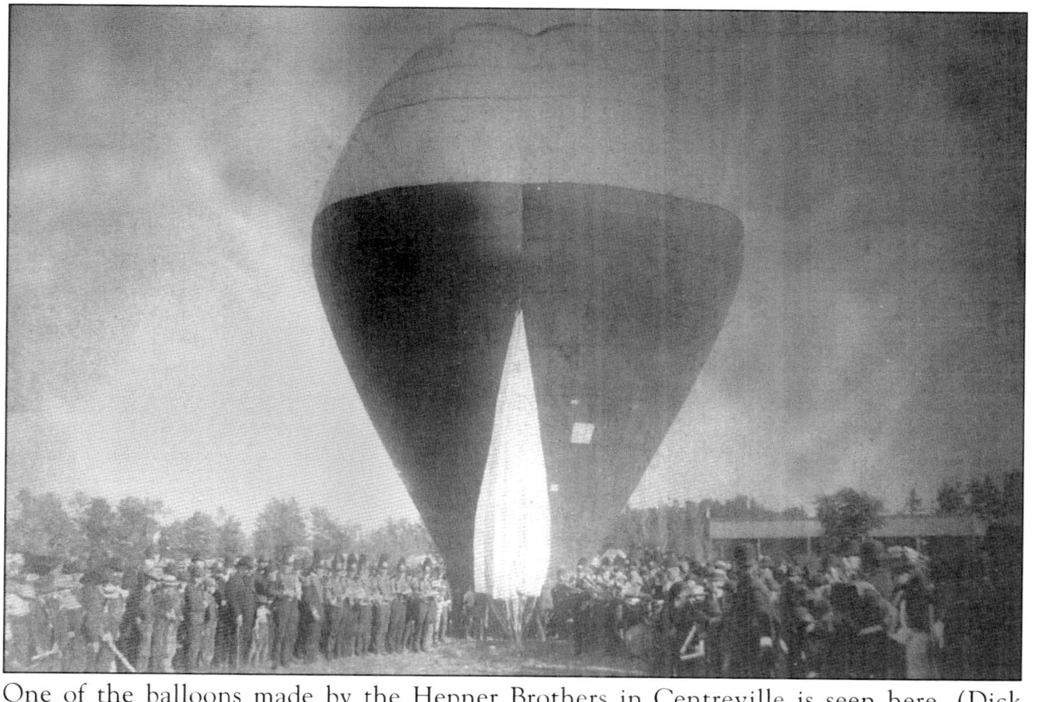

One of the balloons made by the Hepner Brothers in Centreville is seen here. (Dick Cripe Collection.)

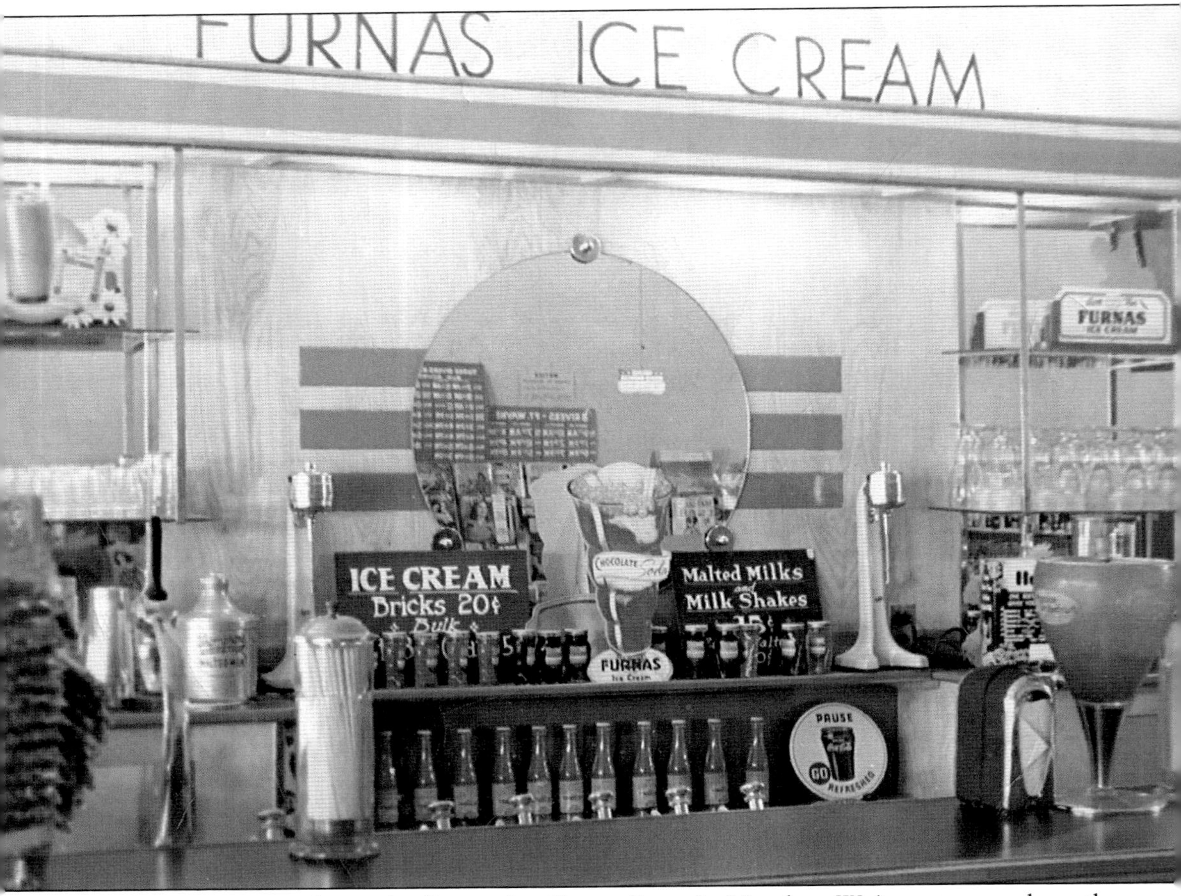

This 1942 image shows the Furans Ice Cream Store in Mendon. We're not sure where they got their ice cream, but we know that Clark Potter Ice Cream, in nearby Three Rivers, produced ice cream and fancy frozen desserts. At Clark Potter, customers were served on the second floor of the building and a dumbwaiter was used to cart the edibles upstairs. (Three Rivers Library Collection.)

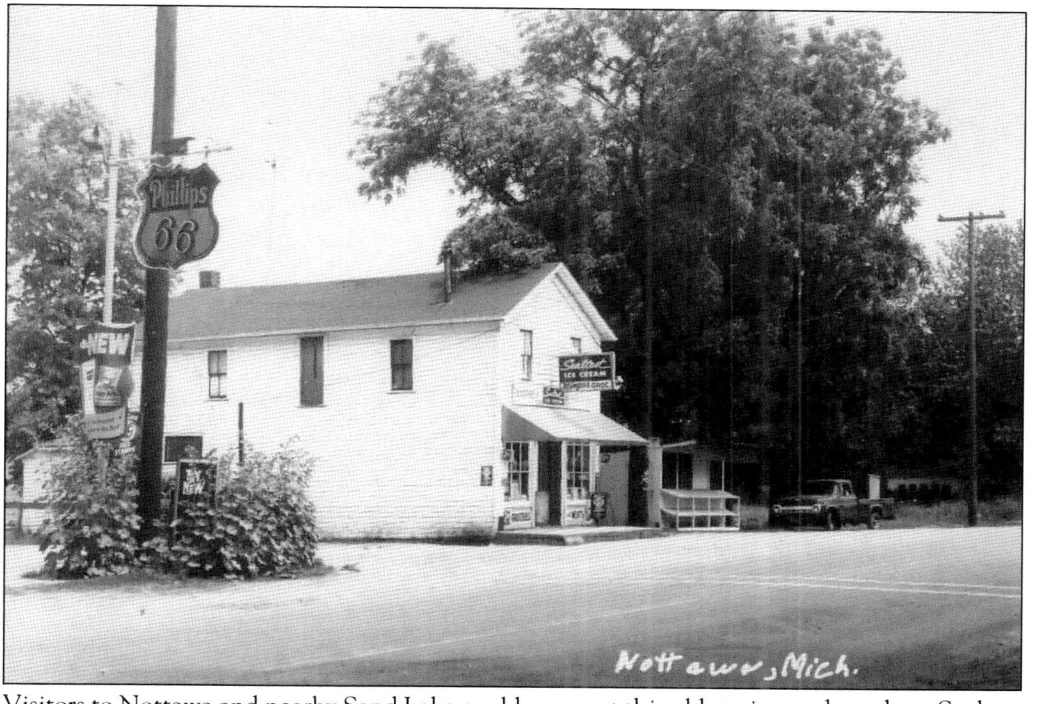

Visitors to Nottawa and nearby Sand Lake could gas up at this old station and purchase Sealtest Ice Cream at the store next door. The image dates to c. 1930s. (Steve Zazra Collection.)

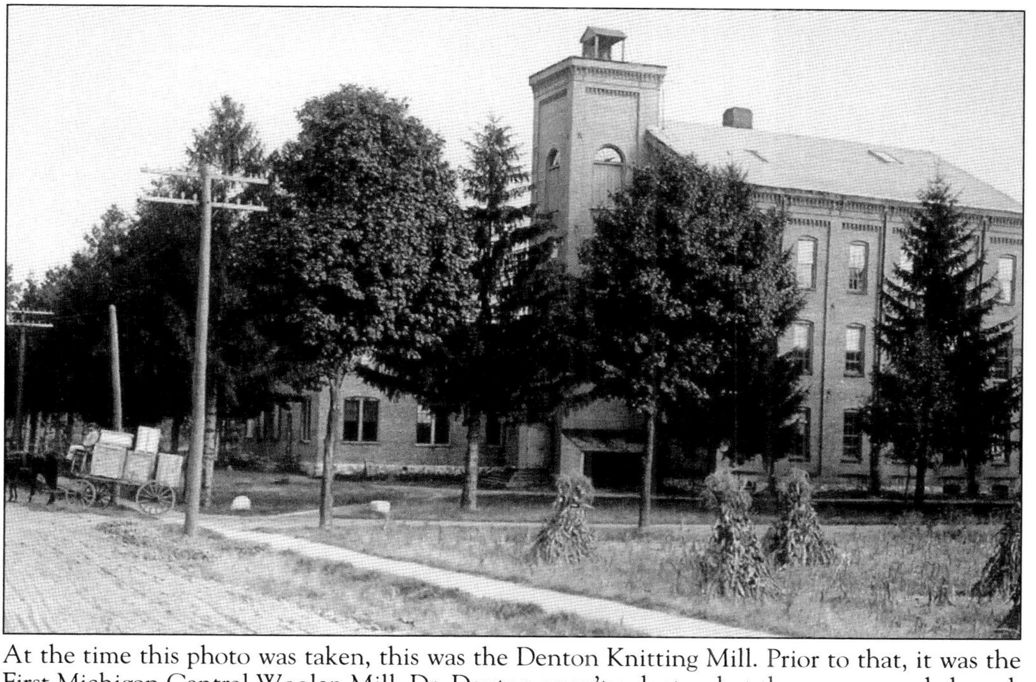

At the time this photo was taken, this was the Denton Knitting Mill. Prior to that, it was the First Michigan Central Woolen Mill. Dr. Denton wasn't a doctor, but the name sounded good. At one time, the mill, located in Centreville, employed 300 people. (Dick Cripe Collection.)

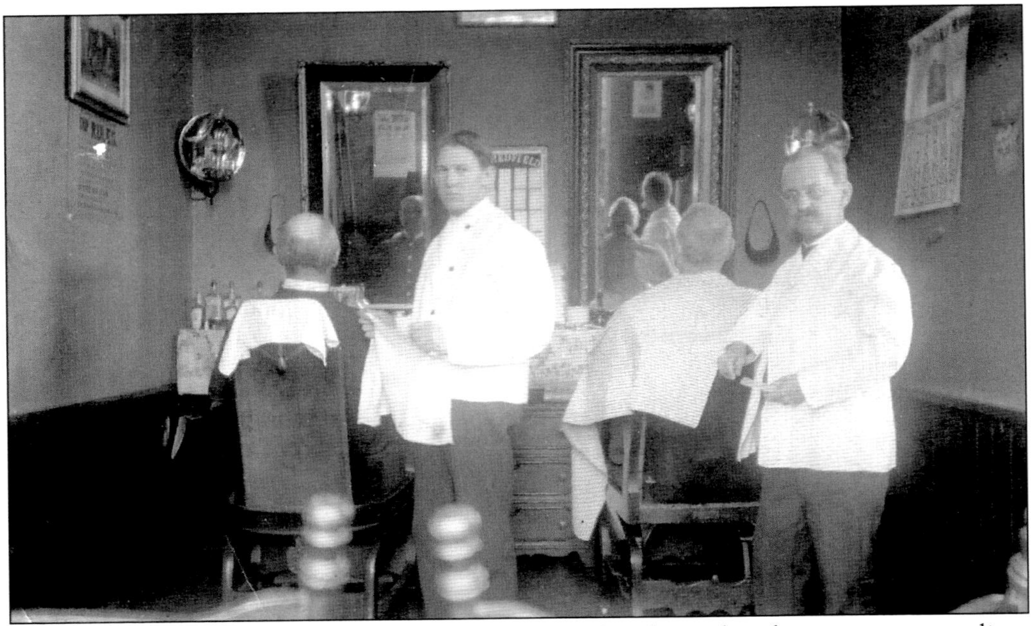

This old postcard depicting a barbershop in Mendon has a handwritten note reading: "Doll Marantette in chair; Myrl Bent, Barber; Johnny Redfield, Barber." (Mendon Country Inn Collection.)

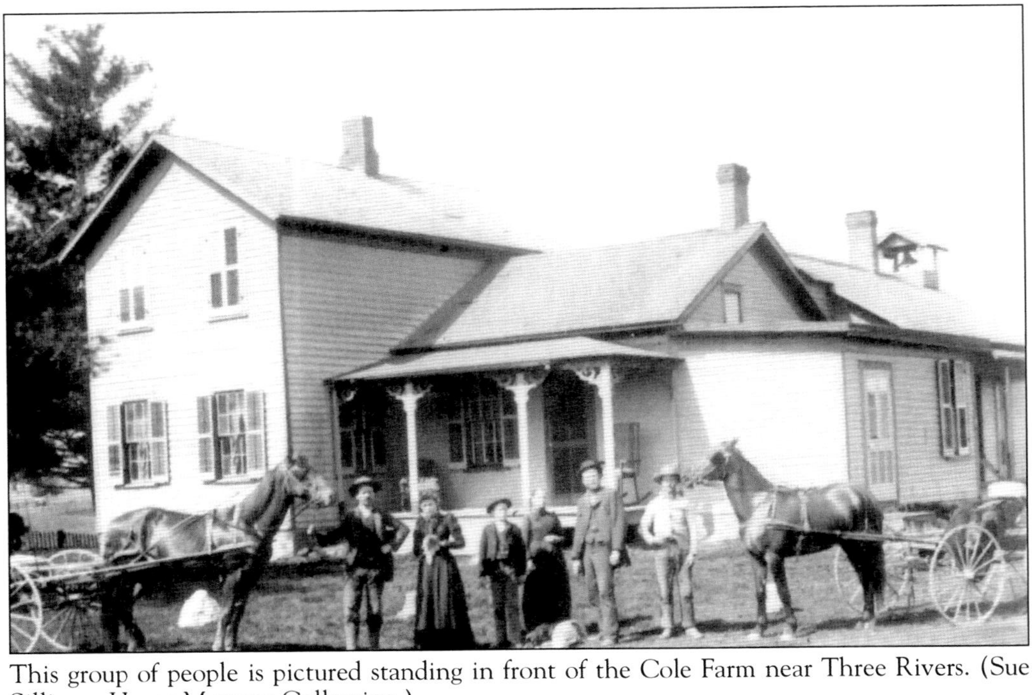

This group of people is pictured standing in front of the Cole Farm near Three Rivers. (Sue Silliman House Museum Collection.)

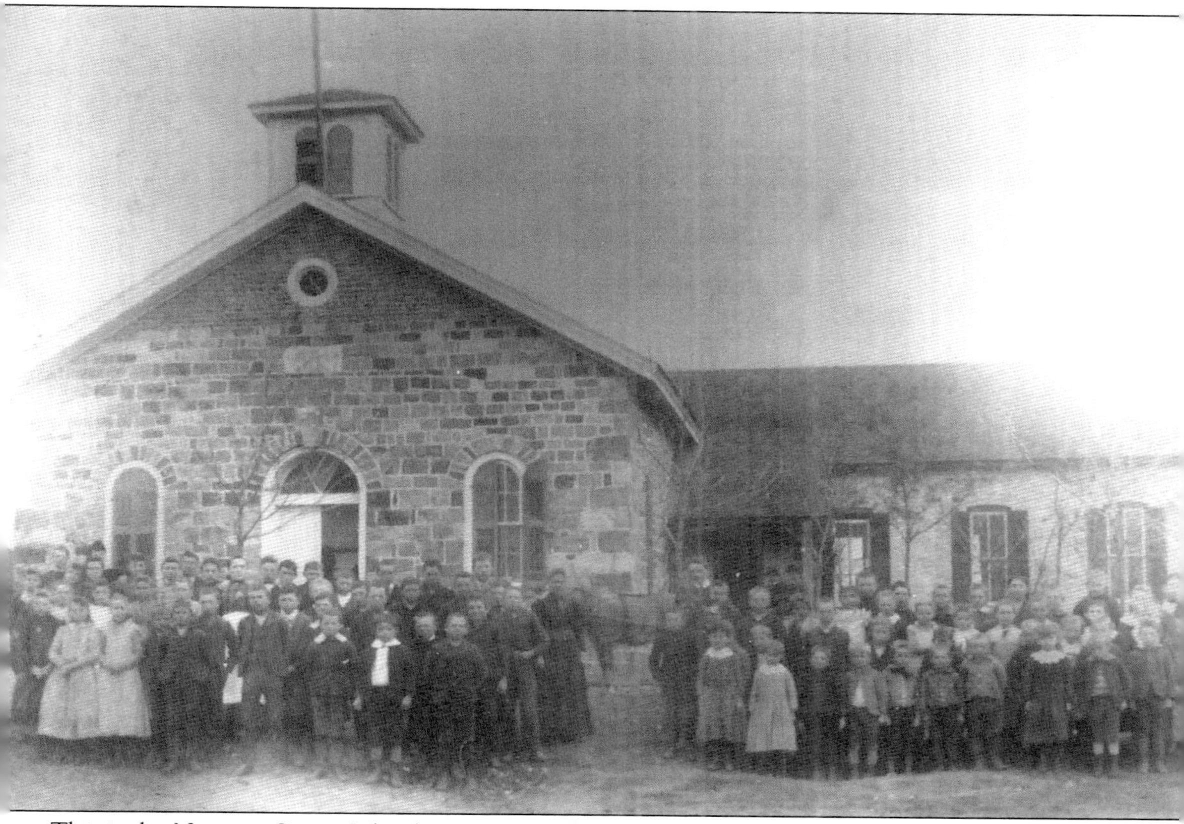

This is the Nottawa Stone School as it appeared *c.* 1900. The school was built out of wood in 1870 and was later covered with stone. An addition had to be built shortly after that because of the increasing population. The population growth at the time was due not only to the success of the A.M. Todd Mint Company, but also the Grand Rapids & Indiana Railroad, which ran north and south into Nottawa, and the Central Michigan Railroad, which ran east and west just north of Nottawa. Local historian Dick Cripe, who rescued the school from being torn down, and converted it into a museum (now overseen by the St. Joseph County Intermediate School District), states that men in Nottawa worked on the railroad in section gangs in the summer, and cut ice on nearby Sand Lake for refrigerated railroad cars in the winter. (Dick Cripe Collection.)

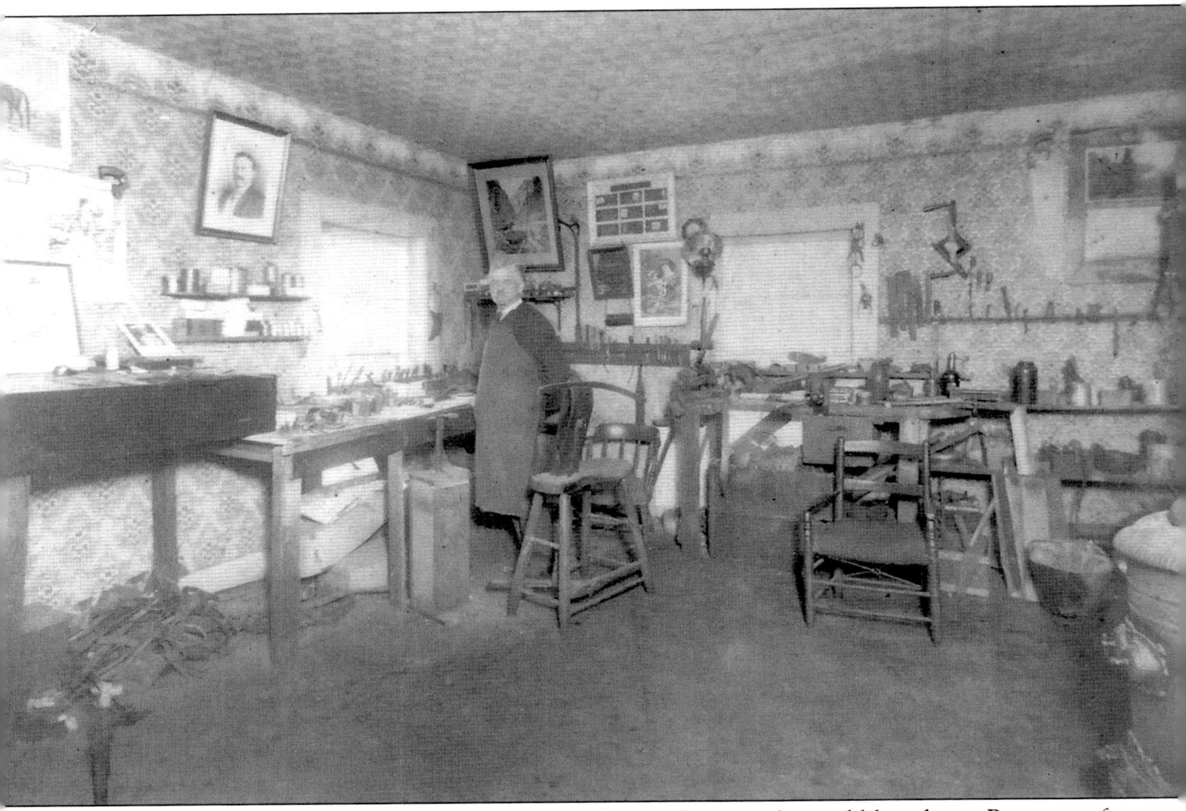

Hiram Wescott, a Civil War veteran, is shown here in his cobbler shop. Because of a miscommunication following the Civil War, Wescott had to walk home from the Sturgis Railroad station to Centreville, because no one knew he was on the train. He lived long enough to take place in Centreville's Centennial Celebration in 1930. (Dick Cripe Collection.)

Nine

CHURCHES

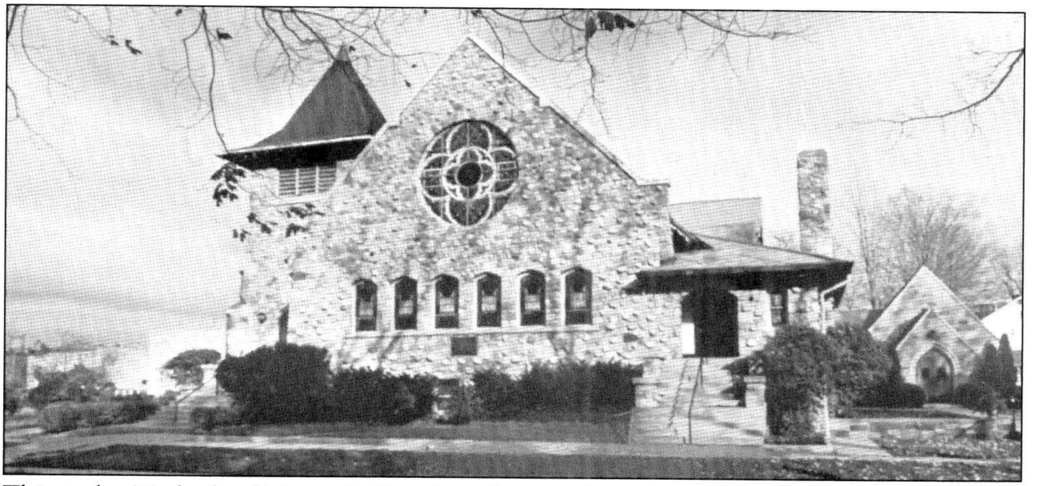

This is the Methodist Episcopal Church in Sturgis. According to Sue Silliman, in her 1931 book *St. Joseph in Homespun*:

> *The first religious society formed in the St. Joseph county territory was a Methodist class at Newville, in 1829; the second one was at White Pigeon village in 1830, with Capt. Alvin Calhoun as leader, Alanson Stewart, local preacher, and with Mr. and Mrs. John Bowers, Mr. and Mrs. John Coates and David Rollins as members. The first Presbyterian church was organized in 1830, the first edifice built in 1834, and from its belfry of modest proportions rang the first church bell installed in Southern Michigan west of Ann Arbor. The first trustees were Elijah White, N.B. Chapin, Dr. Loomis, Charles Kellogg, Lewis B. Judson and William Rowen.*

(Sturgis Historical Society Collection.)

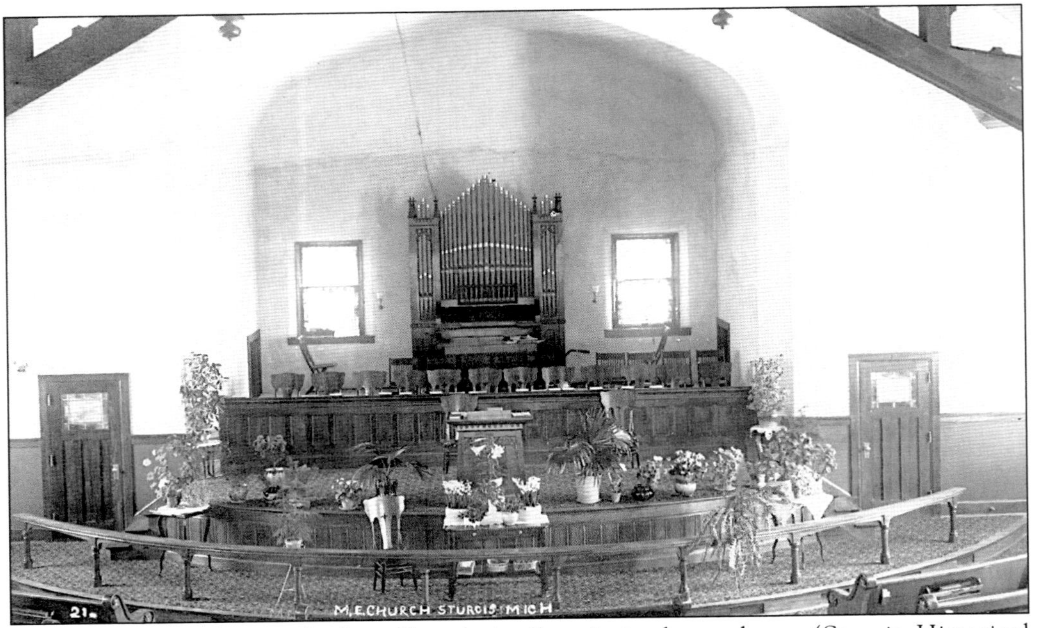

The interior of the Methodist Church in Sturgis is shown here. (Sturgis Historical Society Collection.)

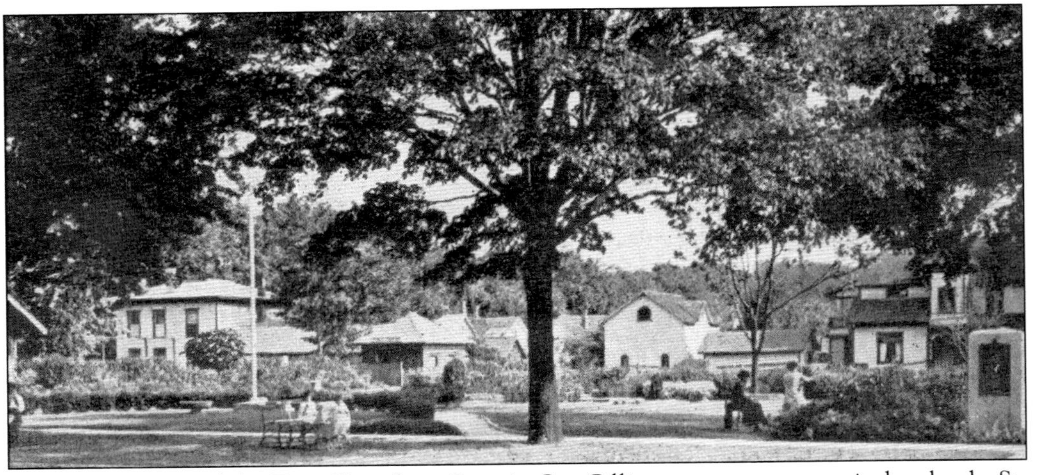

This is an image of the Free Church in Sturgis. Sue Silliman goes on to say in her book, *St. Joseph in Homespun*:

> *In 1858, the Harmonical Society of Sturgis built a Free Church, which was dedicated to religious liberty, where each individual could worship as he chose. A gray granite monument now stands at the intersection of U. S. 112 at Madison Street, Sturgis. On it is a bronze tablet with the inscription: 'The Harmonical Society of Sturgis built on this site a free church dedicated to religious liberty, the first of its kind in the world. To perpetuate the memory of its founders, this ground is granted to the City of Sturgis, to be forever maintained as "The Free Church Park." In accordance with agreement filed with county register of deeds.'*

(Sturgis Historical Society Collection.)

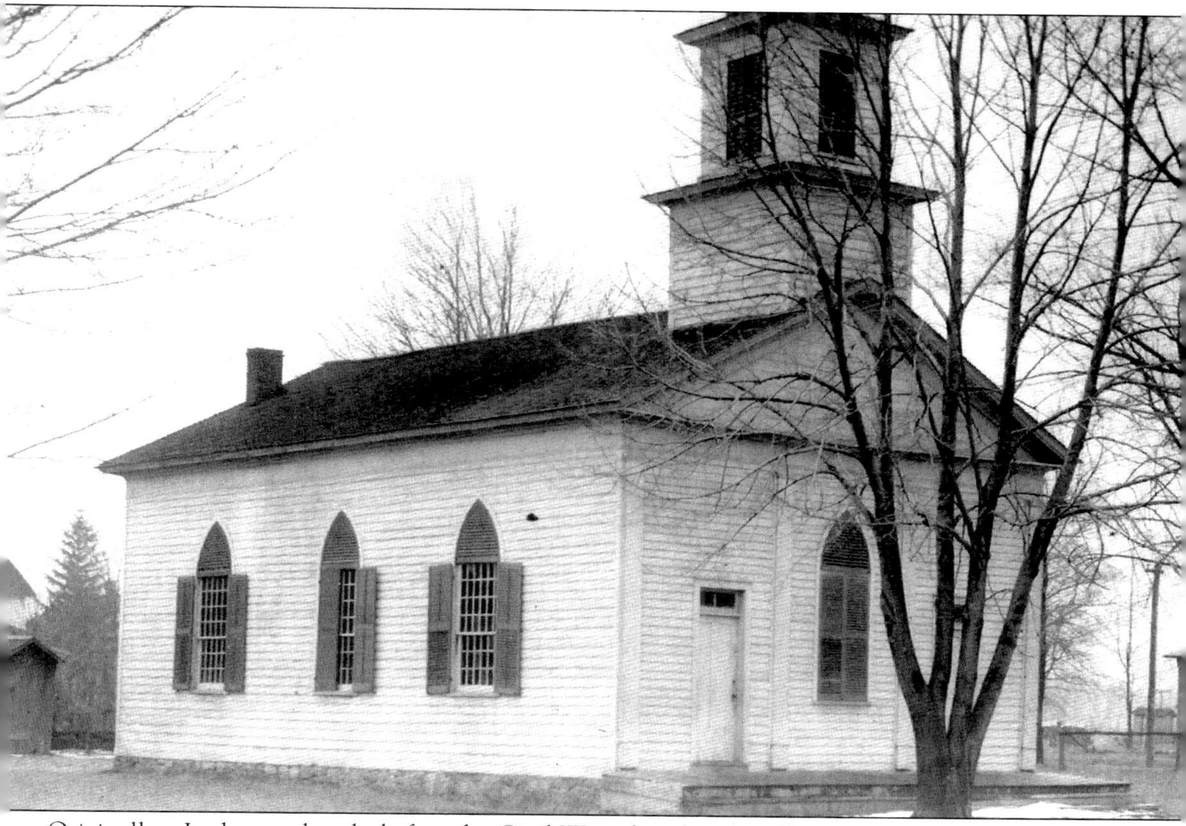

Originally a Lutheran church, before the Civil War, this church still is in operation as the St. Clare Catholic Church in Centreville. (Dick Cripe Collection.)

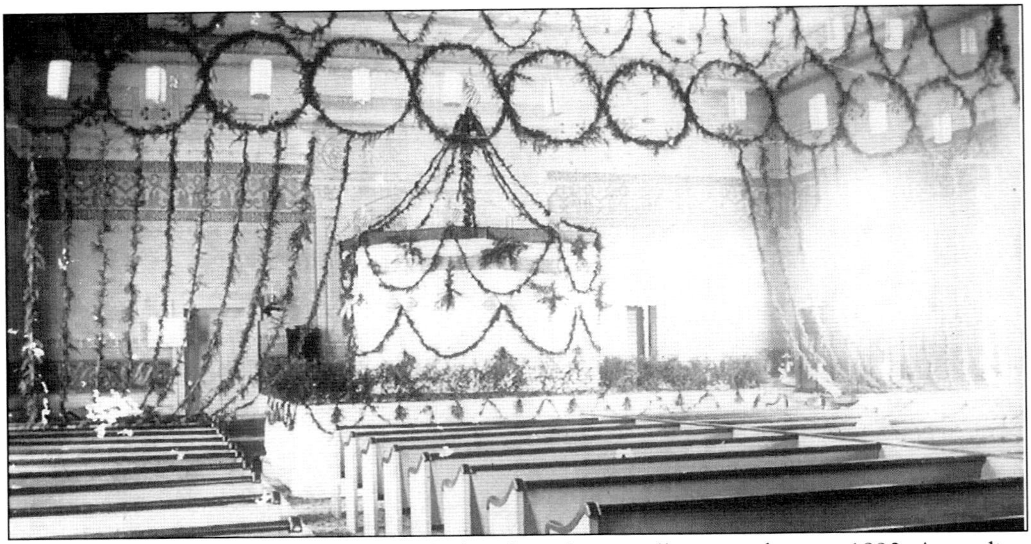

The interior of the Methodist Episcopal Church in Centreville is seen here, c. 1890. According to Sue Silliman's book, the Methodist Church in St. Joseph County got its start with traveling ministers. Here she recounts one example:

> *Rev. T.J. Robe on horseback, and with traditional saddlebags, forded streams, sometimes swimming them on horseback, sometimes mired down nearly all over, following bridle-paths and Indian trails, exploring a wild territory with only here and there a sparsely settled territory, seeking to save souls, established preaching at the following places, viz: at Bronson (now Kalamazoo), Goodrich Prairie, Comstock, Tolen Prairie (now Galesburg), Grand and Genesse Prairies, Climax and Cobb's corners, Judge Harrison's corners on Prairie Ronde, Longwells on the south side of the Prairie, Harris' Prairie (now Three Rivers).*

(Dick Cripe Collection.)

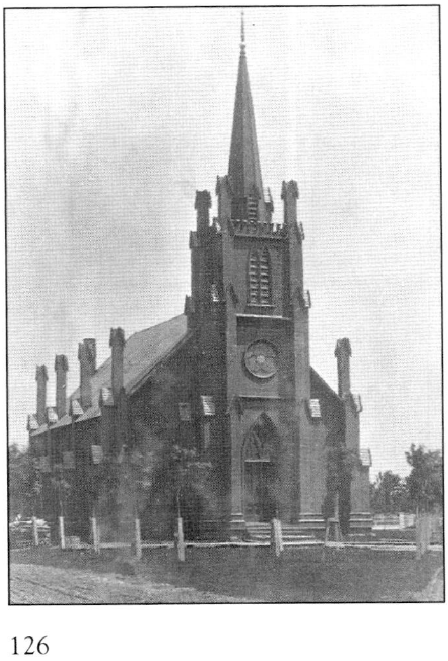

The Three Rivers Episcopal Church was organized in 1862 by Voltaire Spaulding. Trustees included Wm. F. Wheeler, John Cowling, Edwin Murphy, Samuel Chadwick, Isaac Crossett, John M. Baily, S.A. Selleck, William Chart, and Thomas Clark. (Three Rivers Library Collection.)

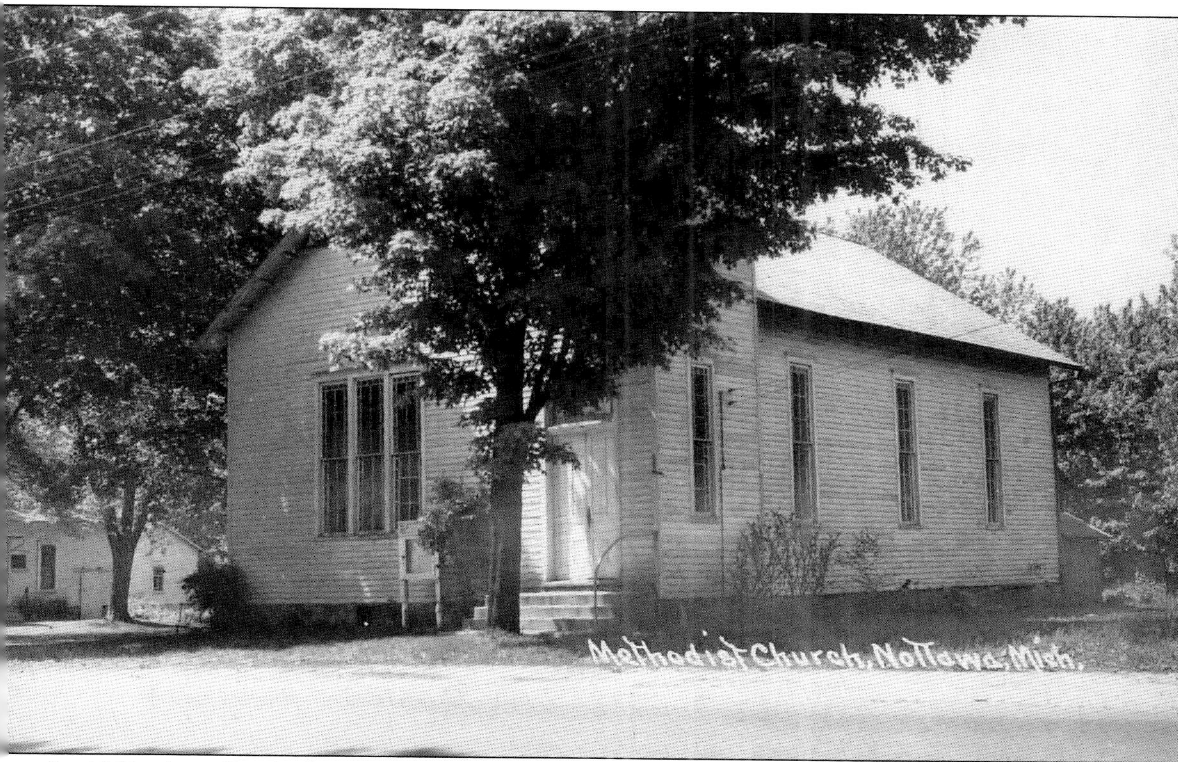

In 1852, the official church board of the Methodist Episcopal Church, located between Centreville and Nottawa, consisted of Phillip Hoffman, William Hazzard, Comfort Tyler, and Luther Goodrich, among others. (Steve Zazra Collection.)

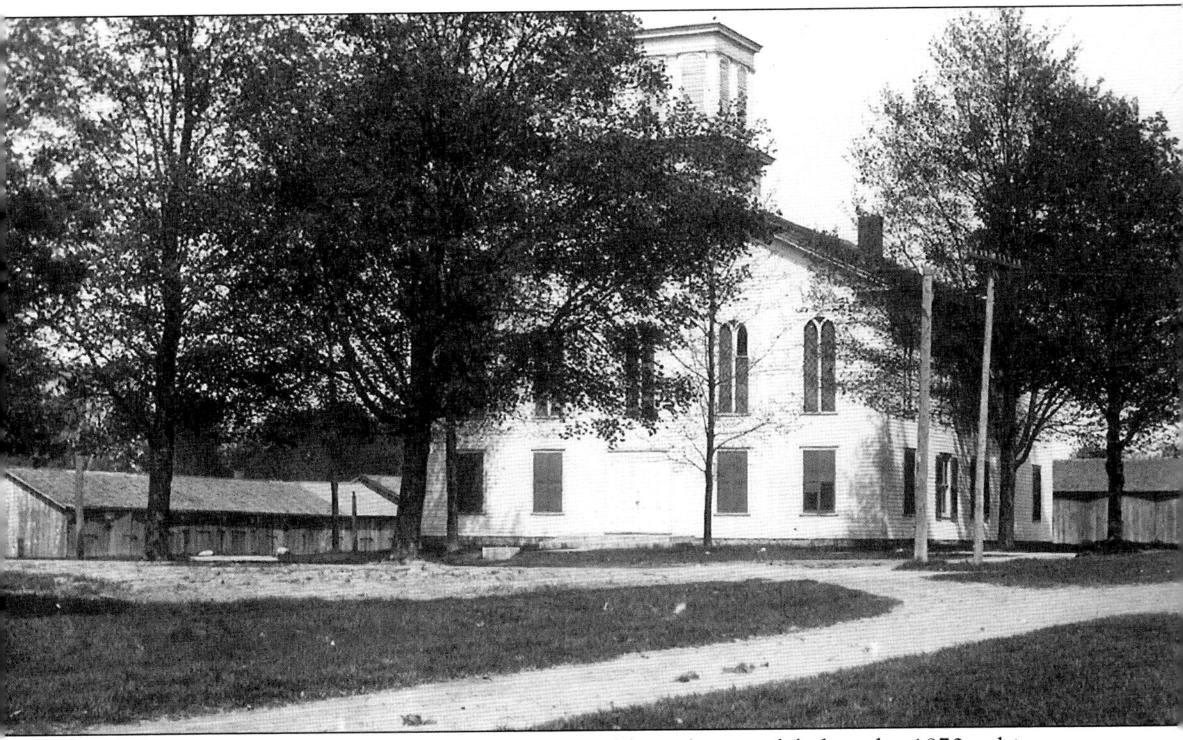

First the Reformed Church, built *c.* 1840s and heavily remodeled in the 1870s, this structure later became the Presbyterian Church, and is now the Masonic Lodge Hall in Centreville. Note the horse sheds in the back. (Dick Cripe Collection.)